Contents

Foreword for language teachers — v

Introduction for students — vi

Glossary of grammar terms — viii

Nouns — 1
Using nouns — 1
Making nouns plural — 9

Articles — 14
Two types of article — 14
The definite article — 14
The indefinite article — 21

Adjectives — 24
Using adjectives — 24
How to make adjectives agree — 25
Comparing people or things — 33
Demonstrative adjectives — 38
Interrogative adjectives — 42
Adjectives used in exclamations — 44
Possessive adjectives — 45
Indefinite adjectives — 50

Pronouns — 53
'What is a pronoun?' — 53
Subject pronouns — 53
Object pronouns — 57
Possessive pronouns — 67
ne and **ci** — 69
Indefinite pronouns — 74
Relative pronouns — 77
Interrogative pronouns — 80
Demonstrative pronouns — 83

Verbs — 85
Overview of verbs — 85
The present tenses — 87
The present simple tense — 88
essere and **stare** — 103
The present continuous tense — 105
The imperative — 107
Reflexive verbs — 115
The future tense — 124
The conditional — 130
The imperfect tense — 136
The perfect tense — 141
The past historic — 150
The pluperfect or past perfect tense — 153
The passive — 159
The gerund — 163
Impersonal verbs — 167
The subjunctive — 171

The infinitive 183
Prepositions after verbs 189
Verbal idioms 194

Negatives **198**

Questions **203**
Different types of questions 203
Question words 206

Adverbs **213**
How adverbs are used 213
How to form adverbs 213
Making comparisons using adverbs 218
Some common adverbs 221
Where to put adverbs 225

Prepositions **228**
Using prepositions 228
a, **di**, **da**, **in**, **su** and **per** 231
Some other common prepositions 239

Conjunctions **244**
e, **ma**, **anche**, **o**, **perché**, **che** and **se** 244
Some other common conjunctions 245
Split conjunctions 246

Spelling **247**

Stress **253**
Which syllable to stress 253

Numbers **257**
Time and date 259

Solutions **263**

Main index **275**

Verb tables **1-25**

Foreword for language teachers

The *Easy Learning Italian Grammar & Practice* is designed to be used with both young and adult learners, as a group revision and practice book to complement your course book during classes, or as a recommended text for self-study and homework/coursework.

The text specifically targets learners from beginners to intermediate or GCSE level, and therefore its structural content and vocabulary have been matched to the relevant specifications up to and including Higher GCSE.

The approach aims to develop knowledge and understanding of grammar and to improve the ability of learners to apply it by:

- defining parts of speech at the start of each major section, with examples in English to clarify concepts
- minimizing the use of grammar terminology and providing clear explanations of terms both within the text and in the **Glossary**
- illustrating all points with examples (and their translations) based on topics and contexts which are relevant to beginner and intermediate course content
- providing exercises which allow learners to practice grammar points

The text helps you develop positive attitudes to grammar learning in your classes by:

- giving clear, easy-to-follow explanations
- highlighting useful **Tips** to deal with common difficulties
- summarizing **Key points** at the end of sections to consolidate learning
- illustrating **Key points** with practice examples

Introduction for students

Whether you are starting to learn Italian for the very first time, brushing up on topics you have studied in class, or revising for your GCSE exams, the *Easy Learning Italian Grammar & Practice* is here to help. This easy-to-use revision and practice guide takes you through all the basics you will need to speak and understand modern everyday Italian.

Learners sometimes struggle with the technical terms they come across when they start to explore the grammar of a new language. The *Easy Learning Italian Grammar & Practice* explains how to get to grips with all the parts of speech you will need to know, using simple language and cutting out jargon.

The text is divided into sections, each dealing with a particular area of grammar. Each section can be studied individually, as numerous cross-references in the text point you to relevant points in other sections of the book for further information.

Every major section begins with an explanation of the area of grammar covered on the following pages. For quick reference, these definitions are also collected together on pages viii-xii in a glossary of essential grammatical terms.

What is a verb?

A **verb** is a word which describes what somebody or something does, what they are, or what happens to them, for example, *play, be, disappear*.

Each grammar point in the text is followed by simple examples of real Italian, complete with English translations, to help you understand the rules. Underlining has been used in examples throughout the text to highlight the grammatical point being explained.

➤ To say *the one* in Italian use **quello** to refer to masculine nouns or **quella** to refer to feminine nouns. The relative pronoun is **che**.

È quello che non funziona.	That's the one which isn't working.
È quello che preferisco.	That's the one I prefer.
È quella che parla di più.	She's the one who talks most.

In Italian, as with any foreign language, there are certain pitfalls which have to be avoided. **Tips** and **Information** notes throughout the text are useful reminders of the things that often trip learners up.

Tip

When you translate an English sentence which starts with a noun, don't forget to use the definite article in Italian.

Le macchine costano caro.	Cars cost a lot.
La frutta fa bene.	Fruit is good for you.

Key points sum up all the important facts about a particular area of grammar, to save you time when you are revising and help you focus on the main grammatical points.

> **KEY POINTS**
> ✔ Most Italian adjectives go after the noun.
> ✔ The meaning of some adjectives changes depending on whether they come before or after the noun.

After each Key point you can find a number of exercises to help you practice all the important grammatical points. You can find the answer to each exercise on pages 263-274.

If you think you would like to continue with your Italian studies to a higher level, look at the **Grammar Extra** sections. These are intended for advanced students who are interested in knowing a little more about the structures they will come across beyond GCSE.

Grammar Extra!
To say that something is getting *better and better*, *worse and worse*, *slower and slower*, and so on, use **sempre** with the comparative adverb.

Le cose vanno sempre meglio.	Things are going better and better.
Mio nonno sta sempre peggio.	My grandfather's getting worse and worse.
Cammina sempre più lento.	He's walking slower and slower.

Finally, the supplement at the end of the book contains **Verb Tables**, where 123 important Italian verbs (both regular and irregular) are declined in full. Examples show you how to use these verbs in your own work.

We hope that you will enjoy using the *Easy Learning Italian Grammar & Practice* and find it useful in the course of your studies.

Glossary of Grammar Terms

ABSTRACT NOUN a word used to refer to a quality, idea, feeling or experience, rather than a physical object, for example, *size, reason, happiness*. Compare with **concrete noun**.

ACTIVE a form of the verb that is used when the subject of the sentence does the action, for example, *A dog bit him* (subject: *a dog*; active verb: *bit*). Compare with **passive**.

ADJECTIVE a 'describing' word that tells you something about a person or thing, for example, a *blue* shirt, a *big* car, a *good* idea.

ADVERB a word used with verbs to give information on where, when or how an action takes place, for example, *here, today, quickly*. An adverb can also add information to adjectives and other adverbs, for example, *extremely* quick, *very* quickly.

AGREEMENT the matching of words or word endings to the person or thing they refer to. For example, the verb *to be* has different forms for *I, you* and *he: I am, you are, he is*. In Italian you use verbs in the form appropriate to the person doing the action, and articles and adjectives have masculine, feminine and plural forms to match (or *agree* with) the noun they go with.

APOSTROPHE S an ending ('s) added to a noun to show ownership, for example, *Peter's car, the company's headquarters*.

ARTICLE a word such as *the, a*, and *an* which goes with nouns: *the sun, a happy boy, an orange*. See also **definite article**, **indefinite article**.

AUXILIARY VERB a verb such as *be, have* and *do* that is used with a main verb to form tenses and questions.

BASE FORM the form of the verb that has no ending added to it, for example, *walk, have, be, go*. Compare with **infinitive**.

CARDINAL NUMBER a number used in counting, for example, *one, seven, ninety*. Compare with **ordinal number**.

CLAUSE a group of words containing a verb.

COMPARATIVE an adjective or adverb with *–er* on the end of it or *more* or *less* in front of it that is used to compare things or people, for example, *faster, more important, less interesting*.

COMPOUND NOUN a word for a living being, thing or idea which is made up of two or more words, for example, *prime minister, mobile phone, home truth*.

CONCRETE NOUN a word that refers to a physical object rather than a quality or idea, for example, *ball, school, apples*. Compare with **abstract noun**.

CONDITIONAL a verb form used to talk about things that would happen or would be true under certain conditions, for example, *I would help you if I could*. It is also used in requests and offers, for example, *Could you lend me some money?; I could give you a lift*.

CONJUGATE (to) to give a verb different endings depending on whether its subject is *I, you, he* and so on, and depending on whether you are referring to the present, past or future, for example, *I have, she has, they listened*.

CONJUGATION a group of verbs that has a particular pattern of endings.

CONJUNCTION a word such as *and, but* or *because* that links two words or phrases, or two parts of a sentence, for example, *Diane and I have been friends for years*.

CONSONANT a sound made by letters such as b, g, m, s and t. In English y is sometimes a consonant, as in *year*, and sometimes a vowel, as in *any*. In Italian i sometimes has a vowel sound (ee) and sometimes the consonant sound of *y* in *year*, for example, **italiano** (eetalyano). Compare with **vowel**.

CONTINUOUS TENSE a verb form made up of *to be* and the *–ing* form, for example, *I'm thinking; They were quarrelling*. Italian continuous tenses are made with **stare** and the gerund.

DEFINITE ARTICLE the word *the*. Compare with **indefinite article**.

DEMONSTRATIVE ADJECTIVE a word used to point out a particular thing or person. There are four demonstrative adjectives in English: *this*, *these*, *that* and *those*.

DEMONSTRATIVE PRONOUN a word used instead of a noun to point out people or things, for example, *That's my brother*. In English the demonstrative pronouns are *this*, *that*, *these* and *those*.

DIRECT OBJECT a noun or pronoun used to show who or what is affected by the verb. For example, in the sentence *He sent flowers*, the subject of the verb is *He* (the person who did the sending) and the direct object of the verb is *flowers* (what he sent). Compare with **indirect object**.

DIRECT OBJECT PRONOUN a word such as *me*, *him*, *us* and *them* used instead of a noun to show who or what is affected by the action of the verb, for example, *His friends helped him*. Compare **indirect object pronoun**.

ENDING something added to the end of a word. In English nouns have plural endings, for example boy → boy<u>s</u>, child → child<u>ren</u> and verbs have the endings *–s*, *–ed* and *–ing*, for example, *walk* → *walks*, *walked, walking*. In Italian there are plural endings for nouns, verb endings, and masculine, feminine and plural endings for adjectives and pronouns.

EXCLAMATION a sound, word or sentence that is spoken suddenly by somebody who is surprised, excited or angry, for example, *Oh!; Look who's coming!; How dare you!*

FEMININE a noun, pronoun, article or form of adjective used to refer to a living being, thing or idea that is not classed as masculine. For example, **una** (feminine indefinite article) **bella** (adjective with a feminine ending) **casa** (feminine noun).

FUTURE a tense used to talk about something that will happen, or be true in the future, for example, *He'll be here soon; I'll give you a call; It will be sunny tomorrow*.

GENDER whether a noun, pronoun or adjective is masculine or feminine.

GERUND in English, a verb form ending in *–ing*, for example, *eating, sleeping*. In Italian the gerund ends in **–ando** or **–endo**.

IMPERATIVE a form of the verb used to give orders and instructions, for example, *Sit down!; Don't go!; Let's start!*

IMPERFECT a tense used to say what was happening, what used to happen and what things were like in the past, for example, *It was sunny at the weekend; They weren't listening; They used to live in Spain*.

IMPERSONAL VERB a verb with the subject *it*, where '*it*' does not refer to any specific thing; for example, *It's going to rain; It's nine o'clock*.

INDEFINITE ADJECTIVE one of a small group of adjectives used to give an idea of amounts and numbers, for example, *several, all, every*.

INDEFINITE ARTICLE the word *a* or *an*. Compare with **definite article**.

INDEFINITE PRONOUN a word like *everything, nobody* and *something* which is used to refer to people or things in a non-specific way.

INDIRECT OBJECT a noun or pronoun used to show who benefits or suffers from an action. For example, in the sentence *He sent Claire flowers*, the <u>direct</u> object (what was sent) is *flowers* and the <u>indirect</u> object is *Claire* (the person the flowers were sent to). An indirect object often has *to* in front of it: *He told lies to everyone*; *He told everyone lies*. In both these sentences the direct object is *lies* and the indirect object is *everyone*. Compare with **direct object**.

INDIRECT OBJECT PRONOUN a pronoun such as *to me* (or *me*), *to you* (or *you*) and *to her* (or *her*). In the sentence *He gave the chocolates to me and the flowers to her*, the direct objects are *the chocolates* and *the flowers* (what he gave), and the indirect object pronouns are *to me* and *to her* (who he gave them to). In the sentence *He gave me the chocolates and her the flowers*, the indirect object pronouns are *me* and *her*.

INDIRECT QUESTION a more roundabout way of asking a question, for example, instead of *Where are you going?* you can say *Tell me where you are going*, or *I'd like to know where you are going*.

INDIRECT SPEECH the words you use to report what someone has said when you aren't using their actual words, for example, *He said that he was going out*. Also called **reported speech**.

INFINITIVE the base form of the verb, for example, *walk*, *see*, *hear*. It is used after other verbs such as *should*, *must* and *can*. The infinitive is often used with *to*: *to speak*, *to eat*, *to live*. Compare with **base form**.

INTERROGATIVE ADJECTIVE a question word such as *which*, *what* or *how much* that is used when asking about a noun, for example, *Which colour?*; *What size?*; *How much sugar?*

INTERROGATIVE PRONOUN one of the following: *who*, *which*, *whose*, *whom* and *what*. These words are used without a noun, when asking questions, for example, *What do you want?*

INTRANSITIVE VERB a verb used without a direct object, for example, *The shop is closing*; *Nothing grows here*. Compare with **transitive verb**.

INVARIABLE the term used to describe an adjective which does not change its form for the feminine or the plural, or a noun which does not change its ending in the plural.

IRREGULAR VERB In Italian, a verb whose forms do not follow one of the three main patterns.

MASCULINE a noun, pronoun, article or form of adjective used to refer to a living being, thing or idea that is not classed as feminine. For example, **il** (masculine definite article) **primo** (adjective with a masculine ending) **treno** (masculine noun).

NEGATIVE a question or statement which contains a word such as *not*, *never* or *nothing*: *Isn't he here?*; *I never eat meat*; *She's doing nothing about it*.

NOUN a naming word for a living being, thing or idea, for example, *woman*, *Andrew*, *desk*, *happiness*.

NUMBER in grammar a verb agrees in number with its subject by being singular with a singular subject and plural with a plural subject, for example, *I am a teacher*; *they are teachers*.

OBJECT a noun or pronoun that, in English, usually comes after the verb and shows who or what is affected by it, for example, *I* (subject) *want* (verb) *a new car* (object); *They* (subject) *phoned* (verb) *him* (object). Compare **direct object**, **indirect object** and **subject**.

OBJECT PRONOUN one of the following: *me, you, him, her, it, us, them*. They are used instead of nouns after prepositions, for example, *for me, with us* and as the object of verbs, for example, *The company sacked him*; *You'll enjoy it*. Compare **subject pronoun**.

ORDINAL NUMBER an adjective used to show where something comes in numerical order, for example, *first, seventh, ninetieth*. Compare with **cardinal number**.

PART OF SPEECH a word with a particular grammatical function, for example, *noun*, *adjective*, *verb*, *preposition*, *pronoun*.

PASSIVE a verb form that is used when the subject of the verb is the person or thing the action is done to, for example, *Shaun was bitten by a dog. Shaun* is the subject of the sentence, but he did not do the action. Compare with **active**.

PAST PARTICIPLE a verb form usually ending –*ed*, for example *lived*, *worked*. Some past participles are irregular, for example, *gone*, *sat*, *broken*. Past participles are used to make the perfect, pluperfect and passive, for example, *They've gone; They hadn't noticed me; Nobody was hurt*. Past participles are also used as adjectives, for example, *a boiled egg*.

PAST PERFECT see **pluperfect**.

PERFECT a tense used in English to talk about what has or hasn't happened, for example, *We've won, I haven't touched it*. Compare **simple past**.

PERSON in grammar one of the following: the first person (*I, we*), the second person (*you*) or the third person (*he, she, it, they*).

PERSONAL PRONOUN a word such as *I, you, he, she, us, them*, which makes it clear who you are talking about or talking to.

PLUPERFECT a tense used to talk about what had happened or had been true at a point in the past, for example, *I had forgotten to send her a card*. Also called **past perfect**.

PLURAL the form of a word which is used to refer to more than one person or thing. In Italian, nouns, adjectives, articles, pronouns and verbs can be plural.

POSITIVE a positive sentence does not contain a negative word such as *not*. Compare with **negative**.

POSSESSIVE ADJECTIVE a word such as *my, your, his* that is used with a noun to show who it belongs to.

POSSESSIVE PRONOUN a word such as *mine, yours, his* that is used instead of a possessive adjective followed by a noun. For example, instead of *My bag is the blue one*, you can say *Mine's the blue one*.

PREPOSITION a word such as *at, for, with, into* or *from*, or a phrase such as *in front of* or *near to*. Prepositions are usually followed by a noun or a pronoun and show how people and things relate to the rest of the sentence, for example, *She's at home; It's for you; You'll get into trouble; It's in front of you*.

PRESENT a verb form used to talk about what is true at the moment, what generally happens and what is happening now; for example, *I'm a student; I travel to college by train; The phone's ringing*.

PRESENT PARTICIPLE a verb form ending in –*ing*, for example, *eating, sleeping*. Compare with **gerund**.

PRONOUN a word you use instead of a noun, when you do not need or want to name someone or something directly, for example, *it, you, somebody*.

PROPER NOUN the name of a person, place or organization. Proper nouns are always written with a capital letter, for example, Kate, New York, the Forestry Commission.

QUESTION WORD a word such as *why, where, who, which* or *how* that is used to ask a question.

REFLEXIVE PRONOUN a word ending in –*self* or –*selves*, such as *myself* and *ourselves*, that is used as the object of a verb, for example *I surprised myself; We're going to treat ourselves*.

REFLEXIVE VERB a verb where the subject and object are the same, and which uses reflexive pronouns such as *myself, yourself* and *themselves*, for example, *I've hurt myself; Look after yourself!; They're enjoying themselves*.

REGULAR VERB in Italian, a verb whose forms follow one of the three main patterns. Compare with **irregular verb**.

RELATIVE PRONOUN one of the following: *who, which, that* and *whom*. They are used to specify exactly who or what is being talked about, for example, *The man who has just come in* is Anna's boyfriend; *The vase that you broke* cost a lot of money.

REPORTED SPEECH see **indirect speech**.

SENTENCE a group of words which usually has a subject and a verb. In writing, a sentence begins with a capital and ends with a full stop, question mark or exclamation mark.

SIMPLE TENSE a verb form made up of one word, for example, *She lives here; They arrived late.* Compare with **Continuous Tense** and **Perfect Tense**.

SIMPLE PAST a tense used in English to say when exactly something happened, for example, *We met last summer; I ate it last night; It rained a lot yesterday.* In Italian the perfect tense is used in this kind of sentence.

SINGULAR the form of a word used to refer to one person or thing. Compare with **plural**.

STEM what is left of an Italian verb when you take away the **–are**, **–ere** or **–ire** ending of the infinitive.

STRESSED PRONOUN an object pronoun used in Italian after prepositions and when you want to stress the word for *me, him, them* and so on. Compare **unstressed pronoun**.

SUBJECT a noun or pronoun that refers to the person or thing doing the action or being in the state described by the verb, for example *Pat likes climbing; The bus is late.* Compare with **object**.

SUBJECT PRONOUN a word such as *I, he, she* and *they* used for the person or thing carrying out the action described by the verb. Pronouns replace nouns when it is clear who is being talked about, for example, *My brother's not here at the moment. He'll be back in an hour.*

SUBJUNCTIVE a verb form often used in Italian to express wishes, thoughts and suppositions. In English the subjunctive is only used occasionally, for example, *If I were you…; So be it; He asked that they be removed.*

SUPERLATIVE an adjective or adverb with *–est* on the end of it or *most* or *least* in front of it that is used to compare things or people, for example, *fastest, most important, least interesting.*

SYLLABLE a unit containing a vowel sound. A word can have one or more syllables, for example, *I, o-pen, ca-the-dral.*

TENSE a particular form of the verb. It shows whether you are referring to the present, past or future.

TRANSITIVE VERB a verb used with a direct object, for example, *Close the door!; They grow wheat.* Compare with **intransitive verb**.

UNSTRESSED PRONOUN an object pronoun used in Italian when you don't want to put any special emphasis on the word for *me, him, them* and so on. Compare **stressed pronoun**.

VERB a word that describes what somebody or something does, what they are, or what happens to them, for example, *play, be, disappear.*

VOWEL one of the sounds made by the letters *a, e, i, o u,* and sometimes *y.* Compare with **consonant**.

grammar & exercises

Nouns

What is a noun?

A **noun** is a naming word for a living being, a thing, or an idea, for example, *woman, Andrew, desk, happiness.*

Using nouns

The basics

➤ In Italian, all nouns, whether referring to living beings or to things and ideas, are either <u>masculine</u> or <u>feminine</u>. This is their <u>gender.</u>

Masculine		Feminine	
olio	oil	**acqua**	water
uomo	man	**donna**	woman
delfino	dolphin	**tigre**	tiger
concetto	concept	**idea**	idea
armadio	wardrobe	**sedia**	chair

➤ The letter a noun ends with is often a reliable guide to its gender. For instance, words ending in **–o** will nearly always be masculine.

➤ When you use an Italian noun you need to know if it is masculine or feminine so that you can make other words that go with it masculine or feminine too:

• how you translate the words for '*the*' or '*a*' depends on the noun's gender. For instance, with masculine nouns you use **il** and **un**, and with feminine nouns you use **la** and **una**.

Masculine		Feminine	
<u>il</u> **giorno**	the day	<u>la</u> **notte**	the night
<u>un</u> **gelato**	an ice cream	<u>una</u> **mela**	an apple

• adjectives describing a noun are masculine or feminine in form.

Masculine	Feminine
un *abito* **car**<u>**o**</u> – an expensive suit	**una** *macchina* **car**<u>**a**</u> – an expensive car
l'Antic<u>**o**</u> **Testamento** – the Old Testament	**l'antic**<u>**a**</u> **Roma** – ancient Rome

• words that replace nouns – called <u>pronouns</u> – must also be masculine or feminine. The translation for *Do you want it?* is **"Lo vuoi?"** if you're offering **un gelato** (*an ice cream*), and **"La vuoi?"** if you're referring to **una mela** (*an apple*).

⇨ *For more information on* **Articles**, **Adjectives** *or* **Pronouns**, *see pages 14, 24 and 53.*

➤ Just like English nouns, Italian nouns can be <u>singular</u> or <u>plural</u>. Most English nouns add **–s** in the plural, for example, *days*, *apples*. Most Italian nouns change their final letter from one vowel to another:

Singular		Plural	
gior<u>no</u>	day	**gior<u>ni</u>**	days
mel<u>a</u>	apple	**mel<u>e</u>**	apples
rivoluzion<u>e</u>	revolution	**rivoluzion<u>i</u>**	revolutions

Tip
When in doubt, you can find out a noun's gender by looking it up in a dictionary. When you come across a new word it's a good idea to memorize the article that goes with it, to help you remember its gender.

KEY POINTS
✔ All nouns in Italian are either masculine or feminine.
✔ This affects the words you use with them.
✔ In most cases it is possible to work out a noun's gender from its ending.

Test yourself

1 **Match the noun on the left with its description on the right.**

a una mela   a piece of furniture; masculine noun

b la notte   a fruit; feminine noun

c un armadio   a liquid; feminine noun

d un delfino   a marine mammal; masculine noun

e l'acqua   opposite of day; feminine noun

2 **Give the gender (use *un* or *una*) for each of the words below.**

a .... tigre

b .... concetto

c .... donna

d .... gelato

e .... giorno

f .... macchina

g .... uomo

h .... casa

i .... sedia

j .... abito

How to recognize what gender a noun is

➤ There are some simple rules that will enable you to work out the gender of a very large number of Italian nouns from their last letter in the singular:

- nearly all words ending in **–o** are <u>masculine</u>.

- nearly all words ending in **–a** are <u>feminine</u>.

- nearly all words ending in **–à**, **–sione** and **–zione** are <u>feminine</u>.

- nearly all words ending with a consonant are <u>masculine</u>.

🛈 Note that words ending in **–e** are masculine in some cases and feminine in others.

➤ The following are typical masculine nouns ending in **–o**: **il treno**   the train

il supermercato	the supermarket
l'aeroporto	the airport
il toro	the bull
un topo	a mouse
un gatto	a (tom) cat
un italiano	an Italian (man)

🛈 Note that a few very common nouns ending in **–o** are feminine.

la mano	the hand
una foto	a photo
la radio	the radio
una moto	a motorbike

➤ The following are typical feminine nouns ending in **–a**: **la casa**   the house

la macchina	the car
una donna	a woman
una regola	a rule
una gatta	a (she) cat
un'italiana	an Italian (woman)

🛈 Note that some very common words ending in **–a** are masculine.

il problema	the problem
il programma	the programme
il sistema	the system
il clima	the climate

- Most words for professions and jobs ending in **–ta** are masculine or feminine, according to whether a male or female is meant.

<u>**un**</u> **giornalista**	a (male) journalist
<u>**una**</u> **giornalista**	a (female) journalist
<u>**un**</u> **dentista**	a (male) dentist
<u>**una**</u> **dentista**	a (female) dentist

➤ The following are typical feminine nouns ending in **–à**, **–sione**, and **–zione**:

Ending	Example	Meaning
-à	**una difficoltà**	a difficulty
	la realtà	the reality
-sione	**la versione**	the version
	un'occasione	an opportunity
-zione	**una lezione**	a lesson
	una conversazione	a conversation

➤ Nouns ending in a <u>consonant</u> are nearly always masculine.

un film   a film
un bar   a bar
un computer   a computer
BUT
una jeep   a jeep

➤ Nouns ending in **–e** can be masculine in some cases and feminine in others.

un mese   a month
il mare   the sea
la gente   the people
la mente   the mind
il mese di giugno   the month of June
una mente logica   a logical mind

[*i*] Note that the names of languages are always masculine, whether they end in **–e** or in **–o**.

Il giapponese è molto difficile.   Japanese is very difficult.
L'italiano è bellissimo.   Italian is beautiful.

Grammar Extra!
Some words have different meanings depending on whether they are masculine or feminine.

Masculine	Meaning	Feminine	Meaning
il fine	the objective	**la fine**	the end
un posto	a place	**la posta**	the mail
un modo	a way	**la moda**	the fashion
il capitale	capital (money)	**una capitale**	a capital city
un bel posto	a nice place	**la posta elettronica**	email

Nouns for males and females

➤ In Italian, just as in English, there are sometimes very different words for male and female people and animals.

<u>un</u> uomo	a man
<u>una</u> donna	a woman
<u>un</u> fratello	a brother
<u>una</u> sorella	a sister
<u>un</u> toro	a bull
<u>una</u> mucca	a cow

➤ In most cases, though, a noun referring to a male can be made to refer to a female by changing the ending:

• Many Italian nouns ending in **–o** can be made feminine by changing the ending to **–a**.

<u>un</u> cuoco	a (male) cook
<u>una</u> cuoca	a (female) cook
<u>un</u> ragazzo	a boy
<u>una</u> ragazza	a girl
<u>un</u> fotografo	a (male) photographer
<u>una</u> fotografa	a (female) photographer
<u>un</u> italiano	an Italian (man)
<u>un</u>'italiana	an Italian (woman)
<u>un</u> gatto	a (tom) cat
<u>una</u> gatta	a (she) cat

• If a noun describing a male ends in **–tore**, the feminine form ends in **–trice**.

<u>un</u> attore	a (male) actor
<u>un</u>'attrice	a (female) actor
<u>un</u> pittore	a (male) painter
<u>una</u> pittrice	a (female) painter
<u>uno</u> scrittore	a (male) writer
<u>una</u> scrittrice	a (female) writer

• Certain nouns describing males ending in **–e** have feminine forms ending in **–essa**.

<u>il</u> professore	the (male) teacher
<u>la</u> professoressa	the (female) teacher
<u>uno</u> studente	a (male) student
<u>una</u> studentessa	a (female) student
<u>un</u> leone	a lion
<u>una</u> leonessa	a lioness

➤ Many nouns ending in **–a** can refer either to males or to females, so there is no change of ending for the feminine.

<u>un</u> turista	a (male) tourist
<u>una</u> turista	a (female) tourist
<u>un</u> collega	a (male) colleague
<u>una</u> collega	a (female) colleague
<u>il mio</u> dentista	my dentist (if it's a man)
<u>la mia</u> dentista	my dentist (if it's a woman)

➤ Many nouns ending in –e can refer either to males or to females, so there is no change of ending for the feminine.

un nipote	a grandson
una nipote	a granddaughter
un cantante	a (male) singer
una cantante	a (female) singer

Grammar Extra!

A few nouns that are feminine refer both to men and women.

una guida	a guide (male or female)
una persona	a person (male or female)
una spia	a spy (male or female)
una star	a star (male or female)
Sean Connery è ancora una star.	Sean Connery's still a star.

KEY POINTS

✔ Most nouns referring to males can be made to refer to females by changing the ending.
✔ Some nouns are the same whether they refer to males or to females, but the words used with them change.
✔ In a few cases the nouns used for male and female are completely different.

Test yourself

3 **Complete the phrase by adding the feminine form of the noun.**

a un gatto e ....

b un attore e ....

c un cuoco e ....

d un fotografo e ....

e un ragazzo e ....

f uno scrittore e ....

g un italiano e ....

h un professore e ....

i un pittore e ....

j un leone e ....

4 **Replace the highlighted masculine nouns with the feminine form.**

a **Il nipote** di Marco arriva stasera. ....

b Abita con **un italiano**. ....

c Abbiamo visto **un leone** allo zoo. ....

d **Il giornalista** mangia sempre in questo ristorante. ....

e Come si chiama **il professore** di francese? ....

f Ha un cane e **un gatto**. ....

g Vado al bar con **un collega**. ....

h È **il dentista** di mia sorella. ....

i **Un turista** ci chiede la strada. ....

j Maria parla con **un ragazzo**. ....

5 **Match each noun with its translation.**

a la fine   the sea

b il programma   the end

c la mano   the opportunity

d l'occasione   the hand

e il mare   the programme

Making nouns plural

➤ There are two main ways of making nouns plural in Italian. In most cases you change the ending, but in a few cases the same form as the singular is used. There are also some plurals which are irregular.

Nouns which you make plural by changing the ending

➤ In English you usually make nouns plural by adding –s. In Italian you usually do it by changing the ending from one vowel to another:

- Change the –o, –a or –e ending of masculine nouns to –i. Nearly all masculine plurals end in –i.

Ending	Example	Meaning
–o	un ann**o**	one year
	due ann**i**	two years
	un ragazz**o**	one boy
	due ragazz**i**	two boys
–a	un ciclist**a**	a (male) cyclist
	due ciclist**i**	two cyclists
	un problem**a**	a problem
	molti problem**i**	lots of problems
–e	un mes**e**	one month
	due mes**i**	two months
	un frances**e**	a Frenchman
	due frances**i**	two Frenchmen

- Change the –a ending of feminine nouns to –e.

una settiman**a**	one week
due settiman**e**	two weeks
una ragazz**a**	one girl
due ragazz**e**	two girls

- Change the –e ending of feminine nouns to –i.

un'ingles**e**	an Englishwoman
due ingles**i**	two Englishwomen
la vit**e**	the vine
le vit**i**	the vines

Nouns you do not change in the plural

- You do not change feminine nouns ending in –à. You show that they are plural by using the plural word for *the*, adjectives in the plural, and so on.

la citt**à**	the city
le citt**à**	the cities
grandi citt**à**	great cities
la loro universit**à**	their university
le loro universit**à**	their universities

⇨ For more information on **Articles** and **Adjectives**, see pages 14 and 24.

- You do not change words ending in a consonant, which are often words borrowed from English and other languages.

il film	the film
i film	the films
il manager	the manager
i manager	the managers
il computer	the computer
i computer	the computers
la jeep	the jeep
le jeep	the jeeps

Nouns with irregular plurals

➤ A small number of common masculine nouns take the ending **–a** in the plural.

il dito	the finger
le dita	the fingers
un uovo	an egg
le uova	the eggs
il lenzuolo	the sheet
le lenzuola	the sheets

i Note that the plural of **uomo** (meaning *man*) is **uomini**. The plural of **la mano** (meaning *hand*) is **le mani**.

➤ All nouns ending in **–ca** and **–ga** add an **h** before the plural ending.

Singular		Plural	
amica	(female) friend	**amiche**	(female) friends
buca	hole	**buche**	holes
riga	line	**righe**	lines
casalinga	housewife	**casalinghe**	housewives

➤ Some nouns ending in **–co** and **–go** also add an **h** before the plural ending.

Singular		Plural	
gioco	game	**giochi**	games
fuoco	fire	**fuochi**	fires
luogo	place	**luoghi**	places
borgo	district	**borghi**	districts

i Note that there are many exceptions: the plurals of **amico** (meaning *friend*) and **psicologo** (meaning *psychologist*) are **amici** and **psicologi**.

⇨ *For more information on **Italian spelling rules**, see page 247.*

Plural or singular?

➤ Bear in mind that some words are <u>plural</u> in Italian but <u>singular</u> in English.

i miei capelli	my hair
gli affari	business
le notizie	the news
consigli	advice
i mobili	the furniture
sciocchezze	nonsense

[i] Note that you use the singular of some of these words to refer to *a piece of* something.

un mobile	a piece of furniture
un consiglio	a piece of advice
una notizia	a piece of news

> *Tip*
> An important word that is <u>singular</u> in Italian but <u>plural</u> in English is **la gente** (meaning *people*). Remember to use a singular verb with **la gente**.
> **È gente molto simpatica.**   They're very nice people.

Grammar Extra!

When nouns are made by combining two words, such as **pescespada** (meaning *swordfish*), **capolavoro** (meaning *masterpiece*), or **apriscatola** (meaning *tin opener*) the plural is often not formed according to the usual rules. You can check by looking in a dictionary.

KEY POINTS

✔ You can make most Italian nouns plural by changing their ending from one vowel to another.
✔ Some nouns are the same in the plural as in the singular.
✔ Some nouns which are singular in English are plural in Italian.

Test yourself

6 **Give the plural form of the noun after the number.**

a 2 .... (mese)

b 2 .... (ragazzo)

c 2 .... (gatto)

d 2 .... (donna)

e 2 .... (francese)

f 2 .... (settimana)

g 2 .... (regola)

h 2 .... (treno)

i 2 .... (mela)

j 2 .... (giorno)

7 **Cross out the noun which the article(s) cannot refer to.**

a	i	film/giorni/luogo/giochi
b	le	righe/ragazze/città/italiani
c	il	manager/ciclisti/problema
d	la	pittore/settimana/ragazza/buca
e	la	rivoluzione/radio/topo/versione
f	il	supermercato/toro/moto/film
g	un	gioco/dita/fuoco/borgo
h	una	jeep/notizia/mobile/macchina
i	il/la	dentista/amiche/turista/collega
j	un/una	cantante/nipote/problemi/giornalista

Test yourself

8 **Write 1 in the gap if the noun is singular, and 2 if it is plural.**

a .... righe

b .... dita

c .... uovo

d .... fuoco

e .... ragazze

f .... problemi

g .... inglese

h .... macchine

i .... colleghi

j .... studentessa

9 **Match the nouns on the left with their translations on the right.**

a i capelli   the news

b i mobili   hair

c un consiglio   the eggs

d le notizie   furniture

e le uova   a piece of advice

Articles

What is an article?

In English, an **article** is one of the words *the*, *a* and *an* which go with nouns:
the sun, *a* happy boy, *an* orange.

Two types of article

➤ There are two types of article: the <u>definite</u> article and the <u>indefinite</u> article.

- The <u>definite</u> article is *the*. You use it to refer to a specified thing or person.
  I'm going to <u>the</u> supermarket.
  That's <u>the</u> woman I was talking to.

- The <u>indefinite</u> article is *a* or *an*. You use it if you are not referring to any particular thing or person.
  Is there <u>a</u> supermarket near here?
  She was talking to <u>a</u> little girl.

The definite article

The basics

➤ There are three questions you need to ask yourself to decide which definite article to use in Italian:

- Is the noun masculine or feminine? (This is known as its <u>gender</u>)

- Is it singular or plural?
  the child   **il bambino** (SINGULAR)
  the children   **i bambini** (PLURAL)

- Does the following word begin with a vowel (*a, e, i, o, u*) or with another letter?

➪ *For more information on **Nouns**, see page 1.*

Which definite article do you use?

➤ The definite article to use for <u>masculine singular nouns</u> is:

- **il** with most nouns starting with a <u>consonant</u>.
  il ragazzo   the boy
  il cellulare   the mobile phone

- **lo** with nouns starting with **z**, or **s** + another <u>consonant</u>, **gn**, **pn**, **ps**, **x** or **y**.
  lo zio   the uncle
  lo studente   the student
  lo pneumatico   the tyre

For further explanation of grammatical terms, please see pages viii-xii.

lo psichiatra	the psychiatrist
lo yogurt	the yoghurt

- **l'** with all nouns starting with a <u>vowel</u>.

l'ospedale	the hospital
l'albergo	the hotel

➤ The definite article to use for <u>masculine plural nouns</u> is:

- **i** with most nouns starting with a <u>consonant</u>.

i fratelli	the brothers
i cellulari	the mobile phones

- **gli** with nouns starting with **z**, **s** + another consonant, **gn**, **pn**, **ps**, **x** or **y**.

gli studenti	the students
gli zii	the uncles
gli gnocchi	the gnocchi
gli pneumatici	the tyres
gli yogurt	the yoghurts

- **gli** with all nouns starting with a <u>vowel</u>.

gli amici	the friends
gli orari	the timetables

➤ The definite article to use for <u>feminine singular nouns</u> is:

- **la** with all nouns starting with a <u>consonant</u>.

la ragazza	the girl
la macchina	the car

- **l'** with all nouns starting with a <u>vowel</u>.

l'amica	the (girl)friend
l'arancia	the orange

➤ The definite article to use for <u>feminine plural nouns</u> is:

- **le** with all nouns, whether they start with a <u>consonant</u> or a <u>vowel</u>.

le ragazze	the girls
le amiche	the (girl)friends

> *Tip*
> When you're learning vocabulary, remember to learn the article that goes with each noun.

🔲 Note that the article you choose depends on the first or first two letters of the following word, which can be an adjective or a noun.

l'amico	the friend
BUT	
il migliore amico	the best friend

lo studente	the student
BUT	
il migliore studente	the best student
gli studenti	the students
BUT	
i migliori studenti	the best students

⇨ *For more information on **Adjectives**, see page 24.*

Combining the definite article with other words

➤ In Italian, when you say *at the cinema, in the cinema*, and so on, the word for *at* and *in* combines with the article. How this works for **a** (meaning *at* or *to*) is shown below:

a + il = al	**al cinema**	at *or* to the cinema
a + l' = all'	**all'albergo**	at *or* to the hotel
a + lo = allo	**allo stadio**	at *or* to the stadium
a + la = alla	**alla stazione**	at *or* to the station
a + i = ai	**ai concerti**	at *or* to the concerts
a + gli = agli	**agli aeroporti**	at *or* to the airports
a + le = alle	**alle partite**	at *or* to the matches

➤ The other words which combine in the same way are: **da**, **di**, **in** and **su**:

- **da** (meaning *from*)

da + il = dal	**dal cinema**	from the cinema
da + l' = dall'	**dall'albergo**	from the hotel
da + lo = dallo	**dallo stadio**	from the stadium
da + la = dalla	**dalla stazione**	from the station
da + i = dai	**dai concerti**	from the concerts
da + gli = dagli	**dagli aeroporti**	from the airports
da + le = dalle	**dalle partite**	from the matches

- **di** (meaning *of*)

di + il = del	**del cinema**	of the cinema
di + l' = dell'	**dell'albergo**	of the hotel
di + lo = dello	**dello stadio**	of the stadium
di + la = della	**della stazione**	of the station
di + i = dei	**dei concerti**	of the concerts
di + gli = degli	**degli aeroporti**	of the airports
di + le = delle	**delle partite**	of the matches

- **in** (meaning *in*)

in + il = nel	**nel cinema**	in the cinema
in + l' = nell'	**nell'albergo**	in the hotel
in + lo = nello	**nello stadio**	in the stadium
in + la = nella	**nella stazione**	in the station
in + i = nei	**nei concerti**	in the concerts
in + gli = negli	**negli aeroporti**	in the airports
in + le = nelle	**nelle partite**	in the matches

For further explanation of grammatical terms, please see pages viii-xii.

- **su** (meaning *on*)

su + il = **sul**	**sul pavimento**	on the floor
su + l' = **sull'**	**sull'orlo**	on the edge
su + lo = **sullo**	**sullo scoglio**	on the rock
su + la = **sulla**	**sulla spiaggia**	on the beach
su + i = **sui**	**sui monti**	on the mountains
su + gli = **sugli**	**sugli scaffali**	on the bookshelves
su + le = **sulle**	**sulle strade**	on the roads

➤ In English, you can use *some* with singular and plural nouns: *some sugar, some students*. One way of expressing the idea of *some* in Italian is to use the word **di** together with the definite article.

del burro	some butter
dell'olio	some oil
della carta	some paper
dei fiammiferi	some matches
delle uova	some eggs
Hanno rotto dei bicchieri.	They broke some glasses.
Ci vuole del sale.	It needs some salt.
Aggiungi della farina.	Add some flour.

When do you use the definite article?

➤ Italian uses the definite article much more than English does. As a rule of thumb, Italian sentences rarely start with a noun that has no article.

I bambini soffrono.	Children are suffering.
Mi piacciono gli animali.	I like animals.
Le cose vanno meglio.	Things are going better.
Il nuoto è il mio sport preferito.	Swimming is my favourite sport.
Non mi piace il riso.	I don't like rice.
Lo zucchero non fa bene.	Sugar isn't good for you.
La povertà è un grande problema.	Poverty is a big problem.
L'Australia è molto grande.	Australia is very big.
La Calabria è bella.	Calabria is beautiful.

ⓘ Note that if the name of a country comes after the Italian word **in**, which means *to* or *in*, the article is **not** used.

Vado in Francia a giugno.	I'm going to France in June.
Lavorano in Germania.	They work in Germany.

> *Tip*
> When you translate an English sentence which starts with a noun, don't forget to use the definite article in Italian.
>
> | **Le macchine costano caro.** | Cars cost a lot. |
> |---|---|
> | **La frutta fa bene.** | Fruit is good for you. |

➤ In the following cases, the article is used rather differently in Italian from in English:

● When you're talking about <u>parts of the body and bodily actions</u>, use the definite article. The English adjectives *my*, *your*, *his* and so on are not translated.

Dammi <u>la</u> mano.	Give me your hand.
Mi fa male <u>il</u> piede.	My foot is hurting.
Soffiati <u>il</u> naso!	Blow your nose!

● Use the definite article when talking about <u>clothes</u>.

Si è tolto <u>il</u> cappotto.	He took off his coat.
Mettiti <u>le</u> scarpe.	Put your shoes on.

● Use the definite article with the <u>time</u>, <u>dates</u> and <u>years</u>.

all'una	at one o'clock
alle due	at two o'clock
Era l'una.	It was one o'clock.
Sono <u>le</u> due.	It's two o'clock.
Sono nata <u>il</u> primo maggio 1990.	I was born on May 1 1990.
Verranno <u>nel</u> 2012.	They're coming in 2012.

● Use the definite article with words such as *my*, *your* and *his*.

<u>la</u> mia casa	my house
<u>le</u> sue figlie	her daughters
<u>i</u> vostri amici	your friends

⇨ *For more information on* **Possessive adjectives**, *see page 45.*

● When you talk about how much something costs <u>per pound</u>, <u>per kilo</u>, and so on; about <u>rates</u>, <u>speeds</u>, and about <u>how often</u> something happens, use the word **a** and the definite article.

Costano 3 euro <u>al</u> chilo.	They cost 3 euros a kilo.
70 km <u>all'</u>ora	70 km an hour
50.000 dollari <u>al</u> mese	50,000 dollars per month
due volte alla settimana	twice a week

● You use the definite article when you are referring to people by using their <u>titles</u>, but NOT when you are speaking to them directly.

<u>La</u> signora Rossi è qui.	Mrs. Rossi is here.
<u>Il</u> dottor Gentile	Doctor Gentile
BUT	
Scusi, signora Rossi.	Excuse me, Mrs. Rossi.

KEY POINTS

✔ Definite articles are used much more in Italian than in English.
✔ Italian sentences rarely start with a noun that has no article.
✔ Sometimes the definite article is used very differently from English. For instance, you use it with parts of the body and the time.

Test yourself

10 **Complete each phrase with the correct form of the definite article.**

a .... ora

b .... bambini

c .... zio

d .... amiche

e .... orari

f .... stazione

g .... luogo

h .... albergo

i .... studenti

j .... macchine

11 **Translate the following into Italian, combining the definite article with another word.**

a in the hotel ....

b to the station ....

c on the floor ....

d from the concert ....

e to the stadiums ....

f on the roads ....

g of the boy ....

h at the cinema ....

i from the airport ....

j on the beach...

Test yourself

12 **Complete each phrase with the Italian word for 'some'.**

    a .... farina

    b .... macchine

    c .... zucchero

    d .... sale

    e .... problemi

    f .... olio

    g .... studenti

    h .... riso

    i .... bambini

    j .... gatte

13 **Complete each sentence with the correct definite article or the combination of the definite article with another word.**

    a Metto .... scarpe.

    b Sono nata .... primo aprile 1991.

    c Le ragazze arrivano.............. una.

    d Mi fa male .... mano.

    e Bisogna soffiare .... naso.

    f Mi metto .... scarpe prima di uscire.

    g Vendono .... loro casa.

    h Invitiamo .... nostri amici alla festa.

    i Usciamo oggi .... tre.

    j Ci vediamo .... 2013.

The indefinite article

The basics

➤ In English the indefinite article is either *a* – *a boy* – or *an* – *an apple*.

➤ In Italian there are four indefinite articles: **un**, **uno**, **una** and **un'**.

➤ Which one you need to choose depends on the gender of the noun it goes with, and the letter the noun starts with.

⇨ *For more information on **Nouns**, see page 1.*

Which indefinite article do you use?

➤ The indefinite article to use for <u>masculine nouns</u> is:

- **un** with nouns starting with <u>most consonants</u> and <u>all vowels</u>.
  un cellulare   a mobile phone
  un uomo   a man

- **uno** with nouns starting with **z**, **s** + <u>another consonant</u>, **z**, **gn**, **pn**, **ps**, **x** and **y**.
  uno studente   a student
  uno zio   an uncle
  uno psichiatra   a psychiatrist

➤ The indefinite article to use for <u>feminine nouns</u> is:

- **una** with nouns starting with a <u>consonant</u>.
  una ragazza   a girl
  una mela   an apple

- **un'** with nouns starting with a <u>vowel</u>.
  un'ora   an hour
  un'amica   a (girl)friend

  ⓘ Note that the article you choose depends on the first or first two letters of the following word, which can be an adjective or a noun.

  <u>un</u> **albergo**   a hotel
  BUT
  <u>uno</u> **splendido albergo**   a magnificent hotel
  <u>uno</u> **scultore**   a sculptor
  BUT
  <u>un</u> **bravo scultore**   a good sculptor

Using the indefinite article

➤ You generally use the indefinite article in Italian when *a* or *an* are used in English.
  Era con un'amica.   She was with a friend.
  Vuoi un gelato?   Do you want an ice cream?

➤ There are some cases where the article is used in English, but <u>not</u> in Italian:

- with the words **cento** and **mille**
  cento volte   a hundred times
  mille sterline   a thousand pounds

- when you translate *a few* or *a lot*
  qualche parola   a few words
  molti soldi   a lot of money

- in exclamations with **che**
  Che sorpresa!   What a surprise!
  Che peccato!   What a pity!

🛈 Note that to say what someone's job is you either leave out the article:

  È medico.   He's a doctor.
  Sono professori.   They're teachers.

Or you use the verb **fare** with the <u>definite</u> article:
  Faccio l'ingegnere.   I'm an engineer.
  Fa l'avvocato.   She's a lawyer.

Plural nouns used without the article

➤ There are some cases where you use plural nouns without any article:

- in negative sentences
  Non ha amici.   He hasn't got any friends.
  Non ci sono posti liberi.   There aren't any empty seats.

- in questions where *any* is used in English
  Hai fratelli?   Have you got any brothers or sisters?
  Ci sono problemi?   Are there any problems?

⇨ *For more information on **Negatives** and **Questions**, see pages 98 and 203.*

- in lists
  Ci vogliono patate, cipolle e carote.   You need potatoes, onions and carrots.
  Vendono giornali, riviste e cartoline.   They sell newspapers, magazines and
                                                 postcards.

- when you are not giving details
  Abbiamo visitato castelli e musei.   We visited castles and museums.
  Ci sono cose da vedere.   There are things to see.
  Hanno problemi.   They've got problems.

> **KEY POINTS**
> ✔ You generally use the indefinite article in a very similar way to English.
> ✔ You do not use it with the numbers **cento** and **mille**, and in exclamations
>   with **che**.
> ✔ The indefinite article is not used when saying what someone's job is.

Test yourself

14 **Complete each of the following with the correct form of the indefinite article.**

   a .... zia

   b .... scultore

   c .... ragazzo

   d .... ora

   e .... uomo

   f .... supermercato

   g .... pneumatico

   h .... radio

   i .... amica

   j .... lenzuolo

15 **Match the questions on the left with their answers on the right.**

   a **Che lavoro fa tuo fratello?**   Non ho soldi.

   b **Hai fratelli?**   No, è medico.

   c **Perché non vieni al cinema?**   Costa mille sterline.

   d **Quanto costa il divano?**   Fa l'avvocato.

   e **Tuo padre è professore?**   Ho un fratello e una sorella.

16 **Translate the following sentences into Italian.**

   a I don't have a car. ....

   b Is there any bread? ....

   c He is an engineer. ....

   d She doesn't have a computer. ....

   e They sell ice cream, eggs and fruit. ....

   f What a surprise! ....

   g My brother has a lot of money. ....

   h How lovely! ....

   i There are one hundred children in the school. ....

   j There are no empty seats. ....

Adjectives

What is an adjective?
An **adjective** is a 'describing' word that tells you more about a person or thing,
for example, *blue*, *big*, *good*.

Using adjectives

➤ You use adjectives like *nice*, *expensive* and *good* to say something about nouns (living beings,
things or ideas). You can also use them with words such as *you*, *he* and *they*. You can use
them immediately in front of a noun, or after verbs like *be*, *look* and *feel*.

    a <u>nice</u> girl
    an <u>expensive</u> coat
    a <u>good</u> idea
    He's <u>nice</u>.
    They look <u>expensive</u>.

   ⇨ *For more information on* **Nouns**, *see page* 1.

➤ In English, adjectives don't change according to the noun they go with.
    a nice boy
    nice girls

➤ In Italian you have to ask:

   ● Is the noun masculine or feminine?

   ● Is it singular or plural?

➤ You then choose the adjective ending accordingly. This is called making the adjective agree.

un ragazzo <u>alto</u>	a tall boy
una ragazza <u>alta</u>	a tall girl
ragazzi <u>alti</u>	tall boys
ragazze <u>alte</u>	tall girls

➤ In English, you put adjectives <u>IN FRONT OF</u> the noun you're describing, but in Italian,
you usually put them <u>AFTER</u> it.
    una casa <u>bianca</u>   a <u>white</u> house

   ⇨ *For more information on* **Word order with adjectives**, *see page* 30.

How to make adjectives agree

The basics

➤ When you look up an adjective in a dictionary you find the <u>masculine singular</u> form.

➤ If you want to use an adjective to describe a feminine noun you <u>often</u> have to change the ending.

➤ If you want to use an adjective to describe a plural noun you <u>nearly always</u> have to change the ending.

How to make adjectives feminine

➤ If the masculine adjective ends in **–o**, change **–o** to **–a**.

un ragazzo <u>simpatico</u>	a nice boy
una ragazza <u>simpatica</u>	a nice girl
un film <u>italiano</u>	an Italian film
una squadra <u>italiana</u>	an Italian team

➤ You don't change the ending for the feminine:

- if the masculine adjective ends in **–e**

un libro <u>inglese</u>	an English book
una famiglia <u>inglese</u>	an English family
un treno <u>veloce</u>	a fast train
una macchina <u>veloce</u>	a fast car

ⓘ Note that adjectives such as **italiano**, **inglese**, **francese** do not start with a capital letter in Italian.

- in the case of some colours

un calzino <u>rosa</u>	a pink sock
una maglietta <u>rosa</u>	a pink T-shirt
un tappeto <u>blu</u>	a blue rug
una macchina <u>blu</u>	a blue car
un vestito <u>beige</u>	a beige suit
una gonna <u>beige</u>	a beige skirt

ⓘ Note that these adjectives don't change in the plural either.

- if the adjective ends with a consonant

un gruppo <u>pop</u>	a pop group
la musica <u>pop</u>	pop music
un tipo <u>snob</u>	a posh guy
una persona <u>snob</u>	a posh person

ⓘ Note that these adjectives don't change in the plural either.

> *Tip*
> If you are female, make sure you always use a feminine adjective when talking about yourself:
> **Sono stanca.**   I'm tired.
> **Sono pronta.**   I'm ready.

How to make adjectives plural

➤ If the masculine singular adjective ends in **–o**, change **–o** to **–i**.

un fiore <u>rosso</u>	a red flower
dei fiori <u>rossi</u>	red flowers
un computer <u>nuovo</u>	a new computer
dei computer <u>nuovi</u>	new computers

➤ If the feminine singular adjective ends in **–a**, change **–a** to **–e**.

una strada <u>pericolosa</u>	a dangerous road
delle strade <u>pericolose</u>	dangerous roads
una gonna <u>nera</u>	a black skirt
delle gonne <u>nere</u>	black skirts

➤ If the adjective ends in **–e**, change **–e** to **–i** for both masculine and feminine plural.

un esercizio <u>difficile</u>	a difficult exercise
degli esercizi <u>difficili</u>	difficult exercises
un sito <u>interessante</u>	an interesting site
dei siti <u>interessanti</u>	interesting sites
una storia <u>triste</u>	a sad story
delle storie <u>tristi</u>	sad stories
una valigia <u>pesante</u>	a heavy case
delle valigie <u>pesanti</u>	heavy cases

➤ Some adjectives do not change in the plural.

un paio di guanti <u>rosa</u>	a pair of pink gloves
delle tende <u>blu</u>	blue curtains
dei gruppi <u>pop</u>	pop groups

➤ Adjectives that do not change for the feminine or plural are called <u>invariable</u>, which is abbreviated to *inv* in some dictionaries.

> *Tip*
> Remember that **spaghetti**, **ravioli**, **lasagne** and so on are plural nouns in Italian, so you must use plural adjectives with them.
> **Sono buoni gli spaghetti?**   Is the spaghetti nice?
> **Le lasagne sono finite.**   The lasagne is all gone.

> ⓘ Note that when you're describing a couple consisting of a man and a woman or a group of people, use a masculine plural adjective unless the group consists entirely of females.

Paolo e Loredana sono pront<u>i</u>.	Paolo and Loredana are ready.
I bambini sono stanch<u>i</u>.	The children are tired.
Le ragazze sono stanch<u>e</u>.	The girls are tired.

For further explanation of grammatical terms, please see pages viii–xii.

Irregular adjectives

➤ There are three very common adjectives which are different from other adjectives – **bello**, **buono** and **grande**.

➤ When the adjective **bello** (meaning *beautiful*) is used in front of a masculine noun it has different forms depending on which letter follows it, just like the definite article.

bello	Masculine Singular	Feminine Singular	Masculine Plural	Feminine Plural
used before a noun	bel	bella	bei	belle
used after a verb or a noun	bello	bella	belli	belle

bel tempo	beautiful weather
bei nomi	beautiful names
Il tempo era bello.	The weather was beautiful.
I fiori sono belli.	The flowers are beautiful.

➤ **bell'** is used before vowels in the masculine and feminine singular forms.
un bell'albero   a beautiful tree

➤ **bello** is used in front of **z** and **s** + another consonant in the masculine singular form.
un bello strumento   a beautiful instrument

➤ **begli** is used in front of vowels, **z** and **s** + another consonant in the masculine plural form.
begli alberi   beautiful trees
begli strument   beautiful instruments

➤ The adjective **buono** (meaning *good*) is usually shortened to **buon** when it comes before a masculine singular noun.
Buon viaggio!   Have a good journey!
un buon uomo   a good man

➤ The shortened form of **buono** is <u>not</u> used in front of nouns that start with **z** or **s** + another consonant.
un buono studente   a good student

➤ The adjective **grande** (meaning *big, large* or *great*) is often shortened to **gran** when it comes before a singular noun starting with a consonant.
la Gran Bretagna   Great Britain
un gran numero di macchine   a large number of cars

KEY POINTS

✔ In Italian, adjectives agree with the person or thing they are describing.
✔ Adjectives ending in **–o** in the masculine have different endings in the feminine and plural forms.
✔ Some adjectives don't have a different feminine or plural form.

Test yourself

17 **Replace the highlighted words with the correct form of the adjective. Note that in some cases the adjective is already correct.**

a una famiglia **italiano** ....

b un ragazzo **simpatico** ....

c delle macchine **bianco** ....

d una gonna **blu** ....

e dei treni **veloce** ....

f un film **francese** ....

g una sciarpa **nero** ....

h dei libri **interessante** ....

i un gruppo **pop** ....

j delle ragazze **alto** ....

18 **Give the plural form of the noun and its adjective after the number.**

a 2 .... (strada pericolosa)

b 2 .... (sito interessante)

c 2 .... (computer nuovo)

d 2 .... (ragazzo alto)

e 2 .... (maglietta rosa)

f 2 .... (fiore rosso)

g 2 .... (macchina veloce)

h 2 .... (persona snob)

i 2 .... (scrittore italiano)

j 2 .... (casa nuova)

PRACTICE PRACTICE PRACTICE PRACTICE PRACTICE PRACTICE

Test yourself

19 **Translate the following phrases into Italian.**

a beautiful flowers...

b a great painter ....

c a good man ....

d a beautiful tree ....

e have a good journey! ....

f a beautiful woman...

g a good instrument ....

h a beautiful dress..

i good students ....

j a big tower ....

Where do you put the adjective?

➤ You put most adjectives <u>AFTER</u> the noun.

un gesto <u>spontaneo</u>	a spontaneous gesture
una partita <u>importante</u>	an important match
capelli <u>biondi</u>	blonde hair

> ⓘ Note that if you have two adjectives you link them with **e** (meaning *and*).

ragazze <u>antipatiche</u> e <u>maleducate</u>   nasty rude girls

➤ The meaning of some adjectives changes depending on whether they come after or before the noun.

gente *povera*	poor people BUT
***Povera* Anna!**	Poor (meaning *unfortunate*) Anna!
un uomo grande	a big man BUT
una grande sorpresa	a great surprise
una macchina nuova	a new car BUT
la sua nuova ragazza	his new (meaning *latest*) girlfriend
una casa vecchia	an old house BUT
un mio vecchio amico	an old (meaning *long-standing*) friend of mine
una borsa cara	an expensive handbag BUT
un caro amico	a dear friend

> ⓘ Note that if you add **molto** (meaning *very*) to an adjective, the adjective always goes after the noun.

una bella casa	a nice house
una casa molto bella	a very nice house

➤ Some types of adjectives always go in front of the noun:

- adjectives that are used to point things out, such as **questo** (meaning *this*) and **quello** (meaning *that*)

<u>Questo</u> cellulare è di mio fratello.	This mobile phone is my brother's.
<u>Quello</u> studente è un mio amico.	That student is a friend of mine.

⇨ *For more information on **Demonstrative adjectives**, see page 38.*

- possessive adjectives such as **mio** (meaning *my*), **tuo** (meaning *your*) and **suo** (meaning *his* or *her*)

<u>mio</u> padre	my father
<u>tuo</u> fratello	your brother
<u>suo</u> marito	her husband

- **ogni** (meaning *each*, *every*), **qualche** (meaning *some*) and **nessuno** (meaning *no*)

<u>ogni</u> giorno	every day
<u>qualche</u> volta	sometimes
Non c'è <u>nessun</u> bisogno di andare.	There's no need to go.

⇨ *For more information on **Indefinite adjectives**, see page 50.*

- question words
  Quali programmi hai?   What plans have you got?
  Quanto pane hai comprato?   How much bread did you buy?

➪ *For more information on **Questions**, see page 203.*

KEY POINTS

✔ Most Italian adjectives go after the noun.
✔ The meaning of some adjectives changes depending on whether they come before or after the noun.

Test yourself

20 **Translate the following phrases into Italian.**

a Poor Maria! ....

b an expensive car...

c poor children ....

d her new job ....

e this boy ....

f a very nice city ....

g a nice handbag ....

h my brother ....

i blonde hair ....

j that student ....

21 **Cross out the adjectives that do not go with the noun.**

a	**un libro**	inglese/buono/interessanti/triste
b	**gli spaghetti**	buoni/caldi/pronta/finiti
c	**la ragazza**	bella/alta/tristi/francese
d	**una macchina**	nera/rosa/blu/bianco
e	**un uomo**	intelligente/interessante/bei/alto
f	**delle storie**	tristi/buona/lunghe/nuove
g	**delle valigie**	pesanti/nere/bianchi/grandi
h	**degli amici**	buoni/cari/vecchie/intelligenti
i	**un albergo**	nuovo/vecchio/buona/grande
j	**un film**	italiano/bello/lungo/inglesi

22 **Match the noun on the left with an appropriate adjective on the right.**

a	**delle storie**	italiane
b	**i ragazzi**	interessanti
c	**una casa**	alti
d	**le città**	molto bravo
e	**un bambino**	molto bella

Comparing people or things

Comparative adjectives

What is a comparative adjective?

In English, a **comparative adjective** is one with *–er* on the end, or *more* or *less* in front of it, for example, *faster, more important, less interesting*. These adjectives are used when you are comparing people or things.

How to make a comparative adjective in Italian

➤ To say that something is *faster, bigger, more important* and so on use **più** in front

una macchina <u>più</u> grande	a bigger car
un film <u>più</u> interessante	a more interesting film
Queste scarpe sono <u>più</u> comode.	These shoes are more comfortable.

➤ To say that something is *less expensive, less interesting* and so on use **meno** in front of the adjective.

un computer <u>meno</u> caro	a less expensive computer
un viaggio <u>meno</u> faticoso	a less tiring journey

How to compare one person or thing with another

➤ Put either **più** or **meno** in front of the adjective and use **di** to translate *than*.

Sono <u>più</u> alto <u>di</u> te.	I'm taller than you.
Milano è <u>più</u> grande <u>di</u> Genova.	Milan is bigger than Genoa.
Carlo è <u>più</u> ambizioso <u>di</u> Luca.	Carlo is more ambitious than Luca.
Il verde è <u>meno</u> caro <u>del</u> nero.	The green one is less expensive than the black one.
La mia borsa è <u>meno</u> pesante <u>della</u> tua.	My bag is less heavy than yours.

[i] Note that **di** combines with the article to make one word: **di + il = del**, **di + la = della**, and so on.

⇨ *For more information on **di**, see **Prepositions** page 228.*

Superlative adjectives

What is a superlative adjective?

In English, a superlative adjective is one with *–est* on the end, or *most* or *least* in front of it, for example, *fastest, most important, least interesting*. The definite article is used with superlative adjectives: *the fastest, the most important, the least interesting*.

How to make a superlative adjective in Italian

➤ Making a superlative adjective is very easy: you simply put a <u>definite article</u> in front of the comparative adjective.

il più alto	the tallest
il meno interessante	the least interesting

➤ The definite article <u>must</u> agree with the person or thing you're describing.

Matteo è <u>il</u> più alto.	Matteo is the tallest.
Lidia è <u>la</u> più alta.	Lidia is the tallest.
Queste scarpe sono <u>le</u> più comode.	These shoes are the most comfortable.
Gianni è <u>il</u> meno ambizioso.	Gianni is the least ambitious.

➤ If there is a definite article in front of the noun, <u>do not</u> put a second definite article in front of **più** or **meno**.

il ragazzo più alto	the tallest boy
la banca più vicina	the nearest bank
lo studente più intelligente	the most intelligent student
i voli più economici	the cheapest flights
i suoi film meno interessanti	his least interesting films

⇨ *For more information on the **Definite article**, see page 14.*

Tip

In phrases like the *most famous in the world*, and *the biggest in Italy*, use **di** to translate *in*.

lo stadio più grande d'Italia	the biggest stadium in Italy
il ristorante più caro della città	the most expensive restaurant in the town

---

Irregular comparatives and superlatives

➤ In English, the comparatives of *good* and *bad* are irregular: *better, best, worse* and *worst*. In Italian, there are regular forms of **buono** and **cattivo**.

Questo è più buono.	This one's better.
I rossi sono i più buoni.	The red ones are the best.
Quello è ancora più cattivo.	That one's even worse.

➤ There are also irregular forms of **buono** and **cattivo**, as there are of **grande**, **piccolo**, **alto** and **basso**:

Adjective	Meaning	Comparative	Meaning	Superlative	Meaning
buono	good	**migliore**	better	**il migliore**	the best
cattivo	bad	**peggiore**	worse	**il peggiore**	the worst
grande	big	**maggiore**	bigger/older	**il maggiore**	the biggest/ oldest
piccolo	small	**minore**	smaller/ younger	**il minore**	the smallest/ youngest
alto	high	**superiore**	higher	**il superiore**	the highest
basso	low	**inferiore**	lower	**l'inferiore**	the lowest

ⓘ Note that these irregular comparatives and superlatives are adjectives ending in **–e**, so their plural ending is **–i**.

il modo <u>migliore</u>	the best way
il mio fratello <u>minore</u>	my younger brother
le mie sorelle <u>maggiori</u>	my older sisters
il labbro <u>inferiore</u>	the lower lip
Il libro è <u>migliore</u> del film.	The book is better than the film.
Giorgia è <u>la peggiore</u> della classe.	Giorgia is the worst in the class.

<u>as ... as ...</u>

➤ Sometimes you want to say that people or things are similar or the same:

I'm <u>as</u> tall <u>as</u> you.

➤ In Italian you use **come** or **quanto** to make this kind of comparison.

Pietro è alto <u>come</u> Michele.	Pietro is as tall as Michele.
La mia macchina è grande <u>come</u> la tua.	My car is as big as yours.
Sono stanca <u>quanto</u> te.	I'm just as tired as you are.

➤ You can make these sentences negative by adding **non**.

| Pietro <u>non</u> è alto come Michele. | Pietro is not as tall as Michele. |
| <u>Non</u> sono stanca quanto te. | I'm not as tired as you are. |

Grammar Extra!

In English, you emphasize adjectives by adding words like *very*, *really* or *terribly*.
You do the same in Italian, using **molto**, **veramente** and **terribilmente**.

Lui è molto ricco.	He's very rich.
I fiori sono veramente belli.	The flowers are really lovely.
Sono terribilmente stanca.	I'm terribly tired.

➤ Another way of adding emphasis to Italian adjectives is to replace the **–o** or **–e** ending with **–issimo**.

bello	beautiful
bellissimo	very beautiful
elegante	smart
elegantissimo	very smart

ⓘ Note that these **-issimo** adjectives change their endings for the feminine and the plural.

Il tempo era bellissimo.	The weather was really beautiful.
Anna è sempre elegantissima.	Anna is always terribly smart.
Sono educatissimi.	They're extremely polite.

KEY POINTS

✔ You make comparative adjectives in Italian by using **più** and **meno**, and translate *than* by **di**.
✔ You add the definite article to the comparative adjective to make a superlative adjective.

Test yourself

23 Build a sentence by making comparisons, using *è* (= is) and *più ... di*, *meno ... di* or *come*, depending on whether you see +, - or =. The first one has been done for you.

a Carlo/Luca/alto/+ .....*Carlo è più alto di Luca.*...

b Luca/Carlo/alto/- ....

c Roma/Siena/grande/+ ....

d Maria/Paola/intelligente/= ....

e Il nero/il verde/bello/+ ....

f Giovanni/suo fratello/ambizioso/- ....

g Il negozio/il ristorante/vicino/= ....

h L'aereo/il treno/economico/- ....

i Lucia/Silvia/simpatica/+ ....

j Silvia/Lucia/simpatica/- ....

24 Fill in the gap in the sentence with the translation of the superlative given in brackets.

a Quella torre è .... della regione. (the highest)

b Questo ristorante è .... della città. (the most expensive)

c Questo studente è .... della classe. (the most intelligent)

d Questa storia è .... del libro. (the most interesting)

e Queste scarpe sono .... (the least comfortable)

f I blu sono .... (the best)

g Ho preso il volo .... (the cheapest)

h Quello è .... (the worst)

i Francesca è .... delle sorelle. (the tallest)

j Paolo è .... dei suoi fratelli. (the least ambitious)

Test yourself

25 **Replace the highlighted words with superlative adjectives ending in –issimo/a/i/e.**

a L'albero è **bello**. ....

b I bambini sono **educati** ....

c Sono **care** amiche. ....

d Luigi è **stanco**. ....

e Mia sorella è **elegante**. ....

f La torre è **alta**. ....

g La mia casa è **grande**. ....

h Il viaggio era **lungo**. ....

i La pasta a pranzo era **buona**. ....

j Le sue mani sono **piccole**. ....

Demonstrative adjectives

What is a demonstrative adjective?
A **demonstrative adjective** is used to point out a particular thing or person. There are four demonstrative adjectives in English: *this, these, that* and *those*.

Using demonstrative adjectives

➤ As in English, Italian demonstrative adjectives go <u>BEFORE</u> the noun. Like other adjectives in Italian, they have to change for the feminine and plural forms.

➤ To say *this*, use **questo**, which has four forms, like any other adjective ending in **–o**.

	Masculine	**Feminine**	**Meaning**
Singular	**questo**	**questa**	this
Plural	**questi**	**queste**	these

Questa gonna è troppo stretta.	This skirt is too tight.
Questi pantaloni mi piacciono.	I like these trousers.
Queste scarpe sono comode.	These shoes are comfortable.

➤ To say *that*, use **quello**, which has several different forms, like the definite article:
- use **quel** with a masculine noun starting with a consonant
  quel ragazzo   that boy

- use **quello** with a masculine noun starting with **z** or **s** + another consonant
  quello zaino   that rucksack
  quello studente   that student

- use **quell'** with nouns starting with a vowel
  quell'*albero*   that tree
  quell'amica   that friend

- use **quella** with a feminine noun starting with a consonant
  quella ragazza   that girl

- use **quei** with a masculine plural noun starting with a consonant
  quei cani   those dogs

- use **quegli** with a masculine plural noun starting with a vowel, with **z** or with **s** + another consonant
  quegli *uomini*   those men
  quegli studenti   those students

- use **quelle** before all <u>feminine plural nouns</u>
  quelle macchine   those cars

> *Tip*
> When you want to say *this one*, don't translate *one*. Use **questo** if what you're referring to is masculine, and **questa** if it's feminine. The same goes when you want to say *that one*: use **quello** or **quella**.
>
> | | |
> |---|---|
> | **Quale casa? – Questa.** | Which house? – This one. |
> | **Quale zaino? – Quello.** | Which rucksack? – That one. |

KEY POINTS

✔ Use **questo** or **questa** for *this*, and **questi** or **queste** for *these*.

✔ Use **quello** for *that*: **quello** behaves like the definite article, **il**.

Test yourself

26 In each of the sentences below, replace the article with the demonstrative adjective *questo* or its feminine or plural forms. The first one has been done for you.

a Il treno è per Milano. ...... *questo* ....

b Non mi piace **la** borsa. ....

c **Gli** alberi sono magnifici. ....

d Voglio comprare **le** scarpe. ....

e **La** valigia è troppo pesante. ....

f Bisogna lavare **i** piatti. ....

g Ci vuole molto tempo per leggere **il** libro. ....

h Ho comprato **la** macchina. ....

i **Gli** studenti sono intelligenti. ....

j Mi piacerebbe visitare **le** città. ....

27 Translate the following into Italian, using the appropriate form of *quello*.

a Those boys are intelligent. ....

b That garden is beautiful. ....

c That tree is big. ....

d Those women are English. ....

e I like that skirt. ....

f Those cars are old. ....

g That rucksack is heavy. ....

h Those students are rude. ....

i That girl is very nice. ....

j Those trousers are expensive. ....

Test yourself

28 **Fill the gap with the correct form of the demonstrative adjective. Note that in some cases, more than one solution may be possible.**

a .... casa è più grande di questa.

b .... libri sono più interessanti di quelli.

c .... scarpe sono più comode delle tue.

d .... studenti sono più bravi di questi.

e .... gonna è più stretta di quella.

f Da dove viene .... ragazzo?

g È in vendita .... casa?

h Quanto costano .... scarpe in vetrina?

i Mia sorella viene a trovarmi .... settimana.

j Mi piacciono .... pantaloni.

Interrogative adjectives

What is an interrogative adjective?
An **interrogative adjective** is a question word such as *which, what* or *how much* that is used when asking about a noun, for example, *Which colour?; What size?; How much sugar?*

➤ In Italian the interrogative adjectives are **che**, **quale** and **quanto**.

➤ **che** and **quale** are used to ask *which* or *what*:

- Use **che** or **quale** with <u>singular nouns</u>.

Che giorno è oggi?	What day is it today?
A che ora ti alzi?	What time do you get up at?
Quale tipo vuoi?	What kind do you want?
Per quale squadra tifi?	Which team do you support?

- Use **che** or **quali** with <u>plural nouns</u>.

Che gusti preferisci?	Which flavours do you like best?
Quali programmi hai?	What plans have you got?

- Use **quanto** with <u>masculine nouns</u> and **quanta** with <u>feminine nouns</u> to ask *how much.*

Quanto pane hai comprato?	How much bread did you buy?
Quanta minestra vuoi?	How much soup do you want?

- Use **quanti** with <u>masculine nouns</u> and **quante** with <u>feminine nouns</u> to ask *how many.*

Quanti bicchieri ci sono?	How many glasses are there?
Quante uova vuoi?	How many eggs do you want?

⇨ *For more information on **Questions**, see page 203.*

KEY POINTS
✔ Use **che** with any noun to mean *which* or *what*.
✔ **quale** has the plural form **quali**.
✔ **quanto** has feminine and plural forms.

Test yourself

29 **Match the question on the left with its answer on the right.**

a	Che giorno è oggi?	Ce ne sono quattro.
b	Quante mele ci sono?	È mercoledì.
c	Quale gusto preferisci?	Alle otto.
d	A che ora si alza la mattina?	Due, per favore.
e	Quanti biscotti vuoi?	Il cioccolato.

30 **Translate the following questions into Italian using the *tu* form of the verb to translate 'you' where appropriate.**

a Which dress do you prefer?

....

b What time do we have to leave at?

....

c How much pasta do you want?

....

d How many cars are there?

....

e Which flights are the cheapest?

....

f Which film did you see?

....

g What plans do they have?

....

h How much sugar does it need?

....

i How many trees do you see?

....

j Which students are the most polite?

....

Adjectives used in exclamations

➤ In Italian **che...!** is often used with a noun where we would say *What a ...!* in English.

Che peccato!	What a pity!
Che disordine!	What a mess!
Che bella giornata!	What a lovely day!
Che brutto tempo!	What awful weather!

➤ **che** can also be used with an adjective when you're commenting on somebody or something.

Che carino!	Isn't he sweet!
Che brutti!	They're horrible!

➤ You can also use an Italian adjective by itself when you are commenting on someone's behaviour.

Furbo!	Cunning devil!
Brava!	Good girl!
Bravi!	Well done!

➤ As in English, you can use an Italian adjective alone when you are commenting on something you see or taste.

Bello!	Lovely!
Buono!	Nice!

> *Tip*
> Remember to make the adjective agree with the person or thing you're commenting on.

➤ You can use **quanto**, **quanta**, **quanti** and **quante** when you are exclaiming about a large amount or number.

Quanto tempo sprecato!	What a waste of time!
Quanta gente!	What a lot of people!
Quanti soldi!	What a lot of money!
Quante storie!	What a fuss!

Possessive adjectives

> ## What is a possessive adjective?
> In English a **possessive adjective** is a word such as *my*, *your*, *his* that is used with a noun to show who it belongs to.

How to use possessive adjectives

The basics

➤ Unlike English you usually put the <u>definite</u> article (**il**, **la**, **i**, **le**) in front of the possessive adjective.

➤ As with all adjectives ending in **–o**, change the ending to:

- **–a** for the feminine singular

- **–i** for the masculine plural

- **–e** for the feminine plural

il mio indirizzo	my address
la mia scuola	my school
i miei amici	my friends
le mie speranze	my hopes

⇨ *For more information on the **Definite article**, see page 14.*

➤ You can also use the <u>indefinite article</u> in front of the possessive adjective in examples like:

una mia amica	a friend of mine
un suo studente	one of her students

➤ You usually put possessive adjectives in front of the noun they describe.

➤ The following table shows all the possessive adjectives:

Singular Masculine	Feminine	Plural Masculine	Feminine	Meaning
il mio	**la mia**	**i miei**	**le mie**	my
il tuo	**la tua**	**i tuoi**	**le tue**	your (belonging to someone you call **tu**)
il suo	**la sua**	**i suoi**	**le sue**	his; her; its; your (belonging to someone you call **lei**)
il nostro	**la nostra**	**i nostri**	**le nostre**	our
il vostro	**la vostra**	**i vostri**	**le vostre**	your (belonging to people you call **voi**)
il loro	**la loro**	**i loro**	**le loro**	their

⇨ *For more information on **How to say 'you' in Italian**, see page 55.*

Dove sono <u>le mie</u> chiavi?	Where are my keys?
Luca ha perso <u>il suo</u> portafoglio.	Luca has lost his wallet.
Ecco <u>i nostri</u> passaporti.	Here are our passports.
Qual è <u>la vostra</u> camera?	Which is your room?
<u>Il tuo</u> amico ti aspetta.	Your friend is waiting for you.

> *Tip*
> Possessive adjectives agree with the noun they go with, <u>NOT</u> with the person who is the owner.
>
> | | |
> |---|---|
> | **Anna ha perso <u>il suo</u> cellulare.** | Anna has lost her mobile phone. |
> | **Marco ha trovato <u>la sua</u> agenda.** | Marco's found his diary. |
> | **Le ragazze hanno <u>i loro</u> biglietti.** | The girls have got their tickets. |

ⓘ Note that possessive adjectives aren't normally used with parts of the body. You usually use **il**, **la**, and so on (the <u>definite article</u>) instead.

Mi sono fatto male all<u>a</u> gamba.	I've hurt my leg.
Si sta lavando <u>i</u> capelli.	She's washing her hair.

⇨ *For more information on the **Definite article**, see page 14.*

> **KEY POINTS**
> ✔ Italian possessive adjectives agree with the nouns they describe.
> ✔ Italian possessive adjectives are usually preceded by an article.
> ✔ Possessive adjectives are not usually used with parts of the body.

Test yourself

31 **Translate the following phrases into Italian.**

a my shoes ....

b his suitcase ....

c their car ....

d your school (*plural*) ....

e my wallet ....

f her address ....

g their tickets ....

h his room ....

i her friends ....

j your keys (*familiar*) ....

32 **Fill the gap with the correct adjective.**

a il mio nome e .... indirizzo

b il suo gatto e .... cane

c la tua famiglia e .... amici

d i miei guanti e .... mani

e la nostra casa e .... giardino

f le loro valigie e .... passaporti

g la vostra camera e .... chiavi

h .... nomi e i nostri indirizzi

i le tue scarpe e .... piedi

j .... giacca e il mio cappello

How to use possessive adjectives when talking about relatives

➤ To say *my mother, your father, her husband, his wife* and so on, use the possessive adjective <u>without</u> the definite article.

mia madre	my mother
tuo padre	your father
suo marito	her husband
sua moglie	his wife
mia sorella	my sister
tuo fratello	your brother

➤ This applies to all family members in the <u>singular</u>, except for the words **mamma** (meaning *mum*) and **babbo** and **papà** (both meaning *dad*).

la mia mamma	my mum
Maria e il suo babbo	Maria and her dad

> ⓘ Note that if you describe a family member with an adjective, for example *my <u>dear</u> wife, her <u>younger</u> sister*, you DO use the definite article with the possessive.

il mio caro marito	my dear husband
il suo fratello maggiore	his older brother

➤ You DO use the definite article with the possessive adjective when you're referring to family members in the <u>plural</u>.

Sandro e i suoi fratelli	Sandro and his brothers
Laura e le sue cognate	Laura and her sisters-in-law

KEY POINTS

✔ Use the possessive adjective without the definite article when talking about family members in the singular.

✔ Use the possessive adjective with the definite article when talking about family members in the plural.

Test yourself

33 **Complete the following sentences with the correct form of the possessive adjective.**

a Hai visto .... fratello? **(her)**

b Arrivano .... figli. **(my)**

c .... mamma è al telefono. **(his)**

d Giovanni è .... cugino. **(our)**

e .... sorella maggiore si chiama Grazia. **(her)**

f .... marito è dentista. **(my)**

g .... genitori sono in vacanza. **(their)**

h Vado al cinema con .... cognata. **(your)**

i Paolo gioca a tennis con .... babbo. **(his)**

j .... padre ha comprato una macchina nuova. **(our)**

34 **Cross out the nouns which the possessive adjective could not refer to.**

a il tuo   cappello/padre/computer/cellulare

b suo   padre/cugino/fratello maggiore/cognato

c i tuoi   pantaloni/genitori/guanti/mani

d la mia   borsa/madre/valigia/amica

e vostro   fratello/cugino/cognato/amico

f i nostri   libri/cugini/sorelle/fratelli

g la sua   indirizzo/borsa/gonna/mamma

h tua   sorella/madre/gonna/moglie

i i loro   biglietti/famiglia/amici/passaporti

j mio   portafoglio/padre/cognato/fratello

Indefinite adjectives

> ## What is an indefinite adjective?
> An **indefinite adjective** is one of a small group of adjectives used to give an idea
> of amounts and numbers, for example, *several*, *all*, *every*.

➤ The indefinite adjectives **ogni** (meaning *each*), **qualche** (meaning *some*) and **qualsiasi**
(meaning *any*) are <u>invariable</u>, that is they do not change their form for the feminine or
plural.

ogni giorno	every day
ogni volta	every time
fra qualche mese	in a few months
qualche volta	sometimes
in qualsiasi momento	at any time
qualsiasi cosa	anything

➤ The following indefinite adjectives end in **–o**, and change their endings in the normal way.

altro	other
tutto	all
molto	much
parecchio	a lot of
poco	a little
tanto	so much
troppo	too much

➤ Put the indefinite or definite article <u>IN FRONT OF</u> **altro**.

un altro giorno	another day
un'altra volta	another time
gli altri studenti	the other students

➤ Put the definite article <u>AFTER</u> **tutto**, even when there is no article in English.

tutta la giornata	all day
tutte le ragazze	all the girls

➤ Use **molto** (masculine) and **molta** (feminine) to talk about large amounts.

Non abbiamo molto tempo.	We haven't much time.
C'è molta roba.	There's a lot of stuff.

➤ Use **molti** (masculine plural) and **molte** (feminine plural) to talk about large numbers.

Abbiamo molti problemi.	We've got a lot of problems.
L'ho fatto molte volte.	I've done it many times.

➤ You can also use **parecchio** and **parecchia** to talk about quite large amounts, and **parecchi**
and **parecchie** to talk about quite large numbers.

Non lo vedo da parecchio tempo.	I haven't seen him for quite some time.
C'era parecchia neve in montagne.	There was quite a lot of snow on the hills.
Ho avuto parecchi guai.	I had quite a few problems.
Ha parecchie amiche inglesi.	She has several English friends.

[i] Note that the masculine singular ending of **parecchio** changes to a single **–i** in the
plural.

➤ Use **poco** and **poca** to talk about small amounts and **pochi** and **poche** to talk about small numbers.

C'è <u>poco</u> tempo.	There's not much time.
Ha <u>pochi</u> amici.	He has few friends.

ⓘ Note that the singular endings **–co** and **–ca** change to **–chi** and **–che** in the plural.

➩ *For more information on* **Spelling**, *see page 247.*

➤ Use **troppo** and **troppa** to say *too much*, and **troppi** and **troppe** to say *too many*.

Questa minestra è <u>troppa</u> per me.	This is too much soup for me.
Ho <u>troppe</u> cose da fare.	I've got too many things to do.

➤ Use **tanto** and **tanta** to talk about very large amounts, and **tanti** and **tante** to talk about very large numbers.

Ho mangiato <u>tanta</u> pasta!	I ate so much pasta!
Abbiamo avuto <u>tanti</u> problemi.	We've had a whole lot of problems.

Grammar Extra!

ciascuno (meaning *each*) and **nessuno** (meaning *no*) have no plural and behave like the indefinite article **uno**.

Before a masculine noun starting with a vowel, or most consonants, use **ciascun** and **nessun**.

<u>**ciascun**</u> candidato	each candidate
<u>**ciascun**</u> amico	each friend
<u>**nessun**</u> irlandese	no Irishman
Non ha fatto <u>nessun</u> commento.	He made no comment.

Before a masculine noun starting with **z** or **s** + another consonant use **ciascuno** and **nessuno**.

<u>**ciascuno**</u> studente	each student
<u>**nessuno**</u> spagnolo	no Spanish person

Before a feminine noun starting with a consonant use **ciascuna** and **nessuna**.

<u>**ciascuna**</u> ragazza	each girl
<u>**nessuna**</u> ragione	no reason

Before a feminine noun beginning with a vowel use **ciascun'** and **nessun'**.

<u>**ciascun'**</u>amica	each friend (*female*)
<u>**nessun'**</u>alternativa	no alternative

KEY POINTS

✔ **ogni**, **qualche** and **qualsiasi** always have the same form.
✔ **altro**, **tutto**, **molto**, **poco**, **parecchio**, **troppo** and **tanto** change their endings in the feminine and plural.

Test yourself

35 **Complete the following sentences with the correct form of the indefinite adjective. The first one has been done for you.**

a Vedo mia sorella ....*ogni*.... giorno. **(every)**

b Ha .... problemi. **(a lot)**

c La ragazza ha .... amici. **(few)**

d Ho mangiato .... frutta. **(so much)**

e Mi piace andare al cinema .... **(sometimes)**

f Ho .... libri da leggere. **(too many)**

g Non abbiamo .... soldi. **(much)**

h C'era .... vento oggi. **(quite a lot)**

i Andiamo a teatro un .... giorno. **(another)**

j Posso fare .... cosa? **(anything)**

36 **Match the columns to create full sentences.**

a **Non abbiamo visto**   ha comprato il libro.

b **Ciascuno studente**   tutta la giornata.

c **Vado a Parigi**   nessun treno.

d **Guarda la televisione**   tanti problemi.

e **Ha avuto**   fra qualche mese.

Pronouns

> ### What is a pronoun?
>
> A **pronoun** is a word you use instead of a noun, when you do not need or want to name someone or something directly, for example, *it, you, somebody, who, that*.

➤ There are many different kinds of pronoun, and all the words underlined in the sentences below are classified as pronouns. As you will see, they are extremely important and versatile words in everyday use.

<u>I</u> liked the black trousers but I couldn't afford <u>them</u>.	(*subject pronoun; direct object pronoun*)
<u>I</u>'m not going to eat it.	(*subject pronoun*)
I know Jack? I saw <u>him</u> at the weekend.	(*direct object pronoun*)
I emailed <u>her</u> my latest ideas.	(*indirect object pronoun*)
It's <u>mine</u>.	(*possessive pronoun*)
<u>Someone</u> came to see you yesterday.	(*indefinite pronoun*)
There's <u>nothing</u> I can do about it.	(*indefinite pronoun*)
<u>This</u> is the book I meant.	(*demonstrative pronoun*)
<u>That's</u> Ian.	(*demonstrative pronoun*)
<u>Who</u>'s he?	(*interrogative pronoun*)
<u>What</u> are those lights over there?	(*interrogative pronoun*)

➤ **Personal pronouns** are words such as *I, you, he, she, us, them*, and so forth, which make it clear who you are talking about or talking to. Personal pronouns replace nouns when it's clear who or what is being referred to, for example, *My brother's not here at the moment. He'll be back in an hour.*

➤ There are two types of personal pronoun:

- <u>subject pronouns</u> for the person or thing performing the action expressed by the verb.
  <u>I</u> like you a lot.
  <u>They</u> always go there on Sundays.

- <u>object pronouns</u> for the person or thing most directly affected by the action.
  I'll help <u>you</u>.
  They sent it to <u>me</u> yesterday.
  He gave <u>us</u> a very warm welcome.

Subject pronouns

➤ Here are the Italian subject pronouns:

Singular	Meaning	Plural	Meaning
io	I	**noi**	we
tu	you (familiar singular)	**voi**	you
lu	he	**loro**	they
lei	she; you (polite singular)		

> *Tip*
> You also use **lei** as a polite word for *you*. You will sometimes see it with
> a capital letter when used in this way.

[i] Note that the pronouns **egli** (meaning *he*), **ella** (meaning *she*), **essi** and **esse** (meaning *they*) are used in literary and formal written Italian, so you may well come across them. However, they are not generally used in speaking.

When to use subject pronouns in Italian

➤ In English we nearly always put a subject pronoun in front of a verb: <u>I</u> know Paul; <u>they</u>'re nice. Without the pronouns it would not be clear who or what is the subject of the verb.

➤ In Italian the verb ending usually makes it clear who the subject is, so generally no pronoun is necessary.

Conosc<u>o</u> Paul.	I know Paul.
Conosc<u>i</u> Paul?	Do you know Paul?
Conosc<u>iamo</u> Paul.	We know Paul.
Cosa sono? – Sono noci.	What are they? – They're walnuts.

⇨ *For more information on* **Verbs**, *see page 85.*

➤ You do <u>not</u> use a subject pronoun in Italian to translate *it* at the beginning of a sentence.

Fa caldo.	It's hot.
Sono le tre.	It's three o'clock.
Che cos'è? – È una sorpresa.	What is it? – It's a surprise.

➤ When you do use subject pronouns, it is for one of the following special reasons:

- for emphasis

Tu cosa dici?	What do you think?
Pago io.	I'll pay.
Ci pensiamo noi.	We'll see to it.

[i] The subject pronoun can come after the verb:

- for contrast or clarity

<u>Io</u> ci vado, <u>tu</u> fai come vuoi.	I'm going, you do what you like.
Aprilo <u>tu</u>, <u>io</u> non ci riesco.	You open it, I can't.

- after **anche** (meaning *too*) and **neanche** (meaning *neither*)

Vengo anch'<u>io</u>.	I'm coming too.
Prendi un gelato anche <u>tu</u>?	Are you going to have an ice cream too?
Non so perché. – Neanch'<u>io</u>.	I don't know why. – Neither do I.

- when there is no verb in Italian

Chi è il più bravo? – <u>Lui</u>.	Who's the best? – He is.
Viene lui, ma <u>lei</u> no.	He's coming, but she isn't.

> *Tip*
> To say it's *me*, for instance when knocking on someone's door, and to say
> who someone is, you use the subject pronoun.
> **Chi è? – Sono io.**   Who's that? – It's me.
> **Guarda! È lui.**   Look, it's him!

How to say *you* in Italian

➤ In English we have one way of saying *you*. In Italian, the word you choose depends on:

- whether you're talking to one person or more than one

- how well you know the person concerned.

➤ Use **tu** when you are speaking to a person you know well, or to a child. If you are a student you can call another student **tu**. If you have Italian relations, of course you call them **tu**.

➤ Use **lei** when speaking to strangers, or anyone you're not on familiar terms with. As you get to know someone better they may suggest that you call each other **tu** instead of **lei**.

➤ Use **voi** when you are speaking to more than one person, whether you know them well or not.

➤ **tu**, **lei** and **voi** are subject pronouns. There are also different forms for *you* when it is not a subject. These are explained in the section of this chapter on object pronouns.

> [*i*] Note that **lei**, the polite word for *you*, also means *she*. This is rarely confusing, as the context makes it clear – if someone speaks directly to you using **lei**, the meaning is obviously *you*.

KEY POINTS
- ✔ You don't generally need to use a subject pronoun in Italian. The verb ending makes it clear who is being referred to.
- ✔ You use subject pronouns in Italian only for emphasis or for contrast.
- ✔ There are two different ways of saying *you* when talking to one person: **tu** for people you know well; **lei** for people you don't know.
- ✔ You use **voi** if you are speaking to more than one person.

Test yourself

37 **Insert the correct subject pronoun in each of the sentences below.**

a Ci penso ....

b Viene anche ....

c Lo facciamo ....

d Vanno al mare anche .... ?

e Noi ci andiamo, ... fate come volete.

f Chi è? — Sono ....

g .... cosa mangi?

h Andiamo in discoteca anche ....

i Lei è simpatica, ... è maleducato.

j Chi è il più bravo? — È ....

38 **Choose which form of 'you' to use in each of the cases below.**

a	your best friend	lei
b	a group of teachers	tu
c	your doctor	tu
d	your grandmother	lei
e	your manager	voi

39 **Translate the following sentences into Italian using the *tu* form of the verb to translate 'you' where appropriate.**

a I'm going to the cinema. ....

b I don't like swimming. — Neither do I.

....

c Who is it? — It's her! ....

d What time is it? — It's two o'clock ....

e He's coming to the party, you do what you like.

....

f They're going too. ....

g She's going to bed, but he isn't. ....

h It's cold today. ....

i They'll see to it. ....

j Maria, what do you think? ....

Object pronouns

What are object pronouns?

➤ Object pronouns are words such as *me*, *him*, *us* and *them* used instead of a noun to show who is affected by the action of the verb.
> Do you like Claire? – Yes I like <u>her</u> a lot.
> I've lost my purse, have you seen <u>it</u>?
> He gave <u>us</u> a fantastic send-off.
> Why don't you send <u>them</u> a note?

➤ In English we use object pronouns in two different ways:

- when the person or thing is <u>directly</u> affected by the action:
> I saw <u>them</u> yesterday.
> They admire <u>him</u> immensely.

➤ In the above examples, *them* and *him* are called <u>direct objects</u>.

- when the person or thing is <u>indirectly</u> affected by the action. In English you often use *to* with the pronoun in such cases.
> I sent it to <u>them</u> yesterday.
> They awarded <u>him</u> a medal.

➤ In the above examples, *them* and *him* are called <u>indirect objects</u>.

➤ For both direct and indirect objects there is one form you use on <u>most</u> occasions. This is called the <u>unstressed</u> form.

Unstressed direct object pronouns

➤ Here are the Italian unstressed object pronouns:

mi	me
ti	you (familiar singular)
lo	him, it
la	her, you (polite singular), it
ci	us
vi	you (plural)
li	them (masculine)
le	them (feminine)

➤ Unlike English, you usually put them <u>before</u> the verb.

<u>**Ti**</u> **amo.**	I love you.
<u>**Lo**</u> **invito alla festa.**	I'm inviting him to the party.
Non <u>**lo**</u> **mangio.**	I'm not going to eat it.
<u>**La**</u> **guardava.**	He was looking at her.
<u>**Vi**</u> **cercavo.**	I was looking for you.
<u>**Li**</u> **conosciamo.**	We know them.

➡ *For more information on* ***Where to place pronouns***, *see page 64.*

> *Tip*
> Remember that you use **ti** only when speaking to someone you know well.

Lo, la, li and le

➤ You need to pay particular attention to how **lo**, **la**, **li** and **le** are used in Italian.

➤ To translate *it* you need to choose between **lo** or **la**. Use **lo** if the noun referred to is masculine, and **la** if it's feminine.

Ho <u>un panino</u>, <u>lo</u> vuoi?	I've got a roll, do you want it?
Ho <u>una mela</u>, <u>la</u> vuoi?	I've got an apple, do you want it?

➤ To translate *them* you choose between **li** or **le**. Use **li** if the noun referred to is masculine, and **le** if it's feminine.

Sto cercando <u>i biglietti</u>. **<u>Li</u> hai visti?**	I'm looking for the tickets, have you seen them?
Dove sono <u>le caramelle</u>? **<u>Le</u> hai mangiate?**	Where are the sweets? Have you eaten them?

➤ When **lo** and **la** are followed by **ho**, **hai**, **ha**, **abbiamo**, **avete** and **hanno**, they drop the vowel and are spelled **l'**.

Non l'ho visto ieri.	I didn't see it yesterday.
L'abbiamo preso con noi.	We took it with us.
L'hanno cercato tutta la giornata.	They looked for it all day.

Grammar Extra!

When you are talking about the past and using the pronouns **lo**, **la**, **li** and **le** you must make the past participle agree with the noun being referred to. Past participles are just like adjectives ending in **–o**. You change the **–o** to **–a** for the feminine singular, to **–i** for the masculine plural, and to **–e** for the feminine plural.

Il suo ultimo film? L'ho vist<u>o</u>.	His new film? I've seen it.
Silvia? L'ho incontrat<u>a</u> ieri.	Silvia? I met her yesterday.
I biglietti? Li ho già pres<u>i</u>.	The tickets? I've already got them.
Queste scarp<u>e</u>? Le ho comprat<u>e</u> anni fa.	These shoes? I bought them years ago.

⇨ *For more information on the **Perfect tense**, see page 41.*

KEY POINTS
✔ You generally use the unstressed direct object pronoun.
✔ Unstressed direct object pronouns usually come before the verb.
✔ You need to pay special attention when translating *it* and *them*.

Test yourself

40 Fill the gap with the correct direct object pronoun.

a Non trovo le mie scarpe. .... hai viste?

b Vedi quel ragazzo? — Sì, ... vedo.

c Ho una sciarpa. .... vuoi?

d Vuoi vedere il film? — No, ... ho visto ieri.

e I suoi genitori? .... ha visti la settimana scorsa.

f Abbiamo i biglietti. .... vuoi?

g Ho delle caramelle. .... volete?

h Senti la musica? — Sì, ... sento.

i Ho perso il mio cellulare. .... vedi?

j Questa gonna? .... ho comprata due settimane fa.

41 Translate the following sentences into Italian.

a She is looking at him.

....

b We're not going to see them.

....

c He is looking for us.

....

d The bag is beautiful. I'll buy it.

....

e Giulia, I have a sandwich, do you want it?

....

f She knows them.

....

g I know her

....

h The dog? We took it with us.

....

i She is inviting you all to the party.

....

j He loves me.

....

Unstressed indirect object pronouns

➤ In English some verbs have to be followed by an indirect object pronoun – *explain to him*, *write to him* – but other similar verbs do not: you say *tell him*, *phone him*.

➤ In Italian you have to use indirect object pronouns with verbs such as **dire** (meaning *to tell*) and **telefonare** (meaning *to phone*).

➤ As with direct object pronouns, there are <u>unstressed</u> and <u>stressed</u> indirect object pronouns.

➤ You will generally need to use <u>unstressed</u> pronouns rather than stressed ones.

➤ Here are the unstressed indirect pronouns.

mi	to me, me	**ci**	to us, us
ti	to you, you (*familiar singular*)	**vi**	to you, you (*plural*)
gli	to him, him	**gli**	to them, them
le	to her, her; to you, you (*polite singular*)		

➤ Unlike English, you usually put these pronouns <u>before</u> the verb.

➤ Just as in English, when you are telling somebody something, giving somebody something and so on, you use an indirect pronoun for the person concerned.

<u>Le</u> **ho detto la verità.**	I told her the truth.
<u>Gli</u> **ho dato la cartina.**	I gave him the map.

➤ Indirect pronouns are also generally used with verbs to do with communicating with people.

<u>Gli</u> **chiederò il permesso.**	I'll ask him for permission. (*literally, I'll ask to him*)
<u>Gli</u> **ho telefonato.**	I phoned him. (*literally, I phoned to him*)
<u>Le</u> **scriverò.**	I'll write to her.
Se li vedi chiedi<u>gli</u> **di venire.**	If you see them ask them to come. (*literally, ...ask to them...*)

➤ You use indirect object pronouns when you are using verbs such as **piacere**, **importare** and **interessare** to talk about what people like, care about or are interested in.

<u>Gli</u> **piace l'Italia.**	He likes Italy.
<u>Le</u> **piacciono i gatti.**	She likes cats.
Non <u>gli</u> **importa il prezzo, sono ricchi.**	They don't care about the price, they're rich.
Se <u>gli</u> **interessa può venire con me.**	If he's interested he can come with me.

> *Tip*
>
> It is worth checking in your dictionary to see if a verb needs a direct or an indirect object. If you look up the verb to *give*, for example, and find the example *to give somebody something*, the <u>**a**</u> in the translation (**dare qualcosa <u>a</u> qualcuno**) shows you that you use an indirect pronoun for the person you give something to.
>
> **Gli ho dato il mio numero di telefono.**   I gave him my phone number.

KEY POINTS

✔ You generally use the unstressed indirect object pronoun.

✔ Unstressed indirect object pronouns are used with many verbs in Italian which do not use them in English such as **chiedere** (meaning to *ask*) and **interessare** (meaning to *interest*).

✔ Unstressed indirect object pronouns usually come before the verb.

For further explanation of grammatical terms, please see pages viii-xii.

Test yourself

42 **Replace the highlighted words with the correct indirect object pronoun, remembering to place it before the verb. The first one has been done for you.**

a Chiedo il permesso **a mio padre**. *Gli chiedo permesso.*

b Scrive **alla sua amica**. ....

c Abbiamo dato le chiavi **ai ragazzi**. ....

d Hanno detto la verità **al professore**. ....

e Telefono **a mia sorella**. ....

f Danno i soldi **ai suoi nipoti**. ....

g Scrivo una lettera **a Paolo**. ....

h Chiedono **a Giovanna** di venire. ....

i Hai dato le notizie **ai tuoi figli**? ....

j Claudio ha dato il suo numero di telefono **alla ragazza**.

....

43 **Translate the following sentences into Italian.**

a She likes dogs. ....

b I don't care about the price. ....

c He's interested in French cinema. ....

d Marta, do you like this bag? ....

e He asked me to come. ....

f They are asking us for permission. ....

g Daniele and Mario, I'll call you tomorrow.

....

h They're not interested in books. ....

i I don't like the rain. ....

j They gave us a present. ....

Stressed object pronouns

➤ You use stressed pronouns for special emphasis. They generally go <u>after</u> the verb.

Cercavo proprio <u>voi</u>.	You're just the people I was looking for.
Invitano <u>me</u> e mio fratello.	They're inviting me and my brother.

➤ They are exactly the same as the <u>subject</u> pronouns, except that **me** is used instead of **io** and **te** is used instead of **tu**.

➤ You use the same words for stressed <u>direct</u> and <u>indirect</u> objects. When you use them as indirect objects you put the word **a** (meaning *to*) before them.

DIRECT		INDIRECT	
me	me	**a me**	(to) me
te	you (*familiar form*)	**a te**	(to) you (*familiar form*)
lui	him	**a lui**	(to) him
lei	her, you (*polite singular*)	**a lei**	(to) her, you (*polite singular*)
noi	us	**a noi**	(to) us
voi	you (*plural*)	**a voi**	(to) you (*plural*)
loro	them	**a loro**	(to) them

➤ You use stressed pronouns:

- when you want to emphasize that you mean a particular person and not somebody else, and for contrast

Amo solo <u>te</u>.	I love only you.
Invito <u>lui</u> alla festa, ma <u>lei</u> no.	I'm inviting him to the party but not her.
Non guardava <u>me</u>, guardava <u>lei</u>.	He wasn't looking at me, he was looking at her.
Ho scritto <u>a lei</u>, <u>a lui</u> no.	I wrote to her, but not to him.
Questo piace <u>a me</u>, ma Luca preferisce l'altro.	I like this one but Luca prefers the other one.

- after a preposition

Vengo con <u>te</u>.	I'll come with you.
Sono arrivati dopo di <u>noi</u>.	They arrived after us.

⇨ *For more information about* **Prepositions**, *see page 228.*

- after **di** when you're comparing one person with another

Sei più alto di <u>me</u>.	You're taller than me.
Sono più ricchi di <u>lui</u>.	They're richer than him.

KEY POINTS

✔ Stressed object pronouns are nearly all the same as subject pronouns.
✔ You use them for emphasis, after prepositions and in comparisons.
✔ You generally put stressed object pronouns after the verb.
✔ You use the same words for direct and indirect objects, but add a before them for indirect objects.

Test yourself

44   **Cross out the pronouns which do not work in the sentence.**

    a Patrizia viene con   io/tu/te

    b Sei più alto di   ti/me/gli

    c Abbiamo scritto a   loro/io/tu

    d Questa gonna piace a   le/gli/me

    e Cercavo proprio   me/tu/lui

    f Carla è più ricca di   io/me/vi

    g Sono arrivati prima di   ci/noi/io

    h Quel film intereressa a   tu/ci/lei

    i Non importa il prezzo a   gli/loro/io

    j Mia sorella telefona a   lui/io/ci

45   **Match the columns to make sentences.**

    a Vuole venire   te.

    b Lei è più intelligente   a loro.

    c Questi pantaloni   con me.

    d Il film non interessa   di lui.

    e Ama solo   piacciono a lei.

Before or after the verb?

➤ Unstressed pronouns generally come <u>before</u> the verb.

Mi aiuti?	Could you help me?
Ti piace?	Do you like it?
Ci hanno visto.	They saw us.
Vi ha salutato?	Did he say hello to you?

➤ In some cases, <u>unstressed</u> pronouns come <u>after</u> the verb:

- when you are using the imperative to tell someone to do something. The pronoun is joined onto the verb.

Aiutami!	Help me!
Lasciala stare.	Leave her alone.
Daglielo.	Give it to him (or her).
Arrivano. Non dirgli niente!	They're coming. Don't tell them anything!

  ⓘ Note that if the verb consists of just one syllable you double the consonant the pronoun starts with, except in the case of **gli**.

Fallo subito!	Do it right away!
Dille la verità!	Tell her the truth!
Dimmi dov'è.	Tell me where it is.
Dacci una mano.	Give us a hand.
Dagli una mano.	Give him a hand.

- when you are using a pronoun with the infinitive (the form of the verb ending in **–re** in Italian). The pronoun is joined onto the verb.

Potresti venire a prendermi?	Could you come and get me?
Non posso aiutarvi.	I can't help you.
Devo farlo?	Do I have to do it?
Dovresti scriverle.	You ought to write to her.
Luigi? Non voglio parlargli.	Luigi? I don't want to talk to him.

  ⓘ Note that the final **e** of the infinitive is dropped: **prendere** + **mi** becomes **prendermi**, **fare** + **ti** becomes **farti** and so on.

➤ <u>Stressed</u> pronouns often come after the verb.

Amo solo te.	I love only you.
Invito lui alla festa, ma lei no.	I'm inviting him to the party but not her.

Using two pronouns together

➤ In English you sometimes use two pronouns together, one referring to the indirect object and the other to the direct object, for example, *I gave <u>him it</u>*.

➤ You often do the same kind of thing in Italian, and must always put the <u>indirect object first</u>.

➤ When you use two pronouns together like this, some of them change:

mi becomes **me**
ti becomes **te**
ci becomes **ce**
vi becomes **ve**

For further explanation of grammatical terms, please see pages viii-xii.

<u>Me</u> la dai?	Will you give me it?
È mia – non <u>te</u> la do.	It's mine, I'm not going to give it to you.
<u>Ce</u> l'hanno promesso.	They promised it to us.
<u>Ve</u> lo mando domani.	I'll send it to you tomorrow.

➤ When you want to use **gli** (meaning *to him* or *to them*) and **le** (meaning *to her*) with **lo**, **la**, **li** or **le**, you add an **–e** to **gli** and join it to **lo**, **la**, and so forth.

gli/le + lo → glielo
gli/le + la → gliela
gli/le + li → glieli
gli/le + le → gliele

<u>Glieli</u> hai promessi.	You promised them to her.
<u>Gliele</u> ha spedite.	He sent them to them.
Carlo? <u>Glielo</u> dirò domani.	Carlo? I'll tell him tomorrow.

➤ When you use two pronouns together to give an order or when using the infinitive (**–re** form of the verb), they join together and are added on to the verb.

Mi piacciono, ma non vuole comprar<u>meli</u>.	I like them but he won't buy me them.
Ecco la lettera di Rita, puoi dar<u>gliela</u>?	Here's Rita's letter, can you give it to her?
Le chiavi? Da<u>gliele</u>.	The keys? Give them to her.
Non abbiamo i biglietti – può mandar<u>celi</u>?	We haven't got the tickets – can you send us them?

[i] Note that the final **e** of the infinitive is dropped: **prendere** + **mi** + **li** becomes **prendermeli**, **mandare** + **ti** + **le** becomes **mandartele** and so on.

Grammar Extra!

In English *you* and *one* are used in general statements and questions such as
You don't do it like that; *Can you park here?*; *One has to be careful*.
Use **si** and the reflexive form of the verb in Italian for these kinds of statements and questions.

<u>Si</u> fa così.	This is how you do it.
<u>Si</u> può nuotare qui?	Can you swim here?
Non <u>si</u> sa mai.	You never know.

⇨ *For more information on **Reflexive verbs**, see page 115.*

KEY POINTS

✔ When you use two pronouns together the indirect object comes first.
✔ Some indirect objects change when used before a direct object.
✔ After orders and the infinitive form, the two pronouns are written as one word and follow the verb.

Test yourself

46 **Change the following orders into questions, by putting them into the present tense of the *tu* form of the verb and moving the pronoun to before the verb. The first one has been done for you.**

a Aiutami!. *Mi aiuti?* ....

b Dammi un bicchiere d'acqua! ....

c Aspettaci! ....

d Dagli la palla! ....

e Finiscilo! ....

f Chiamalo domani! ....

g Dille la verità! ....

h Dacci una mano! ....

i Fallo subito! ....

j Guardami! ....

47 **Replace the highlighted words with the correct pronoun, taking care to change its position in the sentence and to alter the form of the indirect object. The first one has been done for you.**

a Mi dai il portafoglio? *Me lo dai?* ....

b Vi mando la lettera domani. ....

c Ti portiamo i regali. ....

d Gli dico la verità. ....

e Ci spedisce i libri. ....

f Gli dai le chiavi? ....

g Ti do le notizie. ....

h Mi comprano le scarpe. ....

i Vi facciamo vedere la casa. ....

j Gli ha promesso il giocattolo. ....

48 **Match the sentence on the left with its translation on the right.**

a Puoi mandarmelo?   Can you buy them for us?

b Puoi darglieli?   Can you tell her it?

c Puoi comprarceli?   Can you take it for them?

d Puoi prenderglielo?   Can you give them to her?

e Puoi dirglielo?   Can you send me it?

Possessive pronouns

Test Yourself

What is a possessive pronoun?
In English the **possessive pronouns** are *mine*, *yours*, *his*, *hers*, *ours* and *theirs*.
You use them instead of a possessive adjective followed by a noun. For example,
instead of saying *My bag is the blue one*, you say <u>*Mine's* the blue one</u>.

➤ Here are the Italian possessive pronouns; they are exactly the same as Italian possessive adjectives, but with the definite article in front of them.

⇨ *For more information on **Possessive adjectives** and the **Definite article**, see pages 45 and 14.*

Singular Masculine	Feminine	Plural Masculine	Feminine	Meaning
il mio	la mia	i miei	le mie	mine
il tuo	la tua	i tuoi	le tue	yours (*familiar*)
il suo	la sua	i suoi	le sue	his, hers, yours (*polite*)
il nostro	la nostra	i nostri	le nostre	ours
il vostro	la vostra	i vostri	le vostre	yours
il loro	la loro	i loro	le loro	theirs

Tip
There are three ways of saying *yours*, because there are three words for *you* –
tu, **lei** and **voi**.

Questa borsa non è <u>la mia</u>, è <u>la tua</u>.	This bag's not mine, it's yours.
Non è <u>il mio</u>, è <u>il suo</u>, signore.	It's not mine, it's yours, sir.
La nostra casa è piccola, <u>la vostra</u> è grande.	Our house is small, yours is big.
I miei genitori e <u>i suoi</u> si conoscono.	My parents and hers know each other.

ⓘ Note that **i miei**, **i tuoi** and **i suoi** are used to refer to someone's parents.

Vivo con <u>i miei</u>.	I live with my parents.
Cosa hanno detto <u>i tuoi</u>?	What did your parents say?
Lucia è venuta con <u>i suoi</u>.	Lucia came with her parents.

➤ In Italian, possessive pronouns agree with the noun they're used instead of. For example, **il mio** can only be used to refer to a masculine singular noun.

KEY POINTS
✔ Italian possessive pronouns are the same as Italian possessive adjectives.
✔ They are masculine or feminine, singular or plural, depending on what they refer to.

Test yourself

49 **Complete the sentence with the correct form of the possessive pronoun.**

a È la tua macchina? — No, non è ....

b È il suo portafoglio? — Sì, è ....

c Sono i pantaloni di Marta? — No, non sono ....

d Sono le chiavi di tuo marito? — Sì, sono ....

e È il tuo passaporto? — No, non è ....

f È la macchina del tuo amico? — Sì, è ....

g Sono i guanti di Paolo? — No, non sono ....

h È la casa di tua sorella? — Sì, è ....

i Sono i tuoi libri? — No, non sono ....

j È il loro cane? — Sì, è ....

50 **Translate the following sentences into Italian, using the *tu* form of the verb to translate 'you' where appropriate.**

a Is this hat yours, sir? ....

b The black bag is mine. ....

c Our house is bigger than theirs.

    ....

d Which car is hers? ....

e That cat is ours. ....

f Her parents and mine are coming to dinner.

    ....

g He's not my friend, he's yours. ....

h Those shoes are his. ....

i It's not your wallet, it's mine.

    ....

j The children are theirs. ....

ne and ci

> **ne** and **ci** are two extremely useful pronouns which have no single equivalent in English. There are some phrases where you have to use them in Italian.

ne

ne is a pronoun with several meanings.

> It can refer to amounts and quantities.

- It means *some*, and can be used without a noun, just like English.

Ne vuoi?	Would you like some?
Vuoi del pane? – Ne ho grazie.	Would you like some bread? – I've got some, thanks.

> In English, when talking about amounts and quantities, you can say *How much do you want of it?*, or *How much do you want?* and *How many do you want of them?*, or *How many do you want?* **Ne** translates *of it* and *of them* but it is <u>not</u> optional. So you need to remember to use it in sentences of the kind shown below.

Ne ho preso la metà.	I've taken half (of it).
Ne vuoi la metà?	Do you want half (of it/of them)?
Quanti ne vuole?	How many (of them) do you want?
Ne voglio pochi.	I don't want many (of them).

> **Ne** also means *about it/them*, *of it/them*, *with it/them*, and so on, when used with Italian adjectives or verbs which are followed by **di**, for example, **contento di** (meaning *happy about*), **stufo di** (meaning *fed up with*), **aver paura di** (meaning *to be afraid of*), **scrivere di** (meaning *to write about*).

Ne è molto contenta.	She's very happy about it.
Ne sono conscio.	I'm aware of it.
Ne erano stufi.	They were fed up with it.
Ne sei sicura?	Are you sure (of it)?
Ne hai paura?	Are you afraid of it?
Ne ha scritto sul giornale.	She's written about it in the paper.
Non se ne accorge.	He doesn't realize it.

> With adjectives and verbs followed by **di**, **ne** can be used to refer to nouns that have already been mentioned.

Parliamo del futuro. –	Let's talk about the future.
Sì, parliamone	Yes, let's talk about it.
Hai bisogno della chiave? –	Do you need the key?
No, non ne ho più bisogno.	No, I don't need it any more.

> For more information on **di**, see **Prepositions** page 228.

> **Ne** usually comes <u>before</u> the verb, except when the verb is an order or the infinitive (the **–re** form of the verb).

> When it comes after the verb the final **–e** of the infinitive is dropped.

Volevo parlarne.	I wanted to talk about it.

➤ It follows any other pronoun and is written as one word with it and the verb form.

Damme<u>ne</u> uno per favore.	Give me one of them please.
Da<u>glie</u>ne due rossi.	Give him two red ones.

i Note that when joined to **ne**, **mi** becomes **me**, **ti** becomes **te**, **ci** becomes **ce**, **vi** becomes **ve** and **gli** and **le** become **glie**.

KEY POINTS

✔ **ne** can be used to mean *some*.
✔ **ne** can also be used to mean *of it* or *of them* when talking about amounts and quantities. Unlike English, it is not optional.
✔ **ne** is used to mean *about it* or *about them* and so forth with verbs and adjectives followed by **di**.
✔ **ne** usually comes before the verb.

Test yourself

51 **Replace the highlighted words to construct a phrase consisting of *ne* followed by the verb.**

a Quante **pere** vuoi? ....

b Prendo la metà **della torta**. ....

c Volete **del pane**? ....

d Ha paura **dei cani**. ....

e Ho scritto **del viaggio**. ....

f Sono stufi **del tempo**. ....

g È contenta **del nuovo lavoro**. ....

h Sei sicura **della risposta**? ....

i Hai bisogno **della macchina**? ....

j È conscia **della situazione**. ....

52 **Match the statement or question on the left with its reply on the right.**

a **Parliamo del film.**   Ne ero stufo.

b **Quanti fiori vuole, signora?**   Sì, parliamone.

c **Hai bisogno della matita?**   No, no ne ho più bisogno.

d **Perchè non hai finito il libro?**   Ne ho, grazie.

e **Vuoi del vino?**   Ne voglio dieci, per favore.

53 **Translate the following sentences into Italian, using the *tu* form of the verb to translate 'you' where appropriate.**

a She wants to talk about it. ....

b They're scared of it. ....

c He is taking some of it. ....

d Dogs? She has four. ....

e We heard about it. ....

f Give her a black one. ....

g There's cake? I want some! ....

h We are really happy about it. ....

i They don't realize it. ....

j I've got some, thanks. ....

ci

➤ **Ci** is used with certain verbs to mean *it* or *about it*.

Ripensando<u>ci</u> mi sono pentito.	When I thought it over I was sorry.
Non <u>ci</u> credo per niente.	I don't believe it at all.
<u>Ci</u> penserò.	I'll think about it.
Non <u>ci</u> capisco niente.	I can't understand it at all.
Non so che far<u>ci</u>.	I don't know what to do about it.

➤ **Ci** is often used with Italian verbs which are followed by **a**, for example:

- **cr<u>e</u>dere <u>a</u> qualcosa** to believe something, to believe in something
  Non <u>ci</u> credo.　　　　　　　　I don't believe it.

- **pensare <u>a</u> qualcosa** to think about something
  Non voglio nemmeno pensar<u>ci</u>.　I don't even want to think about it.

- **far caso <u>a</u> qualcosa** to notice something
  Non <u>ci</u> ho fatto caso.　　　　I didn't notice.

[i] Note that the equivalent English verb may not be followed by any preposition at all.

➤ With verbs followed by **a**, **ci** can be used to refer to nouns that have already been mentioned.

I fantasmi, non ci credi?	Ghosts – don't you believe in them?
Non pensi mai al futuro? –	Don't you ever think about the future? –
Ci penserò quando sarò più vecchio.	I'll think about it when I'm older.

➤ **ci** is used with the verb **entrare** in some common idiomatic phrases.

Cosa c'entra?	What's that got to do with it?
Io non c'entro.	It's nothing to do with me.

➤ Like **ne**, **ci** usually comes <u>before</u> the verb, except when the verb is an order, the infinitive (the **–re** form of the verb) or the –ing form.

KEY POINTS

✔ **ci** is used to mean *it* or *about it*.
✔ **ci** is used with verbs which can be followed by the preposition **a**.
✔ **ci** usually comes before the verb.

Test yourself

54 **Match the questions on the left with their answers on the right.**

a Maria ha rotto la finestra?	Ci penserò.
b Credi la sua storia?	No, lei non c'entra.
c Prepariamo noi il pranzo?	Non ci credo per niente.
d Parli inglese?	No, ci pensano loro.
e Vuoi venire al cinema?	No, non ci capisco niente.

55 **Translate the following sentences into Italian, using *ci*.**

a She doesn't believe it.

....

b What's that got to do with it?

....

c What's the weather got to do with it?

....

d They don't know what to do about it.

....

e It's nothing to do with them.

....

f Is she coming to the party? — She'll think about it.

....

g We don't want to think about it.

....

h Did she take the car? — I didn't notice.

....

i That film? I didn't understand it at all.

....

j He doesn't think about it any more.

....

Indefinite pronouns

> ### What is an indefinite pronoun?
> An **indefinite pronoun** is a word like *everything, nobody* and *something*
> which is used to refer to people or things in a non-specific way.

➤ Some Italian indefinite pronouns always keep the same form:

- **chiunque** anyone
  Attacca discorso con <u>chiunque</u>.   She'll talk to anyone.

- **niente** nothing
  Cosa c'è? – <u>Niente</u>.   What's wrong? – Nothing.

🗓 Note that **niente** and **nulla** mean exactly the same, but **niente** is used more often.

- **nulla** nothing
  Che cos'hai comprato? – <u>Nulla</u>.   What did you buy? – Nothing.

- **qualcosa** something, anything
  Ho <u>qualcosa</u> da dirti.   I've got something to tell you.
  Ha bisogno di <u>qualcosa</u>?   Do you need anything?
  Voglio <u>qualcos</u>'altro.   I want something else.

⇨ *For more information on **Negatives**, see page 98.*

➤ Other indefinite pronouns are masculine singular words, with a feminine form ending in **–a**:

- **ciascuno, ciascuna** each
  Ne avevamo uno per <u>ciascuno</u>.   We had one each.
  Le torte costano dieci euro <u>ciascuna</u>.   The cakes cost ten euros each.

- **nessuno, nessuna** nobody, anybody; none
  Non è venuto <u>nessuno</u>.   Nobody came.
  Hai visto <u>nessuno</u>?   Did you see anybody?
  <u>Nessuna</u> delle ragazze è venuta.   None of the girls came.

- **ognuno, ognuna** each
  <u>ognuno</u> di voi   each of you

- **qualcuno, qualcuna** somebody; one
  Ha telefonato <u>qualcuno</u>.   Somebody phoned.
  Chiedilo a <u>qualcun</u> altro.   Ask somebody else.
  Conosci <u>qualcuna</u> delle ragazze?   Do you know any of the girls?

- **uno, una** somebody
  Ho incontrato <u>uno</u> che ti conosce.   I met somebody who knows you.
  C'è <u>una</u> che ti cerca.   There's somebody (*meaning a woman*)
                 looking for you.

- **alcuni** and **alcune** (meaning *some*) are always used in the plural.
  Ci sono posti liberi? – Sì, <u>alcuni</u>.   Are there any empty seats? – Yes, some.
  Ci sono ancora delle fragole? –   Are there any strawberries left? –
   Sì, <u>alcune</u>.   Yes, some.

For further explanation of grammatical terms, please see pages viii-xii.

➤ The following pronouns can be singular or plural, masculine or feminine:

- **altro, altra, altri, altre** the other one; another one; other people

L'<u>altro</u> è meno caro.	The other one is cheaper.
Preferisco l'<u>altra</u>.	I prefer the other one.
Non m'interessa quello che dicono gli <u>altri</u>.	I don't care what other people say.
Le <u>altre</u> sono partite.	The others have gone.
Pre**ndine un altro.**	Take another one.

> ⓘ Note that **altro** can also mean *anything else*.

Vuole <u>altro</u>?	Do you want anything else?

- **molto, molta, molti, molte** a lot, lots

Ne ha <u>molto</u>.	He's got lots.
<u>molti</u> di noi	a lot of us

- **parecchio, parecchia, parecchi, parecchie** quite a lot

C'e ancora del pane? – Sì, <u>parecchio</u>.	Is there any bread left? – Yes, quite a lot.
Avete avuto problemi? – Sì, <u>parecchi</u>.	Did you have problems? – Yes, a lot.

- **poco, poca, pochi, poche** not much, not many

C'è pane? – <u>Poco</u>.	Is there any bread? – Not much.
Ci sono turisti? – <u>Pochi</u>.	Are there any tourists? – Not many.

- **tanto, tanta, tanti, tante** lots, so much, so many

Hai mangiato? – Sì, <u>tanto</u>!	Have you eaten? – Yes, lots!
Sono <u>tanti</u>!	There are so many of them!

- **troppo, troppa, troppi, troppe** too much, too many

Quanto hai speso? – <u>Troppo</u>!	How much have you spent? – Too much!
Ci sono errori? – Sì, <u>troppi</u>.	Are there any mistakes? – Yes, too many.

- **tutti, tutte** everybody, all

Ve**ngono <u>tutti</u>.**	Everybody is coming.
Sono arrivate <u>tutte</u>.	They've all arrived (*they're all women*).

> ⓘ Note that in English you can say *Everybody is coming*; *They're all coming* or *All of them are coming*. All three sentences are translated into Italian in the same way, using **tutti** and a plural verb. **tutti** cannot be followed by **di**, so don't try to translate *all of them* – translate *they all*.

- **tutto** everything, all

Va <u>tutto</u> bene?	Is everything okay?
L'ho finito tutto.	I've finished it all.

KEY POINTS

✔ Some indefinite pronouns always have the same form.
✔ Other indefinite pronouns can be masculine or feminine, singular or plural.

Test yourself

56 **Fill the gap with *niente*, *nessuno* or *nessuna*.**

   a Cos' hai comprato? — ....

   b .... dei bambini piange.

   c Quale di queste ragazze conosci? — ....

   d Non ha suonato ....

   e Cos'ha mangiato tua sorella? — ....

   f Non ha telefonato .... ieri sera.

   g Cos'è successo? — ....

   h .... delle donne parla italiano.

   i Avete visto .... nel giardino?

   j Non è venuto .... alla festa.

57 **Translate the following sentences into Italian, using the *tu* form of the verb to translate 'you' where appropriate.**

   a Is everybody coming this evening? ....

   b She ate it all. ....

   c A lot of them are going to the cinema. ....

   d I like this scarf, but I prefer the other one.

      ....

   e Are there any tourists? — Yes, some. ....

   f Are there any cakes? — Yes, quite a lot.

      ....

   g There is a book for each of you. ....

   h The tickets cost twelve euros each.

      ....

   i Sir, would you like anything else? ....

   j Look at the cars! There are so many of them.

      ....

Relative pronouns

What is a relative pronoun?

➤ In English the relative pronouns are *who, which, that* and *whom*. They are used to specify exactly who or what is being talked about, for example, *The man who has just come in is Anna's boyfriend; The vase that you broke cost a lot of money.*

➤ Relative pronouns can also introduce an extra piece of information, for example, *Peter, who is a brilliant painter, wants to study art; Their house, which was built in 1890, needs a lot of repairs.*

che

➤ In English *who, whom* and *that* are used to talk about people and *which* and *that* are used to talk about things. In Italian you use **che** for all of these.

quella signora <u>che</u> ha il piccolo cane nero	that lady who has the little black dog
Mio padre, <u>che</u> ha sessant'anni, va in pensione.	My father, who's sixty, is retiring.
una persona <u>che</u> detesto	a person whom I detest
l'uomo <u>che</u> hanno arrestato	the man that they've arrested
la squadra <u>che</u> ha vinto	the team which *or* that won
il dolce <u>che</u> hai fatto	the pudding you made

➤ In English you can miss out the relative pronoun: *a person I detest; the man they've arrested.* You can <u>never</u> miss out **che**.

the person I admire most → **la persona <u>che</u> ammiro di più**
the money you lent me → **i soldi <u>che</u> mi hai prestato**

➤ Prepositions are sometimes used with relative pronouns: *the man <u>to</u> whom she was talking/ the man that she was talking <u>to</u>; the girl who he's going out <u>with</u>.* In English the preposition often goes <u>at the end</u> of the phrase.

➤ In Italian, when you use a preposition with a relative pronoun, use **cui** instead of **che**, and put the preposition in front of it.

la ragazza <u>di cui</u> ti ho parlato	the girl that I told you about
gli amici <u>con cui</u> andiamo in vacanza	the friends who we go on holiday with
la persona <u>a cui</u> si riferiva	the person he was referring to
il quartiere <u>in cui</u> abito	the area in which I live
il film <u>di cui</u> parlavo	the film which I was talking about

> *Tip*
> In English *who* is used both as a question word, and as a relative pronoun. In Italian **chi** is used in questions, and **che** is used as a relative pronoun: **<u>Chi</u> va al concerto?** — Who's going to the concert?
> **la ragazza <u>che</u> hai visto** — the girl (that) you saw

➤ In English you often use *which* to refer to a fact or situation that you've just mentioned. In Italian use **il che**.

Loro non pagano nulla, <u>il che</u> non mi sembra giusto.	They don't pay anything, which doesn't seem fair to me.
Dice che non è colpa sua, <u>il che</u> è vero.	She says it's not her fault, which is true.

Grammar Extra!

You may come across **il quale** used to mean *who, which, that* and *whom*. **il quale** is more formal than **che**. **il quale** has feminine and plural forms: **la quale**, **i quali** and **le quali**.

suo padre, <u>il quale</u> è avvocato	his father, who is a lawyer
le sue sorelle, <u>le quali</u> studiano a Roma	his sisters, who study in Rome

il quale, **la quale**, **i quali** and **le quali** are used most often with prepositions.

l'albergo <u>al quale</u> ci siamo fermati	the hotel that we stayed at
la signora <u>con la</u> quale parlavi	the lady you were talking to
gli amici <u>ai quali</u> mando questa cartolina	the friends I'm sending this card to
la medicina <u>della quale</u> hanno bisogno	the medicine they need

⇨ *For more information about **Prepositions**, see page 228.*

<u>quello che</u>

➤ In English you can put *the one* or *the ones* in front of a relative pronoun such as *who, which, that* and *whom*. For example, *That's the one that I'd like; They're the ones we need*.

➤ To say *the one* in Italian use **quello** to refer to masculine nouns or **quella** to refer to feminine nouns. The relative pronoun is **che**.

È <u>quello</u> che non funziona.	That's the one which isn't working.
È <u>quello</u> che preferisco.	That's the one I prefer.
È <u>quella</u> che parla di più.	She's the one who talks most.

➤ To say *the ones* in Italian use **quelli** for masculine nouns or **quelle** for feminine nouns. The relative pronoun is **che**.

Sono <u>quelli</u> che sono partiti senza pagare.	They're the ones who left without paying.
Queste scarpe sono <u>quelle</u> che ha ordinato.	These shoes are the ones you ordered.

➤ With a preposition use **cui** instead of **che**. Put the preposition in front of **cui**.

È quello a <u>cui</u> parlavo.	He's the one I was talking to.
Sono quelli a <u>cui</u> ti riferivi?	Are they the ones to whom you were referring?
Sono quelli di <u>cui</u> abbiamo bisogno.	They're the ones we need.

🗓 Note that in English the relative pronoun can be left out, for example, *That's the one I want* instead of *That's the one that I want*. In Italian the relative pronoun **che** can <u>never</u> be left out.

> **KEY POINTS**
>
> ✔ **che** can refer to both people and things in Italian.
> ✔ The relative pronouns *who, which* and *that* can be left out in English, but **che** must always be used.
> ✔ Use **cui** instead of **che** after a preposition.
> ✔ **quello, quella, quelli** and **quelle** are used to say *the one* or *the ones*. They are used with **che**.

For further explanation of grammatical terms, please see pages viii–xii.

Test yourself

58 Fill the gap, using *che*, *cui* or *chi*.

a Il ragazzo .... ha il cappello nero.

b .... va in piscina?

c Il film .... ho visto ieri sera.

d La mia amica, ... parla italiano, è inglese.

e La persona con .... parlavo.

f La casa in .... abitiamo.

g Gli amici con .... andiamo al mare.

h Quella signora .... abita vicino a me.

i .... ha preso la macchina?

j Una persona .... mi piace molto.

59 Match the sentence on the left with its translation on the right.

a The woman I know.   La famiglia con cui andiamo in vacanza.

b The person I was talking about.   Il ragazzo che hai visto.

c Someone I admire.   La persona di cui parlavo.

d The family we go on holiday with.   La signora che conosco.

e The boy that you saw.   Qualcuno che ammiro.

60 Cross out the words that cannot refer to the noun.

a la casa   quello che/quelli che/a cui/quella

b il portafoglio   di cui/quelli che/quello che/quella che

c i bambini   per cui/quelle che/quelli che/ quello che

d lo studente   quella che/quelle che/quello che/di cui

e le scarpe   quelle che/di cui/quelli che/quella che

f gli alberi   quello che/quella che/ a cui/quelli che

g l'uomo   di cui/quella che/quelli che/quello che

h i guanti   quelli che/quelle che/quello che/con cui

i la torta   quello che/quelle che/quella che/di cui

j le sorelle   a cui/quelle che/quelli che/ quella che.

Interrogative pronouns

> **What is an interrogative pronoun?**
> In English the **interrogative pronouns** are *who...?*, *which...?*, *whose...?*, *whom...?*
> and *what...?*. They are used without a noun, to ask questions.

The interrogative pronouns in Italian

> These are the interrogative pronouns in Italian:

Chi?	Who?, Whom?
Che?	What?
Cosa?	What?
Che cosa?	What?
Quale?	Which?, Which one?, What?
Quanto?	How much?
Quanti?	How many?

> **Chi**, **che**, **cosa** and **che cosa** never change their form.

Chi è?	Who is it?
Chi sono?	Who are they?
Che vuoi?	What do you want?
Cosa vuole?	What does he want?
Che cosa vogliono?	What do they want?

i Note that there is no difference between **che**, **cosa** and **che cosa**.

> **Quale** is used for the masculine and feminine singular, and **quali** is used for masculine and feminine plural.

Conosco sua sorella. – Quale?	I know his sister. – Which one?
Ho rotto dei bicchieri. – Quali?	I broke some glasses. – Which ones?

⇨ *For more information on **Question words**, see page 206.*

> **Quanto** and **quanti** have feminine forms.

Farina? Quanta ce ne vuole?	Flour? How much is needed?
Quante di loro passano la sera a leggere?	How many of them spend the evening reading?

che cos'è or qual è?

> **che cos'è?** and **qual è?** both mean *what is?* but are used in different ways:

- Use **che cos'è?** or **che cosa sono?** when you're asking someone to explain or identify something.

Che cos'è questo?	What's this?
Che cosa sono questi? – Sono funghi.	What are these? – They're mushrooms.

- Use **qual è?** or **quali sono?**, not **che**, when you ask *what is?* or *what are?* to find out a particular detail, number, name and so on.

Qual è il suo indirizzo?	What's her address?
Qual è la capitale della Finlandia?	What's the capital of Finland?
Quali sono i loro nomi?	What are their names?

ⓘ Note that **quale** becomes **qual** in front of a vowel.

chi?

➤ Use **chi** for both *who* and *whom*.

Chi ha vinto?	Who won?
Chi hai visto?	Whom did you see?

➤ When there is a preposition in your question put it <u>in front of</u> **chi**.

A chi l'hai dato?	Who did you give it to?
Con chi parlavi?	Who were you talking to?
A chi si riferiva?	To whom was he referring?

➤ Use **di chi è?** or **di chi sono?** to ask who things belong to.

Di chi è questa borsa?	Whose is this bag?
Di chi sono queste chiavi?	Whose are these keys?

KEY POINTS

✔ **chi**, **che cosa**, **quale** and **quanto** are the interrogative pronouns in Italian.
✔ Use **chi** for both *who* and *whom*.

Test yourself

61 **Fill the gap with the correct interrogative pronoun. Note that in some cases, more than one answer may be possible.**

a .... dei ragazzi sono venuti?

b .... vuole venire al parco?

c .... costa questo libro?

d Pane? .... ne vuoi?

e .... vuoi fare stasera?

f .... sono questi bambini?

g Ho comprato la gonna. — .... ?

h .... di queste ragazze studiano all'università?

i .... costano le torte?

j .... hai mangiato?

62 **Match the question on the left with its answer on the right.**

a Quali sono le stagioni dell'anno?   Sono zucche.

b Che cos'è questo?   È 'La Strada'.

c Qual è il tuo film preferito?   È Luca.

d Che cosa sono quelle?   Sono la primavera, l'estate, l'autunno e l'inverno.

e Qual'è il suo nome?   È un giocattolo.

63 **Translate the following sentences into Italian. Use the _tu_ form of the verb to translate 'you' where appropriate.**

a Whose car is that? ....

b Who told you? ....

c Who was she talking to? ....

d Whose are these shoes? ....

e Which team won the match? ....

f What does he want to drink? ....

g Sugar? How much is needed? ....

h How many of those women speak English?

....

i Who did she give it to? ....

j Which scarf do you prefer? ....

Demonstrative pronouns

What is a demonstrative pronoun?

In English the **demonstrative pronouns** are *this*, *that*, *these* and *those*. They are used instead of a noun to point out people or things, for example, *That's my brother*.

Using demonstrative pronouns

➤ These are the demonstrative pronouns in Italian:

	Masculine	**Feminine**	**Meaning**
Singular	questo quello	questa quella	this, this one that, that one
Plural	questi quelli	queste quelle	these, these ones those, those ones

➤ The demonstrative pronoun <u>must</u> agree with the noun it is replacing.

Questo è mio marito.	This is my husband.
Questa è camera mia.	This is my bedroom.
Questi sono i miei fratelli.	These are my brothers.
Quali scarpe ti metti? – **Queste**.	Which shoes are you going to wear? – These ones.
Qual è la sua borsa? – **Quella**.	Which bag is yours? – That one.
Quelli quanto costano?	How much do those cost?

ⓘ Note that **quello** and **quella** can also be used to mean *that man* and *that woman*.

Dice sempre bugie **quello**.	That man is always telling lies.
Conosci **quella**?	Do you know that woman?

⇨ *For more information on **Demonstrative adjectives**, see page 38.*

KEY POINTS

✔ The demonstrative pronouns in Italian are **questo** and **quello**.
✔ **Questo** and **quello** have masculine, feminine, singular and plural forms.
✔ They agree with the nouns they replace.

Test yourself

64 **Fill the gap with the correct form of the demonstrative pronoun _questo_.**

a .... è mia cognata.

b .... sono i miei colleghi.

c .... è mio figlio.

d Qual è la tua macchina? — ....

e .... è la mia casa.

f Quali sono le tue scarpe preferite? — ....

g .... è il mio ufficio.

h .... sono i funghi pericolosi.

i .... sono i miei cugini.

j .... è la mia dentista.

65 **Match the phrase on the left with its translation on the right.**

a **Quella è mia sorella.**   These are my glasses.

b **Quanto costano quelli?**   That woman is an actor.

c **Questo è il mio cane.**   How much do those cost?

d **Questi sono i miei occhiali.**   That's my sister.

e **Quella donna è attrice.**   This is my dog.

Verbs

What is a verb?
A **verb** is a word which describes what somebody or something does, what they are, or what happens to them, for example, *play*, *be*, *disappear*.

Overview of verbs

➤ Verbs are frequently used with a noun or with somebody's name, for example, <u>*Children*</u> like stories; <u>*Jason's*</u> *playing football*. In English, pronouns such as *I*, *you* and *she* often come in front of verbs, for example, <u>*She*</u> *knows my sister*.

➤ Verbs can relate to the present, the past or the future; this is called their <u>tense</u>.

   ⇨ *For more information on **Nouns** and **Pronouns**, see pages 1 and 53.*

➤ Verbs are either:

- <u>regular</u>: their forms follow the normal rules
OR
- <u>irregular</u>: their forms do not follow the normal rules

➤ Almost all verbs have a form called the <u>infinitive</u> that isn't present, past or future, (for example, *walk*, *see*, *hear*). It is used after other verbs, for example, *You should* <u>*walk*</u>; *You can* <u>*see*</u>; *Kirsty wants* <u>*to come*</u>. In English, the infinitive is usually shown with the word *to*, for example, *to speak*, *to eat*, *to live*.

➤ In Italian, the infinitive is always just one word that in most cases ends in either **–are**, **–ere** or **–ire**: for example, **parl<u>are</u>** (meaning *to speak*), **cred<u>ere</u>** (meaning *to believe*) and **dorm<u>ire</u>** (meaning *to sleep*).

➤ Regular English verbs can add three endings to the infinitive: *–s* (*walks*), *–ing* (*walking*) and *–ed* (*walked*).

➤ Italian verbs add endings to the verb <u>stem</u>, which is what is left of the verb when you take away the **–are**, **–ere** or **–ire** ending of the infinitive. This means the stem of **parlare** is **parl-**, the stem of **credere** is **cred-**, and the stem of **dormire** is **dorm-**.

➤ Italian verb endings change according to who or what is doing the action. The person or thing that does the action is called the <u>subject</u> of the verb.

➤ In English, you nearly always put a noun or a pronoun in front of a verb to show who is doing the action, for example, <u>*Jack*</u> *speaks Italian*; <u>*She's*</u> *playing tennis*.

➤ In Italian, <u>nouns</u> are used as the subject of verbs just as they are in English, but <u>pronouns</u> are used much less often. This is because the ending of an Italian verb often shows you who the subject is.

<u>**Mia sorella**</u> **gioca a tennis.**	My sister is playing tennis.
Gioca bene.	She plays well.

⇨ *For more information on **Subject pronouns**, see page* 53.

➤ Italian verb forms also change depending on whether you are talking about the present, past or future: **cred̲o** means *I believe*, **cred̲evo** means *I believed* and **cred̲erò** means *I will believe*.

➤ In English, some verbs are <u>irregular</u>, for example, you do not add *–ed* to *speak*, *go*, or *see* to make the past tense. In the same way, some Italian verbs do not follow the usual patterns. These irregular Italian verbs include some very important and common verbs such as **andare** (meaning *to go*), **essere** (meaning *to be*) and **fare** (meaning *to do* or *to make*).

⇨ *For **Verb tables**, see supplement.*

KEY POINTS

✔ Italian verbs have different endings depending on their subject and their tense.
✔ Endings are added to the verb stem.
✔ You often do not need to use a pronoun before a verb in Italian.

The present tenses

> ## What are the present tenses?
> The **present tenses** are the verb forms that are used to talk about what is true at the moment, what generally happens and what is happening now; for example, *I'm a student; I travel to college by train; The phone's ringing.*

➤ In English there are two tenses you can use to talk about the present:

- the <u>present simple</u> tense
  I <u>live</u> here.
  They always <u>get up</u> early.

- the <u>present continuous</u> tense
  He <u>is eating</u> an apple.
  You <u>aren't</u> <u>listening</u>.

➤ In Italian there is also a <u>present simple</u> and a <u>present continuous</u> tense.

➤ As in English, the <u>present simple</u> tense in Italian is used to talk about:

- things that are generally true
  D'inverno <u>fa</u> freddo.   It'<u>s</u> cold in winter.

- what people and things usually do
  Giulia non <u>mangia</u> la carne.   Giulia <u>doesn't</u> eat meat.
  Queste macchine <u>consumano</u>   These cars <u>use</u> a lot of petrol.
   molta benzina.
  <u>Andiamo</u> spesso al cinema.   We often <u>go</u> to the cinema.

➤ Unlike in English, the <u>present simple</u> tense in Italian can be used to talk about:

- what is happening right now
  <u>Piove</u>.   It'<u>s raining</u>.
  Cosa <u>fai</u>?   What <u>are</u> you <u>doing</u>?

➤ In Italian the <u>present continuous</u> is also used to talk about things that are happening right now.
  Ci <u>sto pensando</u>.   I'm <u>thinking</u> about it.

⇨ *For more information on the use of the **Present tenses**, see pages 88 and 105.*

> *Tip*
> You can use the Italian present simple to translate both the English simple present and the English present continuous.
> **Piove.**   It's raining.
> **Piove molto.**   It rains a lot.
>
> ⇨ *For more information on **How to use the present tense**, see page 100.*

The present simple tense

How to make the present simple tense of regular –are verbs

➤ Verbs that have an infinitive ending in **–are**, such as **parlare**, **abitare** and **studiare** have a particular pattern of endings.

➤ To make the present simple tense of regular **–are** verbs take off the **–are** ending to get the stem of the verb.

Infinitive	Meaning	Stem (without –are)
parlare	to speak	parl-
abitare	to live	abit-
studiare	to study	studi-

➤ Then add the correct ending for the person you're talking about.

➤ Here are the present simple endings for regular **–are** verbs:

Present simple endings	Present simple of parlare	Meaning: *to speak*
–o	(io) parl<u>o</u>	I speak/am speaking
–i	(tu) parl<u>i</u>	you speak/are speaking
–a	(lui/lei) parl<u>a</u> (lei/Lei) parl<u>a</u>	he/she/it speaks/is speaking you speak/are speaking
–iamo	(noi) parl<u>iamo</u>	we speak/are speaking
–ate	(voi) parl<u>ate</u>	you speak/are speaking
–ano	(loro) parl<u>ano</u>	they speak/are speaking

Parli inglese?	Do you speak English?
Chi parla?	Who's speaking?
Parlano bene italiano.	They speak good Italian.

> *Tip*
> When you are talking about a male, a female or a thing, or are using **lei** as the polite word for you, you use the same verb form.
>
> ⇨ For more information on **How to say 'you' in Italian**, see page 55.

[i] Note that in Italian there's often no need to use a subject pronoun such as **io** (meaning *I*) or **tu** (meaning *you*) because the verb ending makes it clear who is doing the action. However, when you're talking about people you can use the pronouns **lui**, **lei** or **loro** with the verb for the sake of emphasis or to make things clearer.

Parla italiano <u>lui</u>?	Does he speak Italian?
<u>Lei</u> parla bene inglese, ma lui no.	She speaks good English, but he doesn't.
<u>Loro</u> non parlano mai.	They never speak.

When you're talking about things you <u>ALWAYS</u> use the verb by itself, with no pronoun.

Vedi l'*autobus*? – Sì, <u>arriva</u>.	Can you see the bus? – Yes, it's coming.
Vuole queste? – No, <u>costano</u> troppo.	Do you want these? – No, they cost too much.

⇨ *For more information on **Subject pronouns**, see page 53.*

KEY POINTS

✔ If you take the **–are** ending off the infinitive of a regular verb you get the stem.

✔ You add one of these endings to the stem: **–o**, **–i**, **–a**, **–iamo**, **–ate** or **–ano**.

✔ You only use a pronoun with the verb for emphasis or to be specially clear, but only when talking about people.

66 **Complete the following sentences with the correct form of the present tense. In some cases, the pronoun is given in brackets at the end of the sentence, to make clear which form to use.**

a I bambini ....con il cane. **(giocare)**

b Tua sorella ....inglese? **(parlare)**

c Il treno ....alle dieci. **(arrivare)**

d Io ....stasera, ma lei no. **(studiare)**

e Cosa ....a pranzo? (*voi*) **(mangiare)**

f I miei genitori ....in Francia. **(abitare)**

g ....le scarpe blu. (*tu*) **(comprare)**

h ....il nuovo film di Scorsese. (*noi*) **(guardare)**

i Mario ....nel ristorante. **(entrare)**

j ....la radio tutto il giorno. (*io*) **(ascoltare)**

67 **Match the two columns to form sentences.**

a Mangiamo	arrivano domani.
b Non	tutti insieme.
c Valentina studia	la televisione?
d I miei	all'università di Bologna.
e Guardate	parlo inglese.

68 **Translate the following sentences into Italian.**

a He studies a lot. ....

b He listens to music, but she doesn't.

....

c They smoke too much. ....

d I work in an office. ....

e Do you all live in that house?..

f Are you buying these shoes? (*tu*) ....

g That bag costs too much..

h My son is playing in the garden. ....

i Will you pass me that book, please? (*Lei*)................................

j We're preparing lunch. ....

How to make the present simple tense of regular –ere verbs

➤ Verbs that have an infinitive ending in **–ere**, such as **credere**, **ricevere** and **ripetere** have their own pattern of endings.

➤ To make the present simple tense of regular **–ere** verbs take off the **–ere** ending to get the stem and then add the correct ending for the person you're talking about.

Infinitive	Meaning	Stem (without –ere)
credere	to believe	cred-
ricevere	to receive	ricev-
ripetere	to repeat	ripet-

➤ The **io**, **tu** and **noi** endings you add to the stem of **–ere** verbs are the same as **–are** verb endings. The other endings are different.

➤ Here are the present simple endings for regular **–ere** verbs:

Present simple endings	Present simple of credere	Meaning: *to believe*
–o	(io) cred<u>o</u>	I believe
–i	(tu) cred<u>i</u>	you believe
–e	(lui/lei) cred<u>e</u> (lei/Lei) cred<u>e</u>	he/she believes you believe
–iamo	(noi) cred<u>iamo</u>	we believe
–ete	(voi) cred<u>ete</u>	you believe
–ono	(loro) cred<u>ono</u>	they believe

Non ci credo.   I don't believe it.
Credi ai fantasmi?   Do you believe in ghosts?
Lo credono tutti.   They all believe it.

> *Tip*
> When you are talking about a male, a female or a thing, or are using **lei** as the polite word for *you*, you use the same verb form.

[i] Note that in Italian there's often no need to use a subject pronoun such as **io** (meaning *I*) or **tu** (meaning *you*) because the verb ending makes it clear who is doing the action. However, when you're talking about people you can use the pronouns **lui**, **lei** or **loro** with the verb for the sake of emphasis or to make things clearer.
Lui non ci crede.   He doesn't believe it.
Lei crede ai fantasmi, io no.   She believes in ghosts, I don't.
Loro lo credono tutti.   They all believe it.

When you're talking about things you <u>ALWAYS</u> use the verb by itself, with no pronoun.
La minestra? Non <u>sa</u> di nulla.   The soup? It doesn't taste of anything.
Le piante? <u>Crescono</u> bene.   The plants? They're growing well.

⇨ *For more information on **Subject pronouns**, see page 53.*

> *Tip*
> Remember that you never use a pronoun in Italian to translate <u>it</u> at the beginning of a sentence.
>
> **Dipende.** It depends.
> **Piove.** It's raining.

KEY POINTS

✔ If you take the **–ere** ending off the infinitive of a regular verb you get the stem.

✔ You add one of these endings to the stem: **–o**, **–i**, **–e**, **–iamo**, **–ete** or **–ono**.

✔ You only use a pronoun with the verb for emphasis or to be specially clear, but only when talking about people.

---

69 **Complete the following sentences with the correct form of the present tense. In some cases, the pronoun is given in brackets at the end of the sentence, to make clear which form to use.**

a ....spesso in inverno. **(piovere)**

b Mia sorella ....la sua macchina. **(vendere)**

c ....la domanda? (*noi*) **(ripetere)**

d Non ci........................? (*tu*) **(credere)**

e Mio marito ....sempre le chiavi di casa. **(perdere)**

f I miei figli ....i loro cugini ogni mese. **(vedere)**

g Mio padre non mi ....di andare in discoteca sabato sera. **(permettere)**

h ....l'autobus per andare a lavoro. (*io*) **(prendere)**

i Il sole ....tutto il giorno. **(splendere)**

j ....la torta tra tutti? (*voi*) **(dividere)**

70 **Make a sentence in the present tense using the elements given. Where it is not obvious, the subject of the verb is given in brackets to show which form of the verb to use. The first one has been done for you.**

a fantasmi/credere/ai/Paolo/non...*Paolo non crede ai fantasmi.*..........

b ricevere/notizia/buona/ragazze/una/le........................

c mai/non/il/prendere/treno? (*tu*) ....

d madre/vendere/mia/casa/sua/la ....

e una/vedere/non/soluzione (*io*)........................

f problema/tempo/con/perdere/questo (*noi*)........................

g ricevere/lo/Lei/quando/stipendio? ....

h tempo/dipendere/dal ....

i strada/prendere/quale? (*voi*) ....

j amica/ci/la/credere/non/mia........................

71 **Match the related sentences.**

a **Non hanno una macchina.**　　Spendi troppi soldi.

b **Perde spesso le chiavi.**　　Fa caldo e splende il sole.

c **Sono povera!**　　Non le vedo.

d **Che tempo fa oggi?**　　Bisogna comprare un portachiavi.

e **Dove sono le mie scarpe?**　　Prendono sempre il treno.

How to make the present simple tense of regular –ire verbs

➤ Most verbs that have an infinitive ending in **–ire**, such as **finire** (meaning *to finish*), **pulire** (meaning *to clean*) and **capire** (meaning *to understand*) follow one pattern of endings in the present. Some common verbs such as **dormire** and **servire** have a different pattern.

➤ To make the present simple tense of <u>all</u> **–ire** verbs take off the **–ire** ending to get the <u>stem</u> of the verb.

Infinitive	Meaning	Stem (without –ire)
finire	to finish	fin-
pulire	to clean	pul-
capire	to understand	cap-
dormire	to sleep	dorm-
servire	to serve	serv-

➤ Here are the present simple endings for regular **–ire** verbs:

Present simple endings	Present simple of finire	Meaning: *to finish*
–isco	(io) fin<u>isco</u>	I finish/am finishing
–isci	(tu) fin<u>isci</u>	you finish/are finishing
–isce	(lui/lei) fin<u>isce</u>	he/she/it finishes/ is finishing
	(lei/Lei) fin<u>isce</u>	you finish/are finishing
–iamo	(noi) fin<u>iamo</u>	we finish/are finishing
–ite	(voi) fin<u>ite</u>	you finish/are finishing
–iscono	(loro) fin<u>iscono</u>	they finish/are finishing

Il film fin<u>isce</u> alle dieci.	The film finishes at ten.
Fin<u>iscono</u> il lavoro.	They're finishing the work.
Non pul<u>isco</u> mai la macchina.	I never clean the car.
Prefer<u>isci</u> l'altro?	Do you prefer the other one?
Non cap<u>iscono</u>.	They don't understand.

ⓘ Note that in Italian there's often no need to use a subject pronoun such as **io** (meaning *I*) or **tu** (meaning *you*) because the verb ending makes it clear who is doing the action. However, when you're talking about people you can use the pronouns **lui**, **lei** or **loro** with the verb for the sake of emphasis or to make things clearer.

<u>Lui</u> **non pulisce mai la macchina.**	He never cleans the car.
<u>Lei</u> **mi capisce sempre.**	She always understands me.
<u>Loro</u> **preferiscono l'altro.**	They prefer the other one.

When you're talking about things you <u>ALWAYS</u> use the verb by itself, with no pronoun.

Il primo treno? – <u>Parte</u> alle cinque.	The first train? It goes at five.
Le lezioni quando finiscono? –	When do lessons finish?
<u>Finiscono</u> alle quattro.	They finish at four.

➤ Some common **–ire** verbs do not add **–isc–** to the stem. The most important ones are **dormire** (meaning *to sleep*), **servire** (meaning *to serve*), **aprire** (meaning *to open*), **partire** (meaning *to leave*), **sentire** (meaning *to hear*) and **soffrire** (meaning *to suffer*).

➤ The endings of these verbs are as follows:

Present simple endings	Present simple of dormire	Meaning: *to sleep*
–o	(io) dorm<u>o</u>	I sleep/am sleeping
–i	(tu) dorm<u>i</u>	you sleep/are sleeping
–e	(lui/lei) dorm<u>e</u> (lei/Lei) dorm<u>e</u>	he/she/it sleeps/is sleeping you sleep/are sleeping
–iamo	(noi) dorm<u>iamo</u>	we sleep/are sleeping
–ite	(voi) dorm<u>ite</u>	you sleep/are sleeping
–ono	(loro) dorm<u>ono</u>	they sleep/are sleeping

ℹ Note that these endings are the same as **–ere** verb endings, except for the second person plural (**voi**).

Dorm<u>o</u> sempre bene.	I always sleep well.
A che cosa serv<u>e</u>?	What's it for?
Quando part<u>ite</u>?	When are you leaving?
Soffr<u>ono</u> molto.	They are suffering a lot.

Tip

When you are talking about a male, a female or a thing, or are using **lei** as the polite word for *you*, you use the same verb form.

KEY POINTS

✔ Take the **–ire** ending off the infinitive of a regular verb to get the stem.

✔ For most **–ire** verbs the endings you add to the stem are: **–isco**, **–isci**, **–isce**, **–iamo**, **–ite** or **–iscono**.

✔ A few common **–ire** verbs add these endings to the stem: **–o**, **–i**, **–e**, **–iamo**, **–ite**, **–ono**.

✔ You only use a pronoun with the verb for emphasis or to be specially clear, but only when talking about people.

72 **Complete the following sentences with the correct form of the present tense. In some cases, the pronoun is given in brackets at the end of the sentence, to make clear which form to use.**

a I soldati ....sempre le loro scarpe. **(pulire)**

b Mio fratello non ....mai il problema. **(capire)**

c ....tutto il giorno? (*voi*) **(dormire)**

d Fortunatamente il bambino non ....molto. **(soffrire)**

e ....delle minestre buonissime nel nostro ristorante. **(servire)**

f Quale torta ....? (*tu*) **(preferire)**

g A che ora ....il prossimo treno per Milano? **(partire)**

h Gli studenti ....le finestre perché fa caldo. **(aprire)**

i Non ....la musica. (*io*) **(sentire)**

j Il concerto ....alle undici. **(finire)**

73 **Translate the following sentences into Italian, using the *tu* form of the verb to translate 'you' where appropriate.**

a She understands everything. ....

b We prefer the other one. ....

c The film finishes at nine o'clock. ....

d Are you all leaving this evening?..

e The dogs sleep under the table.

....

f What's it for?..

g Fortunately we don't hear the traffic from our house.

....

h Giorgio cleans his car every day.

....

i Will you open the bottle for me? ....

j The cats are suffering from the heat. ....

Test yourself

74 **Make a sentence in the present tense using the elements given. Where it is not obvious, the subject of the verb is given in brackets to show which form of the verb to use.**

a mio/sempre/dormire/tardi/fratello/fino a

....

b Paola/il/finire/lavoro

....

c che/il/servire/a/cosa/coltello?

....

d casa/domani/la/pulire (*noi*)

....

e quello/preferire/nero/lui

....

f la/gli/sentire/uccelli/mattina? (*voi*)

....

g persone/la/soffrire/molte/fame

....

h sorella/porta/la/mia/aprire

....

i a/ora/partire/che? (*tu*)

....

j lezioni/alle/finire/cinque/le

....

Infinitives that end in –rre

➤ All regular verbs have infinitives ending in **–are**, **-ere**, or **–ire**.

➤ A few common irregular verbs have infinitives ending in **–rre**. For example:

comporre	to compose	**condurre**	to lead
porre	to put	**produrre**	to produce
proporre	to propose	**ridurre**	to reduce
supporre	to suppose	**tradurre**	to translate

➤ Here are the present simple forms of **comporre**:

	Present simple of comporre	Meaning: *to compose*
(io)	compongo	I compose/I am composing
(tu)	componi	you compose/you are composing
(lui/lei)	compone	he/she/it composes/is composing
(lei/Lei)	compone	you compose/are composing
(noi)	componiamo	we compose/are composing
(voi)	componete	you compose/are composing
(loro)	compongono	they compose/are composing

➤ Here are the present simple forms of **produrre**:

	Present simple of produrre	Meaning: *to produce*
(io)	produco	I produce/I am producing
(tu)	produci	you produce/you are producing
(lui/lei)	produce	he/she/it produces/is producing
(lei/Lei)	produce	you produce/are producing
(noi)	produciamo	we produce/are producing
(voi)	producete	you produce/are producing
(loro)	producono	they produce/are producing

The present tense of all verbs ending in **–porre** follow the pattern of **comporre**, and all verbs ending in **–durre** follow the pattern of **produrre**.

Where to put the stress when saying the infinitive

➤ When you say the infinitives of **–are** and **–ire** verbs the stress goes on the **a**, or **i** of the ending:

Non vuole parlare.	He doesn't want to speak.
Non riesco a dormire.	I can't sleep.

➤ When you say the infinitive of most **–ere** verbs the stress goes on the syllable that comes <u>before</u> the ending.

Devono vendere la casa.	They've got to sell their house.
Può ripetere?	Could you repeat that?

➤ However, there are a number of very important irregular **–ere** verbs which have the stress on the first **e** of the ending.

–ere verb	Meaning
av<u>e</u>re	to have
cad<u>e</u>re	to fall
dov<u>e</u>re	to have to
persuad<u>e</u>re	to persuade
pot<u>e</u>re	to be able
riman<u>e</u>re	to remain
ved<u>e</u>re	to see

Fa' attenzione a non cad<u>e</u>re.   Mind you don't fall.
Non puoi av<u>e</u>re il mio.   You can't have mine.

⇨ *For more information on the* **Infinitive**, *see page 183.*

How to make the present simple tense of common irregular verbs

➤ There are many verbs that do not follow the usual patterns. These include some very common and important verbs such as **avere** (meaning *to have*), **fare** (meaning *to do* or *to make*) and **andare** (meaning *to go*).

➤ Here are the present simple forms of **avere**:

	Present simple of avere	Meaning: *to have*
(io)	ho	I have/have got
(tu)	hai	you have
(lui/lei) (lei/Lei)	ha	he/she/it has you have
(noi)	abbiamo	we have
(voi)	avete	you have
(loro)	hanno	they have

Ho due sorelle.   I've got two sisters.
Hai abbastanza soldi?   Have you got enough money?
Abbiamo tempo.   We've got time.
Hanno i capelli biondi.   They have blonde hair.

➤ Here are the present simple forms of **fare**:

	Present simple of fare	Meaning: *to do, to make*
(io)	faccio	I do/am doing, I make/am making
(tu)	fai	you do/are doing, you make/are making
(lui/lei)	fa	he/she/it does/is doing, he/she/it makes/is making
(lei/Lei)		you do/are doing, you make/are making
(noi)	facciamo	we do/are doing, we make/are making
(voi)	fate	you do/are doing, you make/are making
(loro)	fanno	they do/are doing, they make/are making

<u>Faccio</u> troppi errori. — I make too many mistakes.
Cosa <u>fai</u> sta sera? — What are you doing this evening?
<u>Fa</u> caldo. — It's hot.
<u>Fanno</u> quello che possono. — They're doing what they can.

➤ Here are the present simple forms of **andare**:

	Present simple of andare	Meaning: *to go*
(io)	vado	I go/am going
(tu)	vai	you go/are going
(lui/lei) (lei/Lei)	va	he/she/it goes/is going you go/are going
(noi)	andiamo	we go/are going
(voi)	andate	you go/are going
(loro)	vanno	they go/are going

Ci <u>vado</u> spesso. — I often go there.
Dove <u>vai</u>? — Where are you going?
<u>Va</u> bene. — That's okay.
<u>Vanno</u> tutti al concerto. — They're all going to the concert.

⇨ *For other irregular verbs in the present simple tense, see* **Verb tables** *in the supplement.*

How to use the present simple tense in Italian

➤ The present simple tense is often used in Italian in the same way as in English, but there are also some important differences.

➤ As in English, you use the Italian present simple to talk about:

• things that are generally true
  La frutta <u>fa</u> bene.   Fruit is good for you.

- current situations
  Vivono in Francia.   They live in France.

- what people and things usually do
  Litigano sempre.   They always quarrel.
  Si blocca spesso.   It often jams.

- fixed arrangements
  Comincia domani.   It starts tomorrow.

➤ Unlike in English, the Italian present simple is used to talk about:

- what is happening right now
  Arrivo!   I'm coming!
  Non mangi niente.   You're not eating anything.

- what you are going to do
  È rotto, lo butto via.   It's broken, I'm going to throw it away.
  Ci penso io.   I'll see to it.

- predictions
  Se fai così lo rompi.   If you do that you'll break it.

- offers
  Pago io.   I'll pay.

➤ In English the <u>perfect</u> tense is used to say how long someone has been doing something, or how long something has been happening. In Italian you use **da** and the <u>present simple</u> tense for this kind of sentence.

    Aspetto da tre ore.   I've been waiting for three hours.
    Da quanto tempo studi l'italiano?   How long have you been learning Italian?

⇨ *For more information on the use of tenses with **da**, see page 231.*

KEY POINTS

✔ The present simple tense in Italian is used as in English, and has a few additional uses.
✔ Use the present simple with da to talk about how long something has been going on.

Test yourself

75 **Complete the following sentences with the correct form of the present tense. In some cases, the pronoun is given in brackets at the end of the sentence, to make clear which form to use.**

a Il ragazzo ....il libro sul tavolo. **(porre)**

b ....un testo inglese. (*io*) **(tradurre)**

c ....al cinema stasera? (*noi*) **(andare)**

d I professori ....una soluzione alternativa. **(proporre)**

e ....bisogna di qualcosa? (*voi*) **(avere)**

f La guida ....i turisti nel centro storico della città. **(condurre)**

g Cosa ....domani? (*tu*) **(fare)**

h ....tutti alla festa. (*loro*) **(andare)**

i Tua figlia ....abbastanza soldi? **(avere)**

j ....quello che posso. (*io*) **(fare)**

76 **Match the sentences that are related.**

a Da quanto tempo abiti in Francia? Sì, ci vado spesso.

b Parla bene l'inglese? Ci penso io.

c Claudia, dove sei? Da tre anni.

d È rotta la finestra. Arrivo!

e Conosci Londra? Sì, lo studia da cinque anni.

77 **Translate the following sentences into Italian, using the *tu* form of the verb to translate 'you' where appropriate.**

a I've been waiting for twenty minutes. ....

b Isn't she eating anything? ....

c Vegetables are good for you. ....

d The concert starts in one hour. ....

e If she calls he'll come. ....

f My parents live in Rome. ....

g Which skirt do you prefer? ....

h I've been studying Italian for three years. ....

i What are we doing later? ....

j The children have blonde hair. ....

essere and stare

➤ In Italian there are two irregular verbs, **essere** and **stare**, that both mean *to be*. In the present tense they follow the patterns shown below:

Pronoun	*essere*	*stare*	Meaning: *to be*
(io)	sono	sto	I am
(tu)	sei	stai	you are
(lui/lei) (lei/Lei)	è	sta	he/she/it is you are
(noi)	siamo	stiamo	we are
(voi)	siete	state	you are
(loro)	sono	stanno	they are

➤ **essere** is the verb generally used to translate *to be*:

Cosa <u>sono</u>?	What are they?
<u>È</u> italiana.	She's Italian.
<u>Sono</u> io.	It's me.
<u>È</u> un problema.	It's a problem.
<u>Siete</u> pronti?	Are you ready?

➤ However, **stare** is used for *to be* in some common contexts:

- to say or ask how someone is

Come <u>stai</u>?	How are you?
<u>Sto</u> bene, grazie.	I'm fine thanks.
Mio nonno <u>sta</u> male.	My grandfather isn't well.

- to say where someone is

Luigi <u>sta</u> a casa.	Luigi's at home.
<u>Starò</u> a Roma due giorni.	I'll be in Rome for two days.

- to say where something is situated

La casa <u>sta</u> sulla collina.	The house is on the hill.

- with the adjectives **zitto** and **solo**

Vuole <u>stare</u> solo.	He wants to be alone.
<u>Sta'</u> zitto!	Be quiet!

- to make continuous tenses

<u>Sta</u> studiando.	He's studying.
<u>Stavo</u> andando a casa.	I was going home.

⇨ For more information on the **Present continuous**, see page 105.

KEY POINTS

✔ **essere** is generally used to translate *to be*.
✔ **stare** is used to talk about health, where people and things are and with some adjectives.
✔ **stare** is also used to make continuous tenses.

Test yourself

78 **Complete the following sentences with the correct form of the present tense. In some cases, the pronoun is given in brackets at the end of the sentence, to make clear which form to use.**

   a Marta ....mia cugina. **(essere)**

   b Mio marito ....male. **(stare)**

   c Come ...., signora? **(stare)**

   d ....francese. (*io*) **(essere)**

   e Cosa ....questi? **(essere)**

   f ....a casa tutto il giorno. (*noi*) **(stare)**

   g Oggi ....mercoledì. **(essere)**

   h Gli alberghi ....nel centro storico. **(essere)**

   i ....pronti? (*voi*) **(essere)**

   j ....libero domani sera? (*tu*) **(essere)**

79 **Match the question on the left with its answer on the right.**

   a Dove sei?   Sono dieci.

   b Come sta tuo padre?   Vuole stare solo.

   c Quanti sono i bambini alla festa?   Sono nel soggiorno.

   d Perché non viene?   Sono io.

   e Chi è?   Sta meglio, grazie.

80 **Complete the following sentences with the correct form of *essere* or *stare*.**

   a Mio fratello .... studiando.

   b Giorgio e Anna .... cugini.

   c La mia amica .... tedesca.

   d Mi dispiace, non .... ancora pronta.

   e Il ragazzo .... a casa da solo.

   f Qual .... il problema?

   g I bambini .... dormendo.

   h Questa macchina .... la mia.

   i Dove .... le chiavi?

   j Mia madre .... bene.

The present continuous tense

➤ In Italian the <u>present continuous</u> is used instead of the <u>present simple</u> to talk about what is happening at the moment, when you want to emphasize that it's happening <u>right now</u>.

Arrivano.	They are coming.
Stanno arrivando!	They're coming!

➤ The Italian present continuous is made with the present tense of **stare** and the <u>gerund</u> of the verb. The gerund is a verb form that ends in **–ando** (for **–are** verbs), or **–endo** (for **–ere** and **–ire** verbs) and is the same as the *–ing* form of the verb in English, for example, *walking*, *swimming*.

<u>**Sto cercando** il mio passaporto.</u>	I'm looking for my passport.
<u>**Sta scrivendo.**</u>	He's writing.
<u>**Stanno dormendo.**</u>	They're sleeping.
Cosa <u>**stai facendo**</u>?	What are you doing?

➤ To make the gerund of an **–are** verb, take off the ending and add **–ando**, for example, **mangiando** (meaning *eating*), **cercando** (meaning *looking for*). To make the gerund of an **–ere** or **–ire** verb, take off the ending and add **–endo**, for example, **scrivendo** (meaning *writing*), **partendo** (meaning *leaving*).

⇨ *For more information on the **Gerund**, see page 163.*

> *Tip*
> Only use the Italian present continuous to talk about things that are happening at this very minute. Use the present simple tense to talk about things that are continuing, but not necessarily happening at this minute.
> **Studio medicina.** I'm studying medicine.
>
> ⇨ *For more information on the **Present simple tense**, see page 88.*

KEY POINTS

✔ Only use the present continuous in Italian for actions that are happening right now.
✔ To make the present continuous, use the present tense of **stare** and the gerund of the main verb.

Test yourself

81 **Complete the following sentences with the correct gerund to form the present continuous sense. The first one has been done for you.**

a Non posso venire, sto ..*mangiando*.. (mangiare)

b Cosa stai ....? (cercare)

c Gli ospiti stanno .... (arrivare)

d Sta ....una lettera alla sua mamma. (scrivere)

e Piove, quindi stiamo ....a casa. (tornare)

f Non disturbarlo, sta .... (dormire)

g State ....i libri? (cercare)

h Stai ....al telefono? (parlare)

i Arrivo subito, sto ....questo lavoro. (finire)

j I bambini stanno ....la televisione. (guardare)

82 **Replace the highlighted verb with the present continuous tense. The first one has been done for you.**

a Maria **mangia** la frutta. ...*sta mangiando*...........

b I miei genitori **dormono**. ....

c Il treno **arriva**. ....

d **Parla** con sua moglie. ....

e **Leggi** il giornale? ....

f Mia nipote **studia** medicina. ....

g **Lavoriamo** in un ristorante. ....

h Cosa **cerchi**? ....

i **Puliscono** la casa. ....

j **Ascolta** la radio. ....

83 **Match the reply on the left with its question on the right.**

a È tardi.   Cosa fa la mamma?

b Una biografia politica.   Perché stanno dormendo?

c No, ho finito.   Flavio e Dora sono alla festa?

d Sta comprando il pane.   Stai mangiando?

e No, stanno arrivando.   Cosa stai leggendo?

The imperative

> ## What is the imperative?
> An **imperative** is the form of the verb used to give orders and instructions, for example, *Sit down!*; *Don't go!*; *Let's start!*

Using the imperative

➤ In Italian, you use a different form of the imperative depending on whether you are:

- telling someone to do something

- telling someone not to do something

- speaking to one person or more than one person

- speaking to someone you call **tu**

- speaking formally

➤ The pronouns **tu**, **lei** (the formal way of saying *you*) and **voi** all have their own forms of the imperative, although you don't actually use these pronouns when giving orders and instructions. There is also a formal plural form of the imperative.

- You can also use a form of the imperative to make suggestions. This form is like *let's* in English.

How to tell someone to do something

➤ You make the imperative of regular verbs by adding endings to the verb <u>stem</u>, which is what is left when you take away the **–are**, **–ere** or **–ire**. There are different endings for **–are**, **–ere** and **–ire** verbs:

- The endings for **–are** verb imperatives are **–a** (**tu** form), **–i** (**lei** form), **–iamo** (*let's*), **–ate** (**voi** form) and **–ino** (polite plural). For example, **aspettare → aspett- → aspetta**.

Imperative of aspettare	Example	Meaning: *to wait*
aspett**a**!	**Aspetta Marco!**	Wait Marco!
aspett**i**!	**Aspetti signore!**	Wait Sir!
aspett**iamo**	**Aspettiamo qui.**	Let's wait here.
aspett**ate**!	**Aspettate ragazzi!**	Wait children!
aspett**ino**!	**Aspettino un *attimo* signori!**	Wait a moment ladies and gentlemen!

- The endings for **–ere** verb imperatives are **–i** (**tu** form), **–a** (**lei** form), **–iamo** (*let's*), **–ete** (**voi** form) and **–ano** (polite plural). For example, **prendere → prend-→ prendi**.

Imperative of prendere	Example	Meaning: *to take*
prend**i**	Prendi quello, Marco!	Take that one, Marco!
prend**a**	Prenda quello, signore!	Take that one, Sir!
prend**iamo**	Prendiamo quello.	Let's take that one.
prend**ete**	Prendete quelli, ragazzi!	Take those ones, children!
prend**ano**	Prendano quelli, signori!	Take those ones, ladies and gentlemen!

- The endings for most **–ire** verb imperatives are **–isci** (**tu** form), **–isca** (**lei** form), **–iamo** (*let's*), **–ite** (**voi** form) and **–iscano** (polite plural). For example, **finire → fin-→ finisci**.

☑ Note that **sci** is pronounced like *she*; **sca** is pronounced *ska*.

Imperative of finire	Example	Meaning: *to finish*
fin**isci**	Finisci l'esercizio, Marco!	Finish the exercise, Marco!
fin**isca**	Finisca tutto, signore!	Finish it all, Sir!
fin**iamo**	Finiamo tutto.	Let's finish it all.
fin**ite**	Finite i compiti, ragazzi!	Finish your homework, children!
fin**iscano**	Finiscano tutto, signori!	Finish it all, ladies and gentlemen!

➤ The endings for verbs that do not add **–isc** to the stem, such as **partire** (meaning *to leave*), **dormire** (meaning *to sleep*), **aprire** (meaning *to open*) and **sentire** (meaning *to listen*) are **–i**, **–a**, **–iamo**, **–ite** and **–ano**.

    Dormi Giulia!   Go to sleep Giulia!
    Partiamo.   Let's go.

⇨ *For more information on **Regular –ire verbs**, see page 94.*

➤ Some of the commonest verbs in Italian have irregular imperative forms. Here are the forms for some important verbs:

	dare	dire	*essere*	fare	andare
(tu)	da'! *or* dai!	di'!	sii!	fa'! *or* fai!	va'! *or* vai!
(lei/Lei)	dia!	dica!	sia!	faccia!	vada!
(noi)	diamo	diciamo	siamo	facciamo	andiamo
(voi)	date!	dite!	siate!	fate!	andate!
(loro)	diano!	dicano!	siano!	facciano!	vadano!

Sii bravo, Paolo!　　　Be good Paolo!
Faccia pure, signore!　　Carry on, sir!
Dite la verità, ragazzi!　Tell the truth, children!

⇨ *For more information on the imperatives of* **Irregular verbs***, see Verb tables.*

KEY POINTS
✔ There are familiar and polite forms of the imperative.
✔ The **–iamo** form is used to translate *let's*.

Test yourself

84 **Translate the following commands into Italian.**

a Finish your homework, Riccardo!

....

b Let's wait here!

....

c Be good, boys!

....

d Take this one, sir!

....

e Wait a moment, ladies and gentlemen!

....

f Go to sleep, Giuseppe!

....

g Let's go to the party!

....

h Tell the truth, Mario.

....

i Carry on, madam!

....

j Finish it all, girls!

....

85 **Match the statements that are connected.**

a Ho sonno.	Prenda questo, signore.
b Non sappiamo quali scarpe prendere.	Dormi!
c Vieni, mamma!	Andiamo al mare!
d Ho bisogno di un ombrello.	Aspetta un attimo!
e C'è il sole.	Prendete quelle!

Where do pronouns go?

➤ In English, pronouns such as *me*, *it* and *them* always come after the imperative, for example *Watch me!; Take it!; Give them to me!*

➤ In Italian, pronouns come <u>AFTER</u> the imperative in the **tu** and **voi** forms:

- The pronoun joins with the imperative to make one word.
Guarda<u>mi</u>, mamma!	Look at me, mum!
Aspett*ate<u>li</u>!	Wait for them!

- When the imperative is only one syllable **mi** becomes **–mmi**, **ti** becomes **–tti**, **lo** becomes **–llo** and so on.
Dim<u>mi</u>!	Tell me!
Fal<u>lo</u> s*ubito!	Do it immediately!

- When the pronouns **mi**, **ti**, **ci** and **vi** are followed by another pronoun they become **me-**, **te-**, **ce-** and **ve-**, and **gli** and **le** become **glie-**.
Mand*a<u>meli</u>.	Send me them.
Da<u>glielo</u>.	Give it to him.

> *Tip*
> In Italian you <u>always</u> put the indirect object pronoun first.
>
> ⇨ *For more information on **Indirect object pronouns**, see page 60.*

➤ Pronouns also come <u>AFTER</u> the **–iamo** form of the imperative, joining onto it to make one word.
Provi*a<u>molo</u>!	Let's try it!
Mandi*amo<u>gliela</u>!	Let's send it to them.

➤ Pronouns come <u>BEFORE</u> the **lei** form of the imperative and the polite plural form.
<u>Mi</u> **dia un chilo d'uva, per favore.**	Give me a kilo of grapes please.
<u>La</u> **prenda, signore.**	Take it, sir.
<u>Ne</u> **ass*aggino un po', signori!**	Try a bit, ladies and gentlemen!
<u>Si</u> **acc*omodi!**	Take a seat!

⇨ *For more information on **Reflexive verbs**, see page 115.*

KEY POINTS

✔ Pronouns come after the **tu**, **voi** and **–iamo** forms of the imperative.
✔ Pronouns which come after the imperative join onto it to make one word.
✔ Pronouns come before the polite imperative, and do not join onto it.

86 *Mi dai una mano?* is more polite than using the imperative, *Dammi una mano!*. Change each question into an order in the imperative, remembering that the pronoun may change. The first one has been done for you.

a Mi aspetti, Claudia. *Aspettami, Claudia!*

b Glielo dai? ....

c Lo fai subito? ....

d Ci aspettate? ....

e Lo prendiamo? ....

f Glielo dite? ....

g Ci passa il sale, signore? ....

h Mi guardi, papà? ....

i Mi dà la chiave, signora? ....

j Mi mandate una cartolina? ....

87 Cross out the items the speaker is not likely to be referring to.

a dammelo!   il portafoglio/la tua borsa/il tuo nome

b aspettateli!   i ragazzi/le ragazze/i vostri amici

c mandiamogliela! lo zucchero/la lettera/la cartolina

d dimmela!   la verità/la storia/il tuo indirizzo

e guardami!   mamma/Roberto/signora

f prendile!   le scarpe/i guanti/le chiavi

g datecelo!   l'indirizzo/le lettere/il passaporto

h mangiamola!   la torta/le mele/la pizza

i li prenda!   i soldi/il tuo nome/i pomodori

j portamela!   la carta/le fragole/la penna

88 Match the phrases that are related.

a La torta?   Prendeteli!

b Le scarpe?   Lo aspetti, signore!

c I soldi?   Mangiala!

d Il regalo?   Dagliele!

e L'autobus?   Mandiamoglielo!

How to tell someone NOT to do something

➤ When you are telling someone you call **tu** <u>NOT</u> to do something:

- use **non** with the <u>infinitive</u> (the **–are**, **–ere**, **–ire** form) of the verb
Non <u>dire</u> bugie Andrea!	Don't tell lies Andrea!
Non <u>dimenticare</u>!	Don't forget!

  ⇨ *For more information on the **Infinitive**, see page 183.*

- if there is also a pronoun, join it onto the infinitive, or put it in front
Non toccar<u>lo</u>! OR	
Non <u>lo</u> toccare!	Don't touch it!
Non dir<u>glielo</u>! OR	
Non <u>glielo</u> dire!	Don't tell him about it!
Non far<u>mi</u> ridere! OR	
Non <u>mi</u> far ridere!	Don't make me laugh!
Non preoccupar<u>ti</u>! OR	
Non <u>ti</u> preoccupare!	Don't worry!
Non bagnar<u>ti</u>! OR	
Non <u>ti</u> bagnare!	Don't get wet!

  ⓘ Note that the infinitive usually drops the final **e** when the pronoun joins onto it.

➤ In all other cases, to tell someone not to do something:

- use **non** with the imperative
<u>Non dimenticate</u>, ragazzi.	Don't forget, children.
<u>Non abbia</u> paura, signora.	Don't be afraid, madam.
<u>Non esageriamo</u>!	Don't let's go too far!

- join pronouns onto <u>the end of</u> the **voi** and **–iamo** forms of the imperative
Non <u>guardateli</u>!	Don't look at them.
Non <u>ditemelo</u>!	Don't say it to me!
Non <u>mangiamoli</u> tutti.	Don't let's eat them all.
Non <u>diamoglielo</u>.	Don't let's give it to them.

- put pronouns <u>in front of</u> the **lei** and polite plural forms of the imperative
Non <u>li</u> guardi, signora.	Don't look at them, madam.
Non <u>si</u> preoccupino, signori.	Don't worry, ladies and gentlemen.

KEY POINTS

✔ To tell a person you call **tu** not to do something, use **non** with the infinitive.

✔ To tell all other people not to do something use non with the imperative.

✔ To say *Let's not* use **non** with the **–iamo** form.

Test yourself

89 **Replace the highlighted positive command with a negative one. The first one has been done for you.**

a Mangi tutto! *Non mangiare tutto!* ....

b Dammi la borsa! ....

c Guardate, ragazzi! ....

d Prendilo! ....

e Lasciatemi da sola! ....

f Tocca il disegno! ....

g Li guardino, signori! ....

h Mangiamola! ....

i Parla con i tuoi amici! ....

j Parti senza di loro! ....

90 **Translate the following sentences into Italian using the imperative form. Where appropriate, use the *tu* form of the verb to translate 'you'.**

a Don't touch it! ....

b Do it right now! ....

c Don't speak to me! ....

d Let's go to the cinema! ....

e Don't eat the cake! ....

f Give it to him! ....

g Let's not wait for them! ....

h Don't put it there! ....

i Don't look, ladies and gentlemen! ....

j Don't say it! ....

91 **Match the sentences that are related.**

a È caldo!   Non vi preoccupate!

b Ho sonno!   Mettete le giacche!

c Ho fame!   Vai a dormire!

d Abbiamo freddo!   Mangi un panino!

e Abbiamo paura!   Non toccarlo!

Reflexive verbs

What is a reflexive verb?

Reflexive verbs in English are ones where the subject and object are the same, and which use reflexive pronouns such as *myself, yourself* and *themselves*, for example, *I've hurt myself; Look after yourself!; They're enjoying themselves.*

Using reflexive verbs

The basics

➤ There are more reflexive verbs in Italian than in English. The infinitive form of a reflexive verb has **–si** joined onto it, for example, **divertirsi** (meaning *to enjoy oneself*). This is the way reflexive verbs are shown in dictionaries. **si** is a <u>reflexive pronoun</u> and means *himself, herself, itself, themselves* and *oneself*.

➤ Verbs that are reflexive in English, such as *to hurt oneself* or *to enjoy oneself* are reflexive in Italian. In addition, many verbs that include *get*, for example, *to get up, to get dressed, to get annoyed, to get bored, to get tanned,* are reflexive verbs in Italian. Here are some important Italian reflexive verbs:

accomodarsi	to sit down; to take a seat
addormentarsi	to go to sleep
alzarsi	to get up
annoiarsi	to get bored; to be bored
arrabbiarsi	to get angry
chiamarsi	to be called
chiedersi	to wonder
divertirsi	to enjoy oneself; to have fun
farsi	male to hurt oneself
fermarsi	to stop
lavarsi	to wash; to get washed
perdersi	to get lost
pettinarsi	to comb one's hair
preoccuparsi	to worry
prepararsi	to get ready
ricordarsi	to remember
sbrigarsi	to hurry
svegliarsi	to wake up
vestirsi	to dress; to get dressed

<u>**Si accomodi!**</u>	Take a seat!
<u>**Mi alzo**</u> **alle sette.**	I get up at seven o'clock.
Come <u>**ti chiami?**</u>	What are you called?
Non <u>**vi preoccupate!**</u>	Don't worry!
<u>**Sbrigati!**</u>	Hurry up!
<u>**Ci prepariamo.**</u>	We're getting ready.
Matteo <u>**si annoia.**</u>	Matteo is getting bored.
Lucia <u>**si è fatta**</u> **male.**	Lucia hurt herself.
I bambini <u>**si divertono.**</u>	The children are enjoying themselves.

[i] Note that in English, you can often add a reflexive pronoun to verbs if you want to, for example, you can say *Don't worry yourself!* or *He didn't hurry himself*. Whenever you can do this in English, the Italian equivalent is likely to be a reflexive verb.

➤ Some Italian verbs can be used both as reflexive verbs, and as ordinary verbs with no reflexive pronoun. If you are talking about getting yourself ready you use **prepararsi**; if you are talking about gettting the dinner ready you use **preparare**.

Mi preparo alla maratona.	I'm getting ready for the marathon.
Sto preparando il pranzo.	I'm getting lunch ready.
Mi chiedo cosa stia facendo.	I wonder what he's doing.
Chiedi a Lidia perché piange.	Ask Lidia why she's crying.

[i] Note that **chiedersi** literally means *to ask oneself*.

Grammar Extra!
Some reflexive verbs in Italian add the pronoun **ne** after the reflexive pronoun. The most important of these verbs is **andarsene** (meaning *to go away*, *to leave*).

Me ne vado.	I'm leaving.
Vattene!	Go away!
Ce ne andiamo.	Let's be off.
Se ne sono andati.	They've left.

The pronouns **mi**, **ti**, **si**, **ci** and **vi** become **me**, **te**, **se**, **ce** and **ve** when they are followed by another pronoun, such as **ne**.

How to make the present tense of reflexive verbs

➤ First, decide which reflexive pronoun to use. You can see how the reflexive pronouns correspond to the subject pronouns in the following table:

Subject pronoun	Reflexive pronoun	Meaning
(io)	mi	myself
(tu)	ti	yourself
(lui), (lei), (lei/Lei), (loro)	si	himself, herself, itself, yourself, themselves
(noi)	ci	ourselves
(voi)	vi	yourselves

Mi alzo presto.	I get up early.
Mia sorella si veste.	My sister's getting dressed.
Si lamentano sempre.	They're always complaining.

➤ The present tense forms of a reflexive verb are just the same as those of an ordinary verb, except for the addition of the reflexive pronoun in front of the verb.

⇨ *For more information on the **Present tense**, see page 87.*

➤ The following table shows the reflexive verb **divertirsi** in full.

Reflexive forms of divertirsi	Meaning
mi diverto	I'm enjoying myself
ti diverti	you're enjoying yourself
si diverte	he is enjoying himself she is enjoying herself you are enjoying yourself
ci divertiamo	we're enjoying ourselves
vi divertite	you're enjoying yourselves
si divertono	they're enjoying themselves

Where to put reflexive pronouns

➤ The reflexive pronoun usually goes in front of the verb, but there are some exceptions. The pronoun goes <u>in front</u> if the verb is:

- an ordinary tense, such as the present simple
  Si diverte signora?   Are you enjoying yourself madam?
  Mi abituo al lavoro.   I'm getting used to the work.

⇨ *For more information on the **Present simple tense**, see page 88.*

- the polite imperative
  Si avvicini, signore.   Come closer, sir.

⇨ *For more information on the **Imperative**, see page 107.*

- an imperative telling someone NOT to do something
  Non vi avvicinate troppo ragazzi.   Don't come too close children.
  Non si lamenti, dottore.   Don't complain, doctor.

➤ The pronoun comes <u>after</u> the verb if it is the **tu** or **voi** form of the imperative, used positively:
  Svegliati!   Wake up!
  Divertitevi!   Enjoy yourselves!

➤ In the case of the infinitive, used with **non** to tell someone NOT to do something, the pronoun can either:
  - go <u>in front of</u> the infinitive
  OR
  - join onto the end of the infinitive
    Non ti bruciare! OR   Don't burn yourself!
    Non bruciarti!
    Non ti preoccupare! OR   Don't worry!
    Non preoccuparti!

ⓘ Note that, when telling someone not to do something, you use **non** with the <u>infinitive</u> for people you call **tu**.

➤ There are also two options when you use the infinitive of a reflexive verb after a verb such as *want*, *must*, *should* or *can't*. The pronoun can either:

- go in front of the main verb
OR
- join onto the end of the infinitive

Mi voglio abbronzare. OR **Voglio abbronzarmi.**	I want to get a tan.
Ti devi alzare. OR **Devi alzarti.**	You must get up.
Vi dovreste preparare. OR **Dovreste prepararvi.**	You ought to get ready.
Non mi posso fermare molto. OR **Non posso fermarmi molto.**	I can't stop for long.

➤ In the same way, in <u>continuous tenses</u>, the reflexive pronoun can either:

- go in front of the verb **stare**
OR
- join onto the gerund

Ti stai annoiando? OR **Stai annoiandoti?**	Are you getting bored?
Si stanno alzando? OR **Stanno alzandosi?**	Are they getting up?

🛈 Note that the pronoun is always joined onto the gerund when it is not used in a continuous tense.

Incontrandoci per caso, abbiamo parlato molto.	Meeting by chance, we had a long talk.
Pettinandomi ho trovato un capello bianco.	When I combed my hair I found a white hair.

> **KEY POINTS**
> ✔ Reflexive verbs are commoner in Italian than in English.
> ✔ English verbs that include *get* are often translated by an Italian reflexive verb.
> ✔ Reflexive pronouns usually go in front of the verb.

Test yourself

92 **Fill the gap with the correct reflexive pronoun. The first one has been done for you.**

a A che ora ......*ti*...... alzi?

b .... chiamo Joseph.

c Il treno non .... ferma qui.

d I bambini .... addormentano di solito alle otto.

e .... lamentate sempre.

f Non .... diverti?

g .... accomodi, signora!

h Non .... preoccupare!

i .... prepariamo al viaggio.

j .... abituo al caldo.

93 **Fill the gap with the correct form of the verb.**

a Mio figlio si ....a teatro. **(annoiarsi)**

b Non mi ....dove ho messo il libro. **(ricordarsi)**

c Vi ....presto la mattina? **(svegliarsi)**

d I bambini si........................da soli. **(vestirsi)**

e Lucia si ....dove sia il cane. **(chiedersi)**

f Ci ....le mani prima di mangiare. **(lavarsi)**

g Il gatto si .... **(arrabbiarsi)**

h Come ti ....? **(chiamarsi)**

i Giulia cade e si ....male. **(farsi)**

j Gli autobus si ....qui? **(fermarsi)**

Test yourself

94 **Translate the following sentences into Italian, using the *tu* form of the verb to translate 'you' where appropriate.**

a What time does your daughter wake up?

....

b What's your sister's name?

....

c We must get up.

....

d Are they getting bored?

....

e Don't burn yourself!

....

f We often meet at the market.

....

g Are you enjoying yourselves, boys?

....

h Sit down!

....

i Laura is getting dressed for the party.

....

j We love each other.

....

Using reflexive verbs with parts of the body and clothes

➤ In Italian you often talk about actions to do with your body or your clothing using a reflexive verb.

Mi lavo i capelli ogni mattina.   I wash my hair every morning.
Mettiti il cappotto!   Put your coat on!
Si è rotta la gamba.   She's broken her leg.

ⓘ Note that you do not use possessive adjectives in this kind of sentence. Instead you use the definite article **il**, **la**, **i** and so on with the noun, and a reflexive verb.

Mi lavo le mani.   I'm washing my hands.

⇨ *For more information on **Articles**, see page 14.*

How to use reflexive verbs in the perfect tense

➤ The English perfect tense, for example, I *have burnt* myself, and the English simple past, for example I *burnt* myself yesterday, are both translated by the Italian perfect tense.

⇨ *For more information about the **Perfect tense**, see page 141.*

➤ The perfect tense of reflexive verbs is always made with the verb **essere** and the past participle.

Mi sono fatto male.   I've hurt myself.

➤ The past participle used in the perfect tense of reflexive verbs has to agree with the subject of the sentence. You change the **–o** ending of the participle to **–a** if the subject is feminine. The masculine plural ending is **–i**, and the feminine plural is **–e**.

Silvia si è alzata tardi stamattina.   Silvia got up late this morning.
Vi siete divertiti ragazzi?   Did you have a nice time, children?
Mie sorelle si sono abbronzate.   My sisters have got tanned.

> *Tip*
> If you are female always use a feminine adjective when you are talking about yourself, and always make the past participle feminine when you are talking about what you have done.
> **Mi sono svegliata, mi sono**   I woke up, got up and got dressed.
>   **alzata e mi sono vestita.**

Other uses of reflexive pronouns

➤ **ci**, **vi** and **si** are used to mean *each other* and *one another*.

Ci vogliamo molto bene.   We love each other very much.
Si vede che si odiano.   You can see they hate one another.
Vi conoscete?   Do you know each other?

KEY POINTS

✔ The perfect tense of reflexive verbs is made with **essere**, and the past participle agrees with the subject of the verb.

✔ Reflexive verbs are used with the definite article to talk about washing your hair, breaking your leg, putting on your coat, and so on.

Test yourself

95 **Fill the gap with the correct form of the perfect tense of the verb, remembering that the past participle has to agree with the subject of the sentence. In cases where the gender of the subject isn't obvious, use the masculine form. The reflexive pronoun has been given. The first one has been done for you.**

a I ragazzi si ......*sono alzati*...... alle undici. **(alzarsi)**

b Mia sorella si .... sul divano **(addormentarsi)**

c Vi .... le mani, ragazze? **(lavarsi)**

d Ci .... per caso. **(incontrarsi)**

e Le bambine si .... **(pettinarsi)**

f A che ora ti .... stamattina? **(svegliarsi)**

g Mi .... male. **(farsi)**

h Francesca si .... con suo fratello. **(arrabbiarsi)**

i I miei genitori non si .... molto. **(fermarsi)**

j Gli amici si .... in vacanza. **(abbronzarsi)**

96 **Translate the following sentences into Italian.**

a She washed her hair yesterday morning.

....

b My brother has broken his leg. ....

c How do you say 'dog' in Italian? ....

d The children fell asleep in the car.

....

e I put my coat on. ....

f You don't do it like that. ....

g Our neighbours hate each other. ....

h He burnt his hand. ....

i Do you know each other? ....

j We met at the park. ....

The future tense

What is the future tense?
The **future tense** is a tense used to talk about something that will happen,
or will be true in the future, for example *He'll be here soon*; *I'll give you a call*;
It will be sunny tomorrow.

Using the present tense to talk about the future

➤ Sometimes, both in Italian and in English, you use the <u>present tense</u> to refer to the future.

Il corso <u>comincia</u> domani.	The course <u>starts</u> tomorrow.
Quando <u>partite</u>?	When <u>are you leaving</u>?

➤ In the following cases the <u>present tense</u> is used in Italian, while the <u>future</u> is used in English:

● to say what you're about to do

<u>Pago</u> io.	<u>I'll pay</u>.
<u>Prendo</u> un espresso.	<u>I'll have</u> an espresso.

● to ask for suggestions

Dove lo <u>metto</u>?	Where <u>shall I</u> put it?
Cosa <u>facciamo</u>?	What <u>shall we</u> do?

🛈 *For more information on the **Present simple**, see page 69.*

➤ In Italian the <u>future tense</u> is used after **quando** in cases where *when* is followed by the <u>present</u> in English.

Quando <u>finirò</u>, verrò da te.	When I <u>finish</u> I'll come to yours.
Lo comprerò quando <u>avrò</u> abbastanza denaro.	I'll buy it when <u>I've got</u> enough money.

How to make the future tense

➤ In English we make the future tense by putting *will*, *'ll* or *shall* in front of the verb. In Italian you change the verb endings: **parlo** (meaning *I speak*), becomes **parlerò** (meaning *I will speak*) in the future.

➤ To make the future of regular **–are** and **–ere** verbs take the <u>stem</u>, which is what is left of the verb when you take away the **–are**, **–ere** or **–ire** ending of the infinitive and add the following endings:

● **erò**, **erai**, **erà**, **eremo**, **erete**, **eranno**
For example, **parlare** → **parl-** → **parlerò**.

➤ The following tables show the future tenses of **parlare** (meaning *to speak*) and **credere** (meaning *to believe*).

Pronoun	Future tense of parlare	Meaning: *to speak*
(io)	parl<u>er</u>ò	I'll speak
(tu)	parl<u>er</u>ai	you'll speak
(lui/lei) (lei/Lei)	parl<u>er</u>à	he/she'll speak you'll speak
(noi)	parl<u>er</u>emo	we'll speak
(voi)	parl<u>er</u>ete	you'll speak
(loro)	parl<u>er</u>anno	they'll speak

Gli <u>parlerò</u> domani.　　　　　　I'll speak to him tomorrow.

Pronoun	Future tense of credere	Meaning: *to speak*
(io)	cred<u>er</u>ò	I'll believe
(tu)	cred<u>er</u>ai	you'll believe
(lui/lei) (lei/Lei)	cred<u>er</u>à	he/she'll believe you'll believe
(noi)	cred<u>er</u>emo	we'll believe
(voi)	cred<u>er</u>ete	you'll believe
(loro)	cred<u>er</u>anno	they'll believe

Non ti <u>crederanno</u>.　　　　　　They won't believe you.

[i] Note that there are accents on the first and third person singular forms, to show that you stress the last vowel.

➤ To make the future of regular **–ire** verbs take the *stem* and add the following endings:

● **irò**, **irai**, **irà**, **iremo**, **irete**, **iranno**
   For example, **finire → fin- → finirò**.

➤ The following table shows the future tense of **finire** (meaning *to finish*).

Pronoun	Future tense of finire	Meaning: *to finish*
(io)	fin<u>ir</u>ò	I'll finish
(tu)	fin<u>ir</u>ai	you'll finish
(lui/lei) (lei/Lei)	fin<u>ir</u>à	he/she'll finish you'll finish
(noi)	fin<u>ir</u>emo	we'll finish
(voi)	fin<u>ir</u>ete	you'll finish
(loro)	fin<u>ir</u>anno	they'll finish

Quando <u>finirai</u> il lavoro?　　　　When will you finish the work?

➤ Some verbs do not have a vowel before the **r** of the future ending. Their endings are:

- **rò**, **rai**, **rà**, **remo**, **rete**, **ranno**

➤ The following table shows the future tense of some of these verbs which you should learn.

Verb	Meaning	io	tu	lui/lei	noi	voi	loro
andare	to go	andrò	andrai	andrà	andremo	andrete	andranno
cadere	to fall	cadrò	cadrai	cadrà	cadremo	cadrete	cadranno
dire	to say	dirò	dirai	dirà	diremo	direte	diranno
dovere	to have to	dovrò	dovrai	dovrà	dovremo	dovrete	dovranno
fare	to do/ make	farò	farai	farà	faremo	farete	faranno
potere	to be able	potrò	potrai	potrà	potremo	potrete	potranno
sapere	to know	saprò	saprai	saprà	sapremo	saprete	sapranno
vedere	to see	vedrò	vedrai	vedrà	vedremo	vedrete	vedranno
vivere	to live	vivrò	vivrai	vivrà	vivremo	vivrete	vivranno

Andrò con loro.	I'll go with them.
Pensi che diranno la verità?	Do you think they'll tell the truth?
Non credo che farà bel tempo.	I don't think the weather will be nice.
Lo sapremo domani.	We'll know tomorrow.

➤ Some verbs have no vowel before the future ending, and they also change their stem, for example:

Verb	Meaning	io	tu	lui/lei	noi	voi	loro
rimanere	to remain	rimarrò	rimarrai	rimarrà	rimarremo	rimarrete	rimarranno
tenere	to hold	terrò	terrai	terrà	terremo	terrete	terranno
venire	to come	verrò	verrai	verrà	verremo	verrete	verranno
volere	to want	vorrò	vorrai	vorrà	vorremo	vorrete	vorranno

➤ Verbs with infinitives that end in **–ciare** and **–giare**, for example, **parcheggiare** (meaning *to park*), **cominciare** (meaning *to start*), **mangiare** (meaning *to eat*) and **viaggiare** (meaning *to travel*) drop the **i** from the stem in the future.
For example, **mangiare → mang- → mangerò**.

Comincerò domani.	I'll start tomorrow.
Mangeranno alle otto.	They'll eat at eight o'clock.

➤ Verbs with infinitives that end in **–care** and **–gare**, for example **cercare** (meaning *to look for, to try*), **seccare** (meaning *to annoy*), **pagare** (meaning *to pay*) and **spiegare** (meaning *to explain*) add an **h** before the ending in the future. For example, **pagare → pagh- → pagherò**.

Cercherò di aiutarvi.	I'll try to help you.
Mi pagheranno sabato.	They'll pay me on Saturday.

⇨ *For more information on **Spelling**, see page 247.*

Grammar Extra!

Will you is used in English to ask someone to do something: *Will you hurry up?*; *Will you stop talking!* You use the Italian imperative, or the verb **volere** (meaning *to want*) to translate this sort of request.

Sta' zitto!   Will you be quiet!
Vuoi smetterla!   Will you stop that!

The future tense of *essere* and *avere*

➤ **essere** (meaning *to be*) and **avere** (meaning *to have*) have irregular future forms.

Pronoun	Future tense of *essere*	Meaning	Future tense of *avere*	Meaning
(io)	sarò	I'll be	avrò	I'll have
(tu)	sarai	you'll be	avrai	you'll have
(lui/lei) (lei/Lei)	sarà	he/she/it will be you'll be	avrà	he/she/it will have you'll have
(noi)	saremo	we'll be	avremo	we'll have
(voi)	sarete	you'll be	avrete	you'll have
(loro)	saranno	they'll be	avranno	they'll have

Sarà difficile.   It'll be difficult.
Non ne sarai deluso.   You won't be disappointed by it.
Non avrò tempo.   I won't have time.
Lo avrai domani.   You'll have it tomorrow.

Grammar Extra!

In English we sometimes use *will* or *'ll* to say what we think must be true, for example, *You'll be tired after that long journey*; *It'll be about three miles from here to the town centre*.
The future tense in Italian is used in the same way.

Saranno venti chilometri.   It'll be twenty kilometres.
Avrà cinquant'anni.   He'll be fifty.

KEY POINTS

✔ The future endings of regular **–are** and **–ere** verbs are **erò**, **erai**, **erà**, **eremo**, **erete**, **eranno**.
✔ The future endings of regular **–ire** verbs are **irò**, **irai**, **irà**, **iremo**, **irete**, **iranno**.

97 Replace the highlighted verb with the future tense.

a **Finisco** alle otto. ....

b **Partiamo** in vacanza domani. ....

c Il film **comincia** fra dieci minuti. ....

d **Mangi** al ristorante? ....

e **Dicono** la verità. ....

f **Vado** al supermercato. ....

g **Volete** venire con noi? ....

h Li **vediamo stasera.** ....

i Non **sanno** che fare. ....

j Luca **fa** la spesa. ....

98 Fill the gap with the correct form of the future tense.

a Pensi che le ragazze .... alla festa? **(venire)**

b I miei amici .... tutti alla partita. **(andare)**

c Giulia .... una macchina per suo marito. **(comprare)**

d Ci .... sabato. **(vedere)**

e Mi dispiace, non .... venire. **(potere)**

f Ragazzi, ... fare i compiti prima di uscire. **(dovere)**

g Signora, mi .... piacere accompagnarla? **(fare)**

h I miei genitori non .... l'anno prossimo. **(viaggiare)**

i Il professore gli .... domani. **(parlare)**

j Ragazze, quando .... il lavoro? **(finire)**

Test yourself

99 **Translate the following sentences into Italian. Use the *tu* form of the verb for 'you', where appropriate.**

a It's going to be cold tomorrow.

....

b I'm going to the doctor's next week.

....

c They won't be able to help us.

....

d Will you all come to the cinema?

....

e She'll know this evening.

....

f They'll tell us in a few days.

....

g Will you speak to him about it?

....

h He won't believe you.

....

i I'll eat later.

....

j Sir, when will you send the book?

....

The conditional

> ## What is the conditional?
> The **conditional** is used to talk about things that would happen or would be true under certain conditions, for example, I _would_ help you if I could. It is also used in requests and offers, for example, _Could_ you lend me some money?; I could give you a lift.

Using the conditional

➤ In English, when you're talking about what would happen in certain circumstances, or saying what you could or would like to do, you use _would_, _'d_ or _could_ with the infinitive (the base form of the verb).

  I _would_ pay the money back as soon as possible.
  If you asked him he'_d_ probably say yes.
  You _could_ stay here for a while.

➤ In Italian the _conditional_ is used in this kind of sentence. Like the present and the future tenses, you make it by adding endings to the verb _stem_, which is what is left of the verb when you take away the **–are**, **–ere** or **–ire** ending of the infinitive.

➤ You use the conditional of any Italian verb to say what _would_ happen or _would_ be true.

  Sarebbe difficile.   It would be difficult.
  Farebbe finta di capire.   He'd pretend to understand.
  Mia madre non me lo permetterebbe.   My mother wouldn't let me.

➤ You use the conditional of the verbs **potere** (meaning _to be able_) and **dovere** (meaning _to have to_) to say what _could_ or _should_ happen or _could_ or _should_ be true.

  Potremmo andare in Spagna   We could go to Spain next year.
  il prossimo anno.
  Dovresti studiare di più.   You should study more.

How to make the conditional

➤ To make the conditional of regular **–are** and **–ere** verbs take the _stem_ and add the following endings: **–erei**, **–eresti**, **–erebbe**, **–eremmo**, **–ereste**, **–erebbero**.

➤ The following table shows the conditional of **parlare** (meaning _to speak_) and **credere** (meaning _to believe_).

	Conditional of parlare	Meaning	Conditional of credere	Meaning
(io)	parlerei	I'd speak	crederei	I'd believe
(tu)	parleresti	you'd speak	crederesti	you'd believe
(lui/lei) (lei/Lei)	parlerebbe	he/she'd speak you'd speak	crederebbe	he/she'd believe you'd believe
(noi)	parleremmo	we'd speak	crederemmo	we'd believe
(voi)	parlereste	you'd speak	credereste	you'd believe
(loro)	parlerebbero	they'd speak	crederebbero	they'd believe

For further explanation of grammatical terms, please see pages viii-xii.

| **Con chi <u>parleresti</u>?** | Who would you speak to? |
| **Non ti <u>crederebbe</u>.** | He wouldn't believe you. |

⇨ Note that the same form of the verb is used for the pronouns **lui**, **lei** and **Lei**.

➤ To make the conditional of regular **–ire** verbs take the <u>stem</u> and add the following endings: **–irei**, **–iresti**, **–irebbe**, **–iremmo**, **–ireste**, **–irebbero**.

➤ The following table shows the conditional of **finire** (meaning *to finish*).

(io)	fin<u>irei</u>	I'd finish
(tu)	fin<u>iresti</u>	you'd finish
(lui/lei) (lei/Lei)	fin<u>irebbe</u>	he/she'd finish you'd finish
(noi)	fin<u>iremmo</u>	we'd finish
(voi)	fin<u>ireste</u>	you'd finish
(loro)	fin<u>irebbero</u>	they'd finish

| **Non <u>finiremmo</u> in tempo.** | We wouldn't finish in time. |

🗓 Note that the same form of the verb is used for the pronouns **lui**, **lei** and **Lei**.

The conditionals of volere, potere and dovere

➤ You use the <u>conditional</u> of the verb **volere** (meaning *to want*) to say what you <u>would like</u>.
    <u>Vorrei</u> un'insalata.   I'd like a salad.

➤ You use the conditional of **volere** with an infinitive to say what you <u>would like</u> to do.
    <u>Vorremmo</u> venire con voi.   We'd like to come with you.
    <u>Vorrebbero</u> rimanere qui.   They'd like to stay here.

> *Tip*
> In Italian there are two ways of saying *I'd like to*: **vorrei** and **mi piacerebbe**.
> **Vorrei vedere quel film.** OR   I'd like to see that film.
> **Mi piacerebbe vedere quel film.**

➤ The conditional of **volere** is irregular:

	Conditional of volere	**Meaning**
(io)	vorrei	I'd like
(tu)	vorresti	you'd like
(lui/lei) (lei/Lei)	vorrebbe	he/she'd like you'd like
(noi)	vorremmo	we'd like
(voi)	vorreste	you'd like
(loro)	vorrebbero	they'd like

> *Tip*
> In English, the conditional *What would you like?* is more polite than
> *What do you want?* In Italian there is no difference in politeness.
> **Vuoi un gelato?**   Would you like OR
>   Do you want an ice cream?
> **Vuole altro, signora?**   Would you like anything else, madam?

➤ You use the conditional of the verb **potere** (meaning *to be able*) with an infinitive.

- to say what <u>could</u> be the case, or <u>could</u> happen.
  Potresti avere ragione.   You could be right.
  Potrebbe *essere vero*.   It could be true.
  Potrebbero *vendere la casa*.   They could sell the house.

- to ask if somebody <u>could</u> do something.
  Potresti chiudere la finestra?   Could you close the window?

➤ The conditional of **potere** is as follows:

	Conditional of potere	**Meaning**
(io)	potrei	I could
(tu)	potresti	you could
(lui/lei) (lei/Lei)	potrebbe	he/she/it could you could
(noi)	potremmo	we could
(voi)	potreste	you could
(loro)	potrebbero	they could

➤ You use the conditional of **dovere** (meaning *to have to*):

- to say what you or somebody else <u>should</u> do
  Dovrei fare un po' di ginnastica.   I should do some exercise.
  Dovresti telefonare ai tuoi.   You should phone your parents.

- to talk about what <u>should</u> be the case, or <u>should</u> happen.
  Dovrebbe arrivare verso le dieci. He should arrive at around ten.
  Dovrebbe *essere bello*.   This should be good.

➤ The conditional of **dovere** is as follows:

	Conditional of dovere	**Meaning**
(io)	dovrei	I should
(tu)	dovresti	you should
(lui/lei) (lei/Lei)	dovrebbe	he/she/it should you should
(noi)	dovremmo	we should
(voi)	dovreste	you should
(loro)	dovrebbero	they should

For further explanation of grammatical terms, please see pages viii-xii.

Irregular conditionals

➤ Some common verbs do not have a vowel before the **r** of the conditional ending, their endings are **rei**, **resti**, **rebbe**, **remmo**, **reste**, **rebbero**.

Verb	Meaning	io	tu	lui/lei	noi	voi	loro
andare	to go	andrei	andresti	andrebbe	andremmo	andreste	andrebbero
cadere	to fall	cadrei	cadresti	cadrebbe	cadremmo	cadreste	cadrebbero
sapere	to know	saprei	sapresti	saprebbe	sapremmo	sapreste	saprebbero
vedere	to see	vedrei	vedresti	vedrebbe	vedremmo	vedreste	vedrebbero
vivere	to live	vivrei	vivresti	vivrebbe	vivremmo	vivreste	vivrebbero

> **Non so se _andrebbe_ bene.**   I don't know if it would be okay.
> **_Sapreste_ indicarmi la strada**   Could you tell me the way to the station?
> **per la stazione?**
> **Non _vivrei_ mai in un Paese caldo.**   I'd never live in a hot country.

➤ Some verbs have no vowel before the conditional ending, <u>and</u> change their stem, for example, **rimanere**, **tenere**, **venire**:

Verb	Meaning	io	tu	lui/lei	noi	voi	loro
rimanere	to remain	rimarrei	rimarresti	rimarrebbe	rimarremmo	rimarreste	rimarrebbero
tenere	to hold	terrei	terresti	terrebbe	terremmo	terreste	terrebbero
venire	to come	verrei	verresti	verrebbe	verremmo	verreste	verrebbero

⇨ *For more information on **Verbs which change their stem**, see page 99.*

➤ Verbs such as **cominciare** (meaning *to start*) and **mangiare** (meaning *to eat*), which end in –ciare or –giare, and which drop the **i** in the future tense also drop the **i** in the conditional.
> **Quando _comincerebbe_?**   When would it start?
> **_Mangeresti_ quei funghi?**   Would you eat those mushrooms?

⇨ *For more information on the **Future tense**, see page 124.*

➤ Verbs such as **cercare** (meaning *to look for*) and **pagare** (meaning *to pay*), which end in –care or –gare, and which add an **h** in the future tense also add an **h** in the conditional.
> **Probabilmente _cercherebbe_**   He'd probably look for an excuse.
> **una scusa.**
> **Quanto mi _pagheresti_?**   How much would you pay me?

⇨ *For more information on **Spelling**, see page 247.*

The conditional of *essere* and *avere*

➤ **essere** (meaning *to be*) and **avere** (meaning *to have*) have irregular conditionals.

	Conditional of *essere*	Meaning	Conditional of *avere*	Meaning
(io)	sarei	I'd be	avrei	I'd have
(tu)	saresti	you'd be	avresti	you'd have
(lui/lei) (lei/Lei)	sarebbe	he/she/ it would be you would be	avrebbe	he/she/ it would have you would have
(noi)	saremmo	we'd be	avremmo	we'd have
(voi)	sareste	you'd be	avreste	you'd have
(loro)	sarebbero	they'd be	avrebbero	they'd have

Sarebbe bello.	It would be lovely.
Non so se <u>sarei</u> capace di farlo.	I don't know if I'd be able to do it.
Non <u>avremmo</u> tempo.	We wouldn't have time.
<u>Avresti</u> paura?	Would you be frightened?

Grammar Extra!

The conditional we have looked at so far is the <u>present conditional</u>. There is also the <u>perfect conditional</u>, which is used to talk about what would have happened in the past.

The perfect conditional is made up of the conditional of **avere** or **essere**, and the past participle. Verbs which form their perfect tense with **avere**, such as **fare** (meaning *to do*) and **pagare** (meaning *to pay*) also form their perfect conditional with **avere**. Those forming their perfect with **essere**, such as **andare** (meaning *to go*) also form their perfect conditional with **essere**.

⇨ *For more information about the* **Perfect tense** *and the* **Past participle**, *see pages 141–142.*

Non l'<u>avrei fatto</u> così.	I wouldn't have done it like that.
Non l'<u>avrebbero pagato</u>.	They wouldn't have paid it.
Ci <u>saresti</u> andato?	Would you have gone?

In Italian, unlike in English, the <u>perfect conditional</u> is used to report what somebody said in the past.

Ha detto che mi <u>avrebbe aiutato</u>.	He said he would help me.
Hanno detto che <u>sarebbero venuti</u>.	They said they would come.

KEY POINTS

✔ The Italian conditional is often the equivalent of a verb used with <u>would</u> in English.

✔ *would like, could* and *should* are translated by the conditionals of **volere**, **potere** and **dovere**.

Test yourself

100 Replace the highlighted verb with the conditional tense.

   a **Sarà** difficile. ....

   b **Voglio** andare con loro. ....

   c **Dobbiamo** studiare. ....

   d Mia sorella **potrà** aiutarti. ....

   e **Avete** tempo per mangiare? ....

   f A che ora **cominciano** le lezioni? ....

   g **Mangi** quella pizza? ....

   h Mi **dai** una mano? ....

   i **Vengo** con voi a teatro. ....

   j **Sapete** la strada per Milano? ....

101 Match the related sentences.

   a **Quando comincerebbe il lavoro?**   No, non vivrei mai in un paese freddo.

   b **Vorresti mangiare con noi?**   Probabilmente fra due giorni.

   c **A che ora arriva Domenico?**   No, grazie. Ho già mangiato.

   d **Non hanno soldi.**   Dovrebbe arrivare verso le dieci.

   e **Ti piacerebbe vivere in Islanda?**   Potrebbero vendere la macchina.

102 Translate the following sentences into Italian. Where appropriate, use the *tu* form of the verb for 'you'.

   a It would be lovely to see you. ....

   b Those children would watch TV all day long.

      ....

   c I wouldn't eat these mushrooms. ....

   d How much would they pay for the house?

      ....

   e She doesn't know if she's able to do it. ....

   f You should telephone your mother. ....

   g We would be happy to help them. ....

   h My son would be afraid of the dog. ....

   i She wouldn't be able to finish the work. ....

   j Would you all like to come with us? ....

The imperfect tense

> ## What is the imperfect tense?
> The **imperfect** is a tense used to say what was happening, what used to happen in the past and what things were like in the past, for example, I _was speaking_ to my mother.

When to use the imperfect tense

➤ In English various tenses are used to talk about what things were like in the past, for example, It _was raining_; I _used to like_ her; I _didn't know_ what to do. In Italian the <u>imperfect</u> is the tense you use to translate the verbs in all three of these sentences.

➤ Use the Italian imperfect tense:

- to describe what things were like, what people were doing and how people felt in the past

<u>Faceva</u> caldo.	It was hot.
<u>Aspettavano</u> impazienti.	They were waiting impatiently.
<u>Eravamo</u> tutti felici.	We were all happy.
<u>Avevo</u> fame.	I was hungry.

- to say what people knew, thought or meant in the past

Non <u>sapevo</u> cosa <u>volevi dire</u>.	I didn't know what you meant.
<u>Pensavo</u> che fosse lui.	I thought it was him.

- to say what used to happen or what people used to do in the past

Ci <u>trovavamo</u> ogni venerdì.	We met every Friday.
<u>Vendevano</u> le uova al mercato.	They used to sell eggs in the market.

- to describe what was going on when an event took place

<u>Guardavamo</u> la partita quando è entrato lui.	We were watching the match when he came in.
È successo mentre <u>dormivano</u>.	It happened while they were asleep.
Mentre <u>parlavi</u> mi sono ricordato di qualcosa.	While you were talking I remembered something.

Grammar Extra!
The <u>imperfect continuous</u> is made with the <u>imperfect tense</u> of **stare** and the gerund. The imperfect continuous is used to describe what was going on at a particular moment.

Che <u>stavano</u> facendo?	What were they doing?
Non <u>stava studiando</u>, dormiva.	He wasn't studying, he was asleep.

⇨ _For more information on the **Gerund**, see page 163._

How to make the imperfect tense

➤ You make the imperfect tense of regular **–are**, **–ere** and **–ire** verbs by knocking off the **–re** from the infinitive to form the <u>stem</u> of the verbs and adding **–vo**, **–vi-**, **–va**, **–vamo**, **–vate**, **–vano**.

➤ The following tables show the imperfect tense of three regular verbs: **parlare** (meaning *to speak*), **credere** (meaning *to believe*) and **finire** (meaning *to finish*).

	Imperfect tense of parlare	Meaning	Imperfect tense of credere	Meaning
(io)	parla<u>vo</u>	I was speaking	credevo	I believed
(tu)	parla<u>vi</u>	you were speaking	credevi	you believed
(lui/lei) (lei/Lei)	parla<u>va</u>	he/she was speaking you were speaking	credeva	he/she believed you believed
(noi)	parla<u>vamo</u>	we were speaking	credevamo	we believed
(voi)	parla<u>vate</u>	you were speaking	credevate	you believed
(loro)	parla<u>vano</u>	they were speaking	credevano	they believed

	Imperfect tense of finire	Meaning
(io)	fini<u>vo</u>	I was finishing
(tu)	fini<u>vi</u>	you were finishing
(lui/lei) (lei/Lei)	fini<u>va</u>	he/she was finishing you were finishing
(noi)	fini<u>vamo</u>	we were finishing
(voi)	fini<u>vate</u>	you were finishing
(loro)	fini<u>vano</u>	they were finishing

Con chi <u>parlavi</u>?	Who were you talking to?
<u>Credevamo</u> di aver vinto.	We thought we'd won.
Loro si <u>divertivano</u> mentre io <u>lavoravo</u>.	They had fun while I was working.
Una volta <u>costava</u> di più.	It used to cost more.

Perfect tense or imperfect tense?

➤ The Italian <u>perfect tense</u> is used for what happened on one occasion.

Oggi <u>ho giocato</u> male. — I played badly today.
Ha <u>finto</u> di non conoscermi. — He pretended not to recognize me.

➤ The Italian <u>imperfect tense</u> is used for repeated actions or for a continuing state of affairs.

Da studente <u>giocavo</u> a calcio. — When I was a student I played football.
<u>Fingevano</u> sempre di avere capito tutto. — They always pretended they'd understood everything.
Mi <u>sentivo</u> male solo a pensarci. — I felt ill just thinking about it.
Non <u>sorrideva</u> mai. — She never smiled.
Ci <u>credevi</u>? — Did you believe it?

Verbs with an irregular imperfect tense

➤ The imperfect of **essere** (meaning *to be*) is irregular:

(io)	ero	I was
(tu)	eri	you were
(lui/lei) (lei/Lei)	era	he/she/it was you were
(noi)	eravamo	we were
(voi)	eravate	you were
(loro)	erano	they were

<u>Era</u> un ragazzo molto simpatico. He was a very nice boy.
<u>Eravamo</u> in Italia. We were in Italy.
<u>Erano</u> le quattro. It was four o'clock.

➤ **bere** (meaning *to drink*), **dire** (meaning *to say*), **fare** (meaning *to do, to make*) and **tradurre** (meaning *to translate*) are the most common verbs which have the normal imperfect endings added onto a stem which is irregular. You just have to learn these.

Verb	(io)	(tu)	(lui/lei)	(noi)	(voi)	(loro)
bere	bevevo	bevevi	beveva	bevevamo	bevevate	bevevano
dire	dicevo	dicevi	diceva	dicevamo	dicevate	dicevano
fare	facevo	facevi	faceva	facevamo	facevate	facevano
tradurre	traducevo	traducevi	traduceva	traducevamo	traducevate	traducevano

Di solito <u>bevevano</u> solo acqua. They usually only drank water.
Cosa <u>dicevo</u>? What was I saying?
<u>Faceva</u> molto freddo. It was very cold.
<u>Traducevo</u> la lettera. I was translating the letter.

Grammar Extra!
The Italian imperfect tense is used to translate sentences such as *How long <u>had</u> they known* each other?; *They <u>had been going out</u> together for a year when they got engaged*; *He <u>had been</u> ill since last year*. The words <u>for</u> and <u>since</u> are translated by **da**.

A quel punto <u>aspettava</u> già da tre ore. By then he'd already been waiting for three hours.

<u>Guidavo</u> dalle sei di mattina. I'd been driving since six in the morning.
Da quanto tempo <u>stava</u> male? How long had he been ill?

⇨ *For more information on **da**, see page 231.*

KEY POINTS
✔ You make the imperfect tense of regular verbs by knocking off the final **–re** of the infinitive and adding endings: **–vo**, **–vi**, **–va**, **–vamo**, **–vate**, **–vano**.
✔ The imperfect is used for actions and situations that continued for some time in the past.

For further explanation of grammatical terms, please see pages viii-xii.

Test yourself

103 Replace the highlighted present tense with the imperfect tense.

   a La lezione **comincia** alle dieci. ....

   b Le mie sorelle **giocano** a tennis. ....

   c **Siamo** in vacanza. ....

   d **Fa** freddo. ....

   e **Bevono** solo acqua. ....

   f Cosa **dice**? ....

   g **Parlo** con il professore di mio figlio. ....

   h I bambini **hanno** sete. ....

   i Cosa **stai** facendo? ....

   j **Aspettate** l'autobus? ....

104 Fill the gap with the correct form of the imperfect tense.

   a Tutti ....al concerto. **(divertirsi)**

   b Mio padre ....all'estero. **(lavorare)**

   c Io e Mario ....a calcio. **(giocare)**

   d ....molto caldo quest'estate. **(fare)**

   e Lucia non ....cosa fare. **(sapere)**

   f Voi due ....contenti? **(essere)**

   g I bambini non ....la verità. **(dire)**

   h I miei genitori ....con i tuoi. **(parlare)**

   i Mio fratello non ....abbastanza soldi per andare in vacanza. **(avere)**

   j I ragazzi della squadra ....di aver perso la partita. **(credere)**

Test yourself

105 Translate the following sentences into Italian, using *tu* for 'you' where appropriate.

a While you were talking I saw him arrive.

....

b What was she looking at?

....

c I kissed him while he was sleeping.

....

d I had been waiting for two hours.

....

e It was so hot that we couldn't even go out.

....

f How long had you been studying English?

....

g I was translating the book when Giulia called me.

....

h He was a very nice man.

....

i When she was a student she worked in a bar.

....

j We used to see each other every Saturday.

....

The perfect tense

What is the perfect tense?
In English the **perfect tense** is used to talk about what has or hasn't happened, for example, We've won; I haven't touched it.

Using the perfect tense

➤ In English the perfect tense is made up of the verb *to have* followed by a <u>past participle</u>, such as *done, broken, worked, arrived*. It is used to talk about:

- what you've done at some time in the past, for example, We've <u>been</u> to Australia.

- what you've done so far, for example, I've <u>eaten</u> half of it.

➤ In English the <u>simple past</u>, not the <u>perfect</u> is used to say when exactly something happened, for example, We <u>met</u> last summer; I <u>ate</u> it last night; It <u>rained</u> a lot yesterday.

➤ In Italian there are two ways of making the perfect tense:

- the present tense of **avere** (meaning *to have*) followed by a past participle

- the present tense of **essere** (meaning *to be*), followed by a past participle.

⇨ *For more information on the **Present tense of avere and essere**, see pages 99 and 103.*

➤ The Italian perfect tense is used to say:

- what you've done at some time in the past
  Ho già <u>visto</u> quel film.   I've already <u>seen</u> that film.
  Sono uscita con lui un paio di volte.   I've <u>been out</u> with him a couple of times.

- what you've done so far
  Finora <u>abbiamo fatto</u> solo il presente.   So far we've only <u>done</u> the present.

➤ Unlike in English, the Italian perfect tense is <u>ALSO</u> used to say what you did at some particular time, or when exactly something happened.
  Ho <u>visto</u> quel film sabato scorso.   I <u>saw</u> that film last Saturday.
  Sono uscita con lui ieri sera.   I <u>went out</u> with him last night.
  È successo ieri.   It <u>happened</u> yesterday.

Tip
Do not use the perfect tense to say since when, or how long you've been doing something – **da** and the present tense is used for this in Italian.

⇨ *For more information on **da**, see page 231.*

How to make the past participle

➤ The past participle is <u>always</u> part of the perfect tense.

➤ To make the past participle of a regular **–are** verb, take off the **–are** of the infinitive and add **–ato**.

    parlare (meaning *to speak*) → **parlato** (*spoken*)

➤ To make the past participle of a regular **–ere** verb, take off the **–ere** of the infinitive and add **–uto**.

    credere (meaning *to believe*) → **creduto** (*believed*)

➤ To make the past participle of a regular **–ire** verb, take off the **–ire** of the infinitive and add **–ito**.

    finire (meaning *to finish*) → **finito** (*finished*)

How to make the perfect tense with avere

➤ To make the perfect tense with **avere**:

- choose the present tense form of **avere** that matches the subject of the sentence.

- add the past participle. <u>Do not</u> change the ending of the participle to make it agree with the subject.

➤ The perfect tense of **parlare** (meaning *to speak*) is as follows:

	Present tense of avere	Past participle	Meaning
(io)	ho	parlato	I spoke *or* have spoken
(tu)	hai	parlato	you spoke *or* have spoken
(lui/lei) (lei/Lei)	ha	parlato	he/she spoke *or* has spoken you spoke *or* have spoken
(noi)	abbiamo	parlato	we spoke *or* have spoken
(voi)	avete	parlato	you spoke *or* have spoken
(loro)	hanno	parlato	they spoke *or* have spoken

Non gli <u>ho</u> mai parlato.	I've never spoken to him.
Roberta gli <u>ha parlato</u> ieri.	Roberta spoke to him yesterday.

Verbs with irregular past participles

➤ As in English, some very common verbs have irregular past participles. These are some of the most important ones:

aprire (*to open*)	→	**aperto** (*opened*)
ALSO **coprire** (*to cover*)	→	**coperto** (*covered*)
chiudere (*to close*)	→	**chiuso** (*closed*)
decidere (*to decide*)	→	**deciso** (*decided*)
dire (*to say*)	→	**detto** (*said*)

fare (*to do, to make*)	→	**fatto** (*done, made*)
friggere (*to fry*)	→	**fritto** (*fried*)
leggere (*to read*)	→	**letto** (*read*)
mettere (*to put*)	→	**messo** (*put*)
ALSO **promettere** (*to promise*)	→	**promesso** (*promised*)
morire (*to die*)	→	**morto** (*died*)
offrire (*to offer*)	→	**offerto** (*offered*)
prendere (*to take*)	→	**preso** (*taken*)
ALSO **sorprendere** (*to surprise*)	→	**sorpreso** (*surprised*)
rispondere (*to reply*)	→	**risposto** (*replied*)
ALSO **spendere** (*to spend*)	→	**speso** (*spent*)
rompere (*to break*)	→	**rotto** (*broken*)
scegliere (*to choose*)	→	**scelto** (*chosen*)
scrivere (*to write*)	→	**scritto** (*written*)
vincere (*to win*)	→	**vinto** (*won*)
ALSO **convincere** (*to convince*)	→	**convinto** (*convinced*)
vedere (*to see*)	→	**visto** (*seen*)

(i) Note that, as in English, some Italian past participles are also used as adjectives. When they are adjectives they <u>agree</u> with the noun they go with.

patate fritt<u>e</u>	fried potatoes
È apert<u>a</u> la banca?	Is the bank open?

⇨ *For more information on **Adjectives**, see page 24.*

When to make the perfect tense with avere

➤ You use **avere** to make the perfect tense of most verbs.

Ho preso il treno delle dieci.	I <u>got</u> the ten o'clock train.
L'hai messo in frigo?	<u>Have you put</u> it in the fridge?
Perché l'hai fatto?	Why <u>did you do</u> it?
Carlo ha speso più di me.	Carlo <u>spent</u> more than me.
Abbiamo comprato una macchina.	<u>We've bought</u> a car.
Dove avete parcheggiato?	Where <u>did you park</u>?
Non hanno voluto aiutarmi.	They <u>didn't want</u> to help me.

➤ You <u>do not</u> use **avere** to make the perfect tense of:

• reflexive verbs

• certain verbs that do not take a direct object, such as **andare** (meaning *to go*), **venire** (meaning *to come*) and **diventare** (meaning *to become*).

(i) Note that in English the verb *to have* can be used on its own in replies such as *No, he hasn't*, and question phrases such as *haven't you*? – **avere** <u>cannot</u> be used in this way in Italian.

Te l'ha detto? – No.	Has he told you? – No, he hasn't.
Lo hai fatto, vero?	You've done it, haven't you?

⇨ *For more information on **Questions**, see page 203.*

When to make the past participle agree

➤ When you make the perfect tense with **avere**, the past participle <u>never</u> agrees with the <u>subject</u>.

➤ You <u>must</u> make the past participle agree with the <u>object pronouns</u> **lo** and **la** (meaning *him*, *her* and *it*) when they come in front of the verb.

Hai visto Marco? – Si, <u>l'ho visto</u>.	Have you seen Marco? – Yes, I've seen him.
È un bel film, <u>l'hai visto</u>?	It's a good film, have you seen it?
Hai visto Lucia? – Non <u>l'ho vista</u>.	Have you seen Lucia? – No, I haven't seen her.

➤ You <u>must</u> make the past participle agree with the object pronouns **li** and **le** (meaning *them*) when they come in front of the verb.

I fiammiferi? Non <u>li ho presi</u>.	The matches? I haven't taken them.
Le fragole? <u>Le ho mangiate</u> tutte.	The strawberries? I've eaten them all.

KEY POINTS

✔ The Italian perfect tense is used to translate both the English perfect, and the English simple past.

✔ The Italian perfect tense is made with **avere** or **essere** and the past participle.

✔ The past participle does not agree with the subject when the perfect tense is made with **avere**, except when certain object pronouns come in front of the verb.

For further explanation of grammatical terms, please see pages viii-xii.

Test yourself

106 **Fill the gap with the correct form of the past participle of the verb.**

    a Marco ha .... la finestra. **(chiudere)**

    b Ho .... queste scarpe ieri. **(comprare)**

    c Non hai .... quel libro? **(leggere)**

    d Ha .... venire con noi. **(volere)**

    e Cosa hai ....? **(dire)**

    f La mia borsa? Non so dove l'ho .... **(mettere)**

    g Abbiamo già .... le valigie. **(fare)**

    h Le chiavi? Non le ho .... **(vedere)**

    i Avete .... di mangiare? **(finire)**

    j Ci hanno .... di accompagnarci alla stazione. **(offrire)**

107 **Replace the highlighted present tense with the perfect tense. The first one has been done for you.**

    a Mia sorella **parla** con il dottore. *ha parlato*

    b **Vedo** la luna. ....

    c **Scrivono** le cartoline. ....

    d Chi **apre** la finestra? ....

    e A che ora **finisce** il film? ....

    f Non **credo** la storia. ....

    g **Spendiamo** troppi soldi in vacanza. ....

    h **Rispondono** alla domanda. ....

    i Mio padre **fa** la spesa. ....

    j Cosa **prendete** al bar? ....

Test yourself

108 Translate the following into Italian, using *tu* for 'you' where appropriate.

a Your shoes? I haven't seen them.

....

b Which team won?

....

c Who told you?

....

d We decided to buy the blue car.

....

e Where did I put that book?

....

f Did you call your mother? — No, I haven't called her.

....

g She bought some strawberries from the market.

....

h They haven't written to him yet.

....

i We took the train to go to the mountains.

....

j Did you book, Sir?

....

How to make the perfect tense with *essere*

➤ To make the perfect tense with **essere**:

- choose the present tense form of **essere** that matches the subject of the sentence.

- add the past participle. Make the ending of the participle <u>agree</u> with the subject.

➤ The perfect tense of **andare** (meaning *to go*) is as follows:

	Present tense of *essere*	**Past participle**	**Meaning**
(io)	sono	**andato** *or* **andata**	I went *or* have gone
(tu)	sei	**andato** *or* **andata**	you went *or* have gone
(lui)	è	**andato**	he/it went *or* has gone
(lei)	è	**andata**	she/it went *or* has gone
(lei/Lei)	è	**andato** *or* **andata**	you went *or* have gone
(noi)	siamo	**andati** *or* **andate**	we went *or* have gone
(voi)	siete	**andati** *or* **andate**	you went *or* have gone
(loro)	sono	**andati** *or* **andate**	they went *or* have gone

Tip

You make past participles agree when they follow the verb **essere**, in the same way that you make adjectives agree.

Sei pront<u>a</u>, Maria?   Are you ready Maria?
Sei andat<u>a</u> anche tu, Maria?   Did you go too, Maria?

⇨ *For more information on* **Adjectives**, *see page 24.*

When to make the perfect tense with *essere*

➤ Use **essere** to make the perfect tense of certain verbs that <u>do not</u> take a direct object.

⇨ *For more information on* **Direct objects**, *see page 57.*

➤ The most important of these verbs are:

andare	to go	**arrivare**	to arrive
diventare	to become	**entrare**	to come in
partire	to leave	**rimanere**	to stay
riuscire	to succeed, manage	**salire**	to go up, get on
scendere	to go down	**succedere**	to happen
stare	to be	**tornare**	to come back
uscire	to go out	**venire**	to come

<u>**È rimasta**</u> **a casa tutto il giorno.**   She stayed at home all day.
<u>**Siamo riusciti**</u> **a convincerla.**   We managed to persuade her.
<u>**Sei**</u> **mai** <u>**stata**</u> **a Bologna, Tina?**   Have you ever been to Bologna, Tina?
Le tue amiche sono <u>**arrivate**</u>**.**   Your friends have arrived.
Cos'<u>**è successo**</u>**?**   What happened?

ⓘ Note that **essere** is used to make the perfect tense of **piacere** (meaning literally *to please*). The past participle agrees with the <u>subject</u> of the Italian verb, and not with the subject of the English verb *to like*.

La <u>musica</u> ti è <u>piaciuta</u>, Roberto?	Did you like the music, Robert?
I <u>cioccolatini</u> mi sono <u>piaciuti</u> molto.	I liked the chocolates very much.
<u>Le foto</u> sono <u>piaciute</u> a tutti.	Everyone liked the photos.

➤ Use **essere** to make the perfect tense of all reflexive verbs.

I miei fratelli si <u>sono alzati</u> tardi.	My brothers got up late.
Le ragazze si <u>sono alzate</u> alle sei.	The girls got up at six.

⇨ *For more information on **Reflexive verbs**, see page 115.*

KEY POINTS

✔ When the perfect tense is made with **essere** the past participle agrees with the subject of the sentence.
✔ **essere** is used to make the perfect tense of some very common verbs that do not take a direct object.
✔ **essere** is used to make the perfect tense of all reflexive verbs.

Test yourself

109 Fill the gap with the correct form of the past participle of the verb, remembering to make the ending agree with the subject. If the gender of the subject is not obvious, use the masculine form.

a I miei amici sono .... alle otto. **(arrivare)**

b Sei .... a teatro, Paola? **(andare)**

c Mi sono .... tardi. **(alzarsi)**

d Le ragazze sono .... a scuola fino alle cinque. **(rimanere)**

e Mia madre è .... ieri sera. **(uscire)**

f I bambini sono .... grandi. **(diventare)**

g La torta mi è .... molto. **(piacere)**

h Vi siete ...., ragazzi? **(divertirsi)**

i I miei sono .... a trovarmi. **(venire)**

j Cos'è ....? **(succedere)**

110 Match the answers to the questions.

a Conosci Londra?   Sì, sono riuscita a convincerla.

b Cosa avete fatto ieri?   No, sono tornata a casa mia.

c Viene Maria alla festa?   Sì, è venuto con noi.

d Hai dormito da tua sorella?   Niente, siamo rimasti a casa tutto il giorno.

e È andato anche Luca?   No, non ci sono mai stato.

111 Translate the following into Italian, where appropriate using _tu_ for 'you'.

a I liked the photos very much. ....

b The present arrived yesterday. ....

c The children washed their hands before eating. ....

d My brother went out with some friends last night. ....

e We went to the theatre last week. ....

f Have you ever been to Palermo, Giovanna? ....

g Did you go to school this morning? ....

h I got up at eight o'clock. ....

i How many people came? ....

j He has become very rude. ....

The past historic

> ## What is the past historic?
> The **past historic** is equivalent to the English simple past, except that it is only used in written Italian. In spoken Italian the <u>perfect</u> tense is used to talk about the past.

Recognizing the past historic

➤ You do not need to learn the past historic (**il passato remoto**), since you will never need to use it. However, you may come across it in written Italian. To help you recognize it, here are the past historic forms of **essere** (meaning *to be*), **avere** (meaning *to have*), **parlare** (meaning *to speak*), **credere** (meaning *to believe*) and **partire** (meaning *to leave*).

	Past historic of *essere*	Meaning	Past historic of *avere*	Meaning
(io)	fui	I was	ebbi	I had
(tu)	fosti	you were	avesti	you had
(lui/lei) (lei/Lei)	fu	he/she was you were	ebbe	he/she had you had
(noi)	fummo	we were	avemmo	we had
(voi)	foste	you were	aveste	you had
(loro)	furono	they were	ebbero	they had

Ci <u>fu</u> un improvviso silenzio quando <u>entrai</u> nella stanza.

There was a sudden silence when I came into the room.

Non <u>ebbero</u> nessuna speranza.

They had no hope.

	Past historic of *parlare*	Meaning	Past historic of *credere*	Meaning
(io)	parlai	I spoke	credei *or* credetti	I believed
(tu)	parlasti	you spoke	credesti	you believed
(lui/lei) (lei/Lei)	parlò	he/she spoke you spoke	credé *or* credette	he/she believed you believed
(noi)	parlammo	we spoke	credemmo	we believed
(voi)	parlaste	you spoke	credeste	you believed
(loro)	parlarono	they spoke	crederono *or* credettero	they believed

	Past historic of partire	Meaning
(io)	partii	I left
(tu)	partisti	you left
(lui/lei) (lei/Lei)	partì	he/she left you left
(noi)	partimmo	we left
(voi)	partiste	you left
(loro)	partirono	they left

Parlò piano.
Non lo credettero.
Partì in fretta.

He spoke slowly.
They did not believe it.
He left hastily.

> **KEY POINTS**
> ✔ You will come across the past historic in written Italian.
> ✔ It is translated by the English simple past.

Test yourself

112 **Replace the highlighted perfect tense with the past historic.**

a **È stato** nel giardino. ....

b Il dottore **ha parlato** con lui. ....

c Gli ospiti **sono partiti** alle otto. ....

d **Hanno avuto** un incidente stradale. ....

e Non **ho creduto** la sua storia. ....

f **Abbiamo parlato** con il suo professore. ....

g I bambini **sono stati** bravi. ....

h Giovanna **è partita** presto. ....

i Non **ho parlato** con gli studenti. ....

j **Hai avuto** il tempo di vederlo? ....

113 **Translate the following sentences into Italian, using the past historic tense. Where appropriate, translate 'you' with** *tu*.

a We left in the morning. ....

b There was a problem. ....

c She didn't believe it. ....

d He had a fever. ....

e You spoke to the girl. ....

f The houses were built in 1920. ....

g They left in a hurry. ....

h I believed him. ....

i My mother was ill. ....

j She had no hope. ....

The pluperfect or past perfect tense

> **What is the pluperfect tense?**
> The **pluperfect tense** is used to talk about what had happened or had been true at a point in the past, for example, *I'd forgotten to send her a card.*

Using the pluperfect tense

➤ When talking about the past we sometimes refer to things that had already happened previously. In English we use *had* followed by a <u>past participle</u> such as *done, broken, worked, arrived* to do this. This tense is called the <u>pluperfect</u> or <u>past perfect</u>.

➤ The Italian pluperfect tense is used in a similar way, but like the perfect tense, it can be made with either **avere** or **essere**, and the past participle.

⇨ *For more information on **Past participles**, see page 142.*

Avevamo già **mangiato** quando è arrivato.	We'd already eaten when he arrived.	
Ovviamente *erano* *riusciti* a risolvere il problema.	They'd obviously managed to solve the problem.	

How to make the pluperfect tense with avere

➤ To make the pluperfect tense with **avere**:

- choose the <u>imperfect</u> form of **avere** that matches the subject of the sentence.

- add the past participle. <u>Do not</u> change the ending of the participle to make it agree with the subject.

⇨ *For more information on the **Imperfect tense** of avere and **Past participles**, see pages 136 and 142.*

➤ The pluperfect tense of **parlare** (meaning *to speak*) is as follows:

	Imperfect tense of avere	Past participle	Meaning
(io)	avevo	parlato	I had spoken
(tu)	avevi	parlato	you had spoken
(lui/lei) (lei/Lei)	aveva	parlato	he/she had spoken you had spoken
(noi)	avevamo	parlato	we had spoken
(voi)	avevate	parlato	you had spoken
(loro)	avevano	parlato	they had spoken

Non gli <u>avevo</u> mai <u>parlato</u> prima. I'd never spoken to him before.
Sara gli <u>aveva parlato</u> il giorno prima. Sara had spoken to him the day before.

ⓘ Note that you use the same form of **avere** for **lui**, **lei** and **Lei**.

⇨ *For more information on **Verbs with irregular past participles**, see page 142.*

> *Tip*
> Do not use the pluperfect tense to say since when, or how long you had been doing something – **da** and the imperfect tense is used for this in Italian.
>
> **Abitavamo lì dal 1990.**   We'd lived there since 1990.
>
> ⇨ *For more information on **da**, see **Prepositions** page 231.*

When to make the pluperfect tense with avere

> As with the perfect tense, you use **avere** to make the <u>pluperfect</u> tense of most verbs.

> You do <u>not</u> use **avere** to make the pluperfect tense of:

- reflexive verbs

- certain verbs that do not take a direct object, such as **andare** (meaning *to go*), **venire** (meaning *to come*), **diventare** (meaning *to become*).

   Ovviamente <u>avevo sbagliato</u>.   I'd obviously made a mistake.
   <u>Avevano lavorato</u> molto il giorno prima.   They'd worked hard the day before.

ⓘ Note that, as with the perfect tense, the past participle agrees with the <u>object pronouns</u> **lo** and **la**, (meaning *him*, *her* and *it*) and **li** and **le** (meaning *them*) when they come before the verb.

   Non l'avevo vista.   I hadn't seen her.
   Le lettere? Non <u>le aveva</u> mai <u>lette</u>.   The letters? He'd never read them.

⇨ *For more information on **Object pronouns** and the **Perfect tense**, see pages 57 and 141.*

> **KEY POINTS**
> ✔ The pluperfect tense is used to talk about what had already happened in the past.
> ✔ The Italian pluperfect tense is made with the imperfect of **avere** or **essere**, and the past participle.
> ✔ **avere** is used to make the pluperfect tense of most verbs.

Test yourself

114 Fill the gap with the correct form of the past participle of the verb, to make the pluperfect tense.

a Non avevano .... prima di venire da noi. **(mangiare)**

b Avevo .... il compleanno di mio fratello. **(dimenticare)**

c Aveva .... tutta la notte. **(dormire)**

d Giulia? Non l'avevo .... **(vedere)**

e Avevamo .... molto il mese di giugno. **(lavorare)**

f Non gli aveva mai .... **(parlare)**

g Claudia aveva .... il libro la settimana prima. **(leggere)**

h Le lettere? Non le avevi .... prima? **(scrivere)**

i Avevo .... per le otto e mezza. **(prenotare)**

j Marco sapeva che aveva .... **(sbagliare)**

115 Replace the highlighted present tense with the pluperfect tense.

a Mia sorella **parla** con il dottore. ....

b **Vedo** la luna. ....

c **Scrivono** le cartoline. ....

d La ragazza **apre** la finestra. ....

e Il film **finisce** alle nove. ....

f Non **credo** la storia. ....

g **Spendiamo** troppi soldi in vacanza. ....

h **Rispondono** alla domanda. ....

i Mio padre **fa** la spesa. ....

j Il mio amico **prende** l'autobus per andare a Milano. ....

Test yourself

116 Translate the following into Italian, where appropriate using *tu* for 'you'.

a Your shoes? I hadn't seen them.

....

b She told me which team had won.

....

c Who had told you?

....

d We had decided to buy the blue car.

....

e Where had I put that book?

....

f Had you called your mother? — No, I hadn't called her.

....

g She had bought some strawberries from the market.

....

h They had never written to him.

....

i We had taken the train to go to the mountains.

....

j Had you read the book, Sir?

....

How to make the pluperfect tense with *essere*

➤ To make the pluperfect tense with *essere*:

- choose the <u>imperfect</u> form of **essere** that matches the subject of the sentence.

- add the past participle. Make the ending of the participle <u>agree</u> with the subject.

➤ The pluperfect tense of **andare** (meaning *to go*) is as follows:

	Imperfect tense of *essere*	Past participle	Meaning
(io)	ero	**andato** *or* **andata**	I had gone
(tu)	eri	**andato** *or* **andata**	you had gone
(lui)	era	**andato**	he/it had gone
(lei)	era	**andata**	she/it had gone
(lei/Lei)	era	**andato** *or* **andata**	you had gone
(noi)	eravamo	**andati** *or* **andate**	we had gone
(voi)	eravate	**andati** *or* **andate**	you had gone
(loro)	erano	**andati** *or* **andate**	they had gone

Silvia <u>era andata</u> con loro.	Silvia had gone with them.
Tutti i miei amici <u>erano andati</u> alla festa.	All my friends had gone to the party.

When to make the pluperfect tense with *essere*

➤ When **essere** is used to make the perfect tense of a verb, you also use **essere** to make the pluperfect.

⇨ *For more information on **Making the perfect tense with essere**, see page 147.*

➤ Use **essere** to make the pluperfect of all reflexive verbs, and of certain verbs that do not take a direct object, such as **andare** (meaning *to go*), **venire** (meaning *to come*), **riuscire** (meaning *to succeed*), **diventare** (meaning *to become*) and **piacere** (meaning to like).

Ovviamente non gli <u>erano</u> piaciuti i quadri.	He obviously hadn't liked the pictures.
Sono arrivata alle cinque, ma <u>erano</u> già <u>partiti</u>.	I arrived at five, but they'd already gone.
Fortunatamente non si <u>era fatta</u> male.	Luckily she hadn't hurt herself.

KEY POINTS

✔ Verbs that make their perfect tense with **essere** also make their pluperfect tense with **essere**.

✔ When the pluperfect tense is made with **essere** the past participle agrees with the subject of the sentence.

✔ **essere** is used to make the pluperfect tense of reflexive verbs and certain verbs that do not take a direct object.

Test yourself

117 Fill the gap with the correct form of the past participle of the verb, remembering to make the ending agree with the subject. If the gender of the subject is not obvious, use the masculine form.

a I miei amici erano .... alle otto. **(venire)**

b Ti eri .... a teatro, Paola? **(divertirsi)**

c Mi ero .... tardi. **(addormentarsi)**

d Lo studente era .... a scuola fino alle cinque. **(rimanere)**

e Mia sorella era .... la mattina. **(arrivare)**

f Mio figlio era .... grande. **(diventare)**

g Il film non mi era .... per niente. **(piacere)**

h I ragazzi erano .... in vacanza. **(andare)**

i La mia amica era .... a trovarmi. **(venire)**

j Cos'era .... alla festa? **(succedere)**

118 Translate the following into Italian, where appropriate using *tu* for 'you'.

a I had liked the flowers very much. ....

b The present had arrived earlier. ....

c The children had washed their hands before eating.

....

d My husband had gone out with some friends that evening.

....

e We had gone to the cinema. ....

f Had you ever been to London, Marta? ....

g Had your daughter gone to school that day?

....

h I had got up at ten o'clock. ....

i How many people had come to the party?

....

j He had become very rude. ....

The passive

> **What is the passive?**
> The **passive** is a verb form that is used when the subject of the verb is the person or thing that is affected by the action, for example, *Everyone was shocked by the incident*; *Two people were hurt*; *The house is being demolished*.

Using the passive

➤ Verbs can be <u>active</u> or <u>passive</u>.

➤ In a sentence with an <u>active verb</u> the subject of the sentence does the action:

Subject	Active verb	Object
She	does	most of the work.
A dog	bit	him.

➤ In a sentence with a <u>passive</u> verb the action is done by someone or something that is not the subject of the sentence.

Subject	Passive verb	Who/what the action is done by
Most of the work	is done	by her.
He	was bitten	by a dog.

➤ To show who or what is responsible for the action in a passive sentence you use *by* in English.

➤ You use passive rather than active verbs:

- when you want to focus on the person or thing <u>affected</u> by the action
  <u>John</u> was injured in an accident.

- when you don't know who is responsible for the action
  My car was stolen last week.

How to make the passive

➤ In English we use the verb *to be* with a <u>past participle</u> (*is done, was bitten*) to make the passive.

➤ In Italian the passive is made in exactly the same way, using **essere** (meaning *to be*) and a <u>past participle</u>.

➡ *For more information on the **Past participle**, see page 142.*

Siamo invitati ad una festa a casa loro.	We're invited to a party at their house.
L'elettricità è stata tagliata ieri.	The electricity was cut off yesterday.
La partita è stata rinviata.	The match has been postponed.
È stato costretto a ritirarsi dalla gara.	He was forced to withdraw from the competition.

➤ When you say who or what is responsible for the action you use **da** (meaning *by*).

I ladri sono stati catturati dalla polizia.   The thieves were caught by the police.

[i] Note that the past participle agrees with the subject of the verb **essere** in the same way an adjective would.

⇨ *For more information on **Adjectives**, see page 24.*

➤ Here is the perfect tense of the **–are** verb **invitare** (meaning *to invite*) in its passive form.

(Subject pronoun)		Perfect tense of *essere*	Past Participle	Meaning
(io)	– masculine	**sono stato**	**invitato**	I was, have been
	– feminine	**sono stata**	**invitata**	invited
(tu)	– masculine	**sei stato**	**invitato**	you were, have been
	– feminine	**sei stata**	**invitata**	invited
(lui)		**è stato**	**invitato**	he was, has been invited
(lei)		**è stata**	**invitata**	she was, has been invited
(lei/Lei)	– masculine	**è stato**	**invitato**	you were, have been invited
	– feminine	**è stata**	**invitata**	you were, have been invited
(noi)	– masculine	**siamo stati**	**invitati**	we were, have been invited
	– feminine	**siamo state**	**invitate**	we were, have been invited
(voi)	– masculine	**siete stati**	**invitati**	you were, have been invited
	– feminine	**siete state**	**invitate**	you were, have been invited
(loro)	– masculine	**sono stati**	**invitati**	they were, have been invited
	– feminine	**sono state**	**invitate**	they were, have been invited

➤ You can change the tense of the verb **essere** to make whatever passive tense you want. *For more information on Irregular past participles, see page 110.*

Sarete tutti **invitati.** You'll all be invited.

Non so se sarebbe invitata. I don't know if she would be invited.

➤ Some past participles are irregular.

⇨ *For more information on **Irregular past participles**, see page 142.*

Grammar Extra!

venire (meaning *to come*) and **rimanere** (meaning *to remain*) are sometimes used instead of **essere** to make the passive.

venire is used in the present, imperfect, future and conditional to make passives, but not in the perfect or pluperfect.

Quando <u>vengono cambiate</u>?	When <u>are they changed</u>?
<u>Venivano controllati</u> ogni sei mesi.	They <u>were checked</u> every six months.
<u>Verrà criticato</u> da tutti.	He<u>'ll be criticized</u> by everyone.
<u>Verrebbe scoperto</u>.	It <u>would be</u> discovered.

rimanere is used very often with **ferito** (meaning *injured*), and with participles describing emotion, such as **stupefatto** (meaning *amazed*) and **deluso** (meaning *disappointed*).

<u>È rimasto ferito</u> in un incidente stradale.	He <u>was injured</u> in a car accident.
<u>È rimasta stupefatta</u> dalla scena.	She <u>was amazed</u> by the scene.

Avoiding the passive

➤ Passives are not as common in Italian as they are in English. In many cases, where we would use a passive verb, one of the following alternatives would be used in Italian:

- an active construction

Due persone sono morte.	Two people were killed.
Mi hanno rubato la macchina la settimana scorsa.	My car was stolen last week.
C'erano delle microspie nella stanza.	The room was bugged.
Dicono che sia molto ambizioso.	He's said to be very ambitious.

- an ordinary verb made passive by having **si** put in front (this is known as the **si passivante**)

Qui <u>si vende</u> il pane.	Bread is sold here.
<u>Si parla</u> inglese.	English spoken.
Dove <u>si trovano</u> i migliori vini?	Where are the best wines to be found?
In Italia il prosciutto <u>si mangia</u> col melone.	In Italy ham is eaten with melon.
Gli spaghetti non <u>si mangiano</u> con le dita!	Spaghetti should not be eaten with one's fingers!
"comodo" <u>si scrive</u> con una solo m.	"comodo" is spelled with only one m.

📖 Note that wherever the subject comes in the sentence the verb has to agree with it.

- an impersonal construction with **si**

Si dice che non vada molto bene.	It's said not to be going very well.
Non si fa così.	That's not how it's done.

> *Tip*
> When you want to say something like *I was told*, or *She was given* use an active construction in Italian: **Mi hanno detto** (meaning *they told me*); **Le hanno dato** (meaning *they gave her*).

KEY POINTS
✔ The passive is made using **essere** with the past participle.
✔ The past participle must agree with the subject of **essere**.
✔ Alternatives to the passive are often used in Italian.

Test yourself

119 **Fill the gap with the correct form of the past participle of the verb. If the gender of the subject is not obvious, use the masculine form.**

    a La casa è stata .... nel 1860. **(costruire)**

    b I bambini non sarebbero .... **(invitare)**

    c Questa partita sarà .... da tutta la famiglia. **(guardare)**

    d L'uscita per il nostro volo è stata .... **(cambiare)**

    e I lavoratori sono .... delusi dalla decisione. **(rimanere)**

    f Le lettere sono state .... cento anni fa. **(scrivere)**

    g I cioccolatini sono stati .... a mano. **(fare)**

    h Questa canzone è .... da tutti. **(conoscere)**

    i Il suo compleanno sarà .... sabato prossimo. **(festeggiare)**

    j Il formaggio è stato .... ieri. **(comprare)**

120 Match the active and passive sentences.

    a Ha mandato la lettera stamattina.   È stato cambiato.

    b Mi hanno rubato la borsa ieri.   Tutti sono invitati.

    c Si invitano tutti alla festa.   È mangiato col melone.

    d Hanno cambiato l'indirizzo.   È stata rubata ieri.

    e Si mangia il prosciutto col melone.   È stata già mandata.

121 Translate the following sentences into Italian, using the passive. Where appropriate translate 'you' with *tu*.

    a The party has been postponed. ....

    b The tickets will be checked later. ....

    c They had been injured by the explosion. ....

    d The house was sold last month. ....

    e These eggs were bought yesterday. ....

    f They will be criticized by their family. ....

    g He was killed by his friend. ....

    h English is spoken in many countries. ....

    i Have you been invited? ....

    j We will be forced to go home. ....

The gerund

What is a gerund?

In English the **gerund** is a verb form ending in *–ing* which is used to make continuous tenses, for example, *What are you <u>doing</u>?* It can also be used as a noun or an adjective, for example, *I love <u>swimming</u>; a <u>skating</u> rink*.

Using the gerund

➤ In Italian the gerund is a verb form ending in **–ando** or **–endo**. It is used to make continuous tenses.

Sto <u>lavorando</u>.	I'm working.
Cosa stai <u>facendo</u>?	What are you doing?

- The gerund follows the present tense of **stare** to make the <u>present continuous</u>.

<u>Sto scrivendo</u> una lettera.	I'm writing a letter.
<u>Stai cercando</u> lavoro?	Are you looking for a job?

⇨ *For more information on the **Present continuous**, see page 105.*

- The gerund follows the imperfect tense of **stare** to make the <u>past continuous</u>.

Il bambino <u>stava piangendo</u>.	The little boy was crying.
<u>Stavo lavando</u> i piatti.	I was washing the dishes.

i Note that the Italian <u>past participle</u> is sometimes used where the gerund is used in English: **essere disteso** means *to be lying*; **essere seduto** means *to be sitting* and **essere appoggiato** means *to be leaning*.

<u>Era disteso</u> sul divano.	He was lying on the sofa.
<u>Era seduta</u> accanto a me.	She was sitting next to me.
La scala <u>era appoggiata</u> al muro.	The ladder was leaning against the wall.

➤ The gerund can be used by itself:

- to say when something happened

<u>Entrando</u> ho sentito odore di pesce.	When I came in I could smell fish.
<u>Ripensandoci</u>, credo che non fosse colpa sua.	Thinking about it, I don't reckon it was his fault.

- to say why something happened

<u>Sentendomi</u> male sono andato a letto.	Because I felt ill I went to bed.
<u>Vedendolo</u> solo, è venuta a parlargli.	Seeing that he was on his own she came to speak to him.

- to say in what circumstances something could happen

<u>Volendo</u>, potremmo comprarne un altro.	If we wanted to, we could buy another one.

> Tip
> The gerund never changes its form to agree with the subject of the sentence.

How to make the gerund

➤ To make the gerund of –**are** verbs, take off the –**are** ending of the infinitive to get the stem, and add –**ando**.

Infinitive	Stem	Gerund	Meaning
lavorare	lavor-	lavorando	working
andare	and-	andando	going
dare	d-	dando	giving
stare	st-	stando	being

ⓘ Note that the only –**are** verb that does not follow this rule is **fare**, and verbs made of **fare** with a prefix, such as **rifare** (meaning *to do again*) and **disfare** (meaning *to undo*). The gerund of **fare** is **facendo**.

➤ To make the gerund of –**ere** and –**ire** verbs, take off the –**ere** or –**ire** ending of the infinitive to get the stem, and add –**endo**.

Infinitive	Stem	Gerund	Meaning
credere	cred-	credendo	believing
essere	ess-	essendo	being
dovere	dov-	dovendo	having to
finire	fin-	finendo	finishing
dormire	dorm-	dormendo	sleeping

ⓘ Note that the only –**ire** verb that does not follow this rule is **dire** (and verbs made of **dire** with a prefix, such as **disdire** (meaning *to cancel*) and **contraddire** (meaning *to contradict*). The gerund of **dire** is **dicendo**.

When not to use the gerund

➤ In English the –*ing* form can follow other verbs, for example, *She started crying; He insisted on paying; They continued working*.

➤ In Italian the gerund is not used in this way. A construction with a preposition and the infinitive is used instead.

| **Ha cominciato a ridere.** | She started laughing. |
| **Hai finito di mangiare?** | Have you finished eating? |

⇨ *For more information on **Prepositions after verbs**, see page 189.*

➤ In English we often use –*ing* forms as nouns, for example, *driving, skating, cleaning*.

➤ In Italian you cannot use the **–ando** and **–endo** forms like this. When talking about activities and interests you use nouns, such as **il giardinaggio** (meaning *gardening*), **la pulizia** (meaning *cleaning*) and **il fumo** (meaning *smoking*).

A mia madre piace molto <u>**il giardinaggio**</u>**.**	My mother loves gardening.
Facciamo un po' di <u>**pulizia**</u>**.**	Let's do a bit of cleaning.
<u>**Il fumo**</u> **fa male.**	Smoking is bad for you.

➤ In English you can put an *-ing* noun in front of another noun, for example, *skating rink*.

➤ In Italian you can never put one noun in front of another noun.

- Often you link two words together with a preposition:

calzoncini <u>**da**</u> **bagno**	swimming trunks
una borsa <u>**per**</u> **la spesa**	a shopping bag
un istruttore <u>**di**</u> **guida**	a driving instructor

- Sometimes there is one word in Italian for two English words:

la <u>**patente**</u>	the <u>driving licence</u>
una <u>**piscina**</u>	a <u>swimming pool</u>

> *Tip*
> When you want to translate this kind of English two-word combination it's a good idea to look it up in a dictionary.

Where to put pronouns used with the gerund

➤ Pronouns are usually joined onto the end of the gerund.

Vedend<u>oli</u> è scoppiata in lacrime.	When she saw them she burst into tears.
Ascoltand<u>olo</u> mi sono addormentato.	Listening to him, I fell asleep.
Incontrand<u>osi</u> per caso sono andati al bar.	Meeting each other by chance, they went to a café.

➤ When the gerund is part of a continuous tense the pronoun can either come before **stare** or be joined onto the gerund.

<u>**Ti**</u> **sto parlando** OR **Sto parland<u>oti</u>.**	I'm talking to you.
<u>**Si**</u> **sta vestendo** OR **Sta vestend<u>osi</u>.**	He's getting dressed.
<u>**Me lo**</u> **stavano mostrando** OR **Stavano mostrand<u>omelo</u>.**	They were showing me it.

> **KEY POINTS**
> ✔ Use the gerund in continuous tenses with **stare**, and by itself to say when or why something happened.
> ✔ *-ing* forms in English are not always translated by the gerund.

Test yourself

122 **Replace the following infinitives with the gerund.**

a entrare ....

b credere ....

c dire ....

d vedere ....

e parlare ....

f fare ....

g essere ....

h andare ....

i cominciare ....

j spendere ....

123 **Complete the following sentences with the gerund.**

a Cosa stai ....? **(cercare)**

b .... ho visto Marco. **(entrare)**

c La ragazza stava .... **(cantare)**

d Gli stavo .... **(parlare)**

e La bambina sta .... **(piangere)**

f Cosa stavi ....? **(dire)**

g Gli studenti non stavano .... **(ascoltare)**

h Mio figlio sta .... i compiti. **(finire)**

i Stavo .... quando è arrivato. **(dormire)**

j .... il ragazzo solo, è andata a parlargli. **(vedere)**

124 **Match the two halves of the sentence.**

a Sentendosi male,   siamo andati a bere un caffè.

b Stavo leggendo il giornale,   è andato a letto.

c Volendo,   è venuto ad abbracciarmi.

d Vedendomi piangere,   potrebbe vendere la casa.

e Incontrandoci alla stazione,   quando mi ha chiamato.

Impersonal verbs

What is an impersonal verb?
In English an **impersonal verb** has the subject *it*, but this *'it'* does not refer to any specific thing; for example, *It's going to rain; It's nine o'clock.*

Verbs that are always impersonal

➤ Verbs such as **piovere** (meaning *to rain*) and **nevicare** (meaning *to snow*), are always impersonal because there is no person, animal or thing doing the action.

➤ They are used only in the *'it'* form, the infinitive, and as a gerund (the *–ing* form of the verb).

Piove.	It's raining.
Sta piovendo?	Is it raining?
Ha iniziato a piovere.	It started to rain.
Nevicava da due giorni.	It had been snowing for two days.
Pensi che nevicherà?	Do you think it'll snow?

⚘ Note that the perfect and pluperfect tenses of verbs to do with the weather such as **piovere**, **nevicare**, **grandinare** (meaning *to hail*) and **tuonare** (meaning *to thunder*) can be made either with **avere** or **essere**.

<u>Ha</u> piovuto or <u>è</u> piovuto molto ieri.	It rained a lot yesterday.
<u>Aveva</u> nevicato or <u>era</u> nevicato durante la notte.	It had snowed during the night.

Verbs that are sometimes impersonal

➤ **fare** is used impersonally to talk about the weather and time of day:

<u>Fa</u> caldo.	It's hot.
<u>Fa</u> freddo.	It's cold.
<u>Faceva</u> bel tempo.	It was good weather. OR The weather was good.
<u>Fa</u> sempre brutto tempo.	The weather's always bad.
<u>Fa</u> notte.	It's getting dark.

Tip
Fa niente means *It doesn't matter.*

➤ **è**, and other tenses of **essere** are used impersonally, like *it's* and other tenses of *to be* in English.

<u>È</u> tardi.	It's late.
<u>Era</u> presto.	It was early.
<u>È</u> da tre ore che aspettano.	It's three hours now that they've been waiting.
<u>Era</u> Pasqua.	It was Easter.
Non <u>era</u> da lei fare così.	It wasn't like her to act like that.

> Tip
> Just use the verb by itself when talking about the time or the weather.
> There is no Italian equivalent for 'it'.

➤ **essere** is used in impersonal constructions with adjectives, for example:

- with an adjective followed by an infinitive

  È _facile_ capire che qualcosa non va.   It's easy to see that something's wrong.
  Mi è impossibile andar via adesso.   It's impossible for me to leave now.
  È stato stupido buttarli via.   It was stupid to throw them away.
  Sarebbe bello andarci.   It would be nice to go there.

- with an adjective followed by **che**

  È vero che sono stato impaziente.   It's true that I've been impatient.
  Era bello che c'eravamo tutti.   It's nice that we were all there.

Grammar Extra!
When an impersonal construction with **che** is used to refer to something that is a possibility rather than a fact, the following verb must be in the <u>subjunctive</u>.
The following impersonal expressions refer to what might, should, or could be the case, rather than what <u>is</u> the case, and therefore they are always followed by the subjunctive:

- **È possibile che...**   It's possible that...
  È possibile che _abbia_ sbagliato tu.   It's possible that you made a mistake.
- **Non è possibile che...**   It's impossible that...
  Non è possibile che _sappiano_   It's impossible that they should know. OR
  They can't possibly know.

- **È _facile_ che...**   It's likely that...
  È _facile_ che piova.   It's likely that it'll rain. OR
  It'll probably rain.

  È difficile che...   It's unlikely that...
  È difficile che venga.   It's unlikely that he'll come.

⇨ _For more information on the **Subjunctive**, see page 171._

➤ **parere** and **sembrare** (both meaning _to seem_) are often used impersonally.

  Sono contenti? – Pare di sì.   Are they happy? – It seems so.
  L'ha creduto? – Pare di no.   Did he believe it? – Apparently not.
  Forse va tutto bene, ma non sembra.   Maybe everything's okay, but it doesn't look like it.

  Pare che sia stato lui.   Apparently it was him.
  Sembra che tu abbia ragione.   Seemingly you're right.

[i] Note that the Italian construction with a verb can often be translated by the adverbs _apparently_ and _seemingly_.

➤ Other verbs used impersonally are **bastare** (meaning _to be enough_), **bisognare** and **occorrere** (both meaning _to be necessary_), **importare** (meaning _to be important_).

  Basta?   Is that enough?
  Bisogna prenotare?   Is it necessary to or do you have to book?

For further explanation of grammatical terms, please see pages viii-xii.

Bisogna arrivare un'ora prima.	You have to get there an hour before.
Occorre farlo subito.	It should be done at once.
Oggi o domani, non importa.	Today or tomorrow, it doesn't matter.

ⓘ Note that these verbs can be replaced by impersonal constructions with **essere** and an adjective.

È necessario prenotare?	Is it necessary to book?
Sarebbe opportuno farlo subito.	It would be best to do it at once.

> *Tip*
> **può darsi** (meaning *it's possible*), can be used like **forse** (meaning *maybe*).
>
> **Vieni? – Può darsi.**   Are you coming? – Maybe.
> **Può darsi che vincano.**   It's possible or maybe they'll win.

KEY POINTS

✔ Impersonal verbs and expressions can only be used in the '*it*' form, the infinitive and the gerund.

✔ Impersonal verbs are often used when talking about the weather.

Test yourself

125 Translate the following sentences into Italian, using impersonal verbs or constructions.

a It had been raining for a week.

....

b Was it raining?

....

c The weather is always bad in January.

....

d It's true that she's angry.

....

e Do you need to book?

....

f Are they coming? — Apparently not.

....

g It would be nice to see them.

....

h It was Christmas.

....

i It's late.

....

j I forgot the book. — It doesn't matter.

....

126 Match the related sentences.

a Basta?	Bisogna accendere la luce.
b Che tempo faceva?	Sì, grazie.
c Perché vuoi andare a letto?	Pare di sì.
d Fa notte.	È tardi.
e Vendono la casa?	Nevicava da due giorni quando siamo arrivati.

The subjunctive

What is the subjunctive?

The **subjunctive** is a verb form that is often used in Italian to express wishes, thoughts and beliefs. In English the subjunctive is only used occasionally, mainly in formal language, for example, *If I were you...; So be it; He asked that they be removed.*

Using the subjunctive

➤ If you have the word **che** (meaning *that*) in an Italian sentence you often have to use the subjunctive.

➤ The subjunctive is used after **che**:

- following verbs such as **pensare** (meaning *to think*), **credere** (meaning *to believe/think*) and **sperare** (meaning *to hope*).

Penso che <u>sia</u> giusto.	I think it's fair.
Credo che <u>partano</u> domani.	I think they're leaving tomorrow.
Spero che Luca <u>arrivi</u> in tempo.	I hope Luca arrives in time.

  > *Tip*
  > Whereas in English you can say either *I think...* or *I think <u>that</u>...* in Italian you <u>always</u> say **che**.

- following the verb **volere** (meaning *to want*).

Voglio che i miei ragazzi <u>siano</u> felici.	I want my children to be happy.
Vuole che la <u>aiuti</u>.	She wants me to help her.

How to make the present subjunctive

➤ To make the present subjunctive of most verbs, take off the **–o** ending of the **io** form and add endings.

➤ For **–are** verbs the endings are **–i, –i, –i, –iamo, –iate, –ino**.

➤ For **–ere** and **–ire** verbs the endings are **–a, –a, –a, –iamo, –iate, –ano**.

🛈 Note that in the case of **–ire** verbs which add **–isc** in the **io** form, for example **finisco** (meaning *I finish*) and **pulisco** (meaning *I clean*), **–isc** is <u>not</u> added in the **noi** and **voi** forms.

> *Tip*
> The **io**, **tu**, **lui** and **lei** forms of the present subjunctive are all the same.
> The **noi** form of the present subjunctive is the same as the present simple.
>
> ⇨ *For more information on the **Present simple**, see page 88.*

➤ The following table shows the present subjunctive of three regular verbs: **parlare** (meaning *to speak*), **credere** (meaning *to believe*) and **finire** (meaning *to finish*).

Infinitive	io, tu, lui, lei	noi	voi	loro
parlare	parli	parliamo	parliate	parlino
credere	creda	crediamo	crediate	credano
finire	finisca	finiamo	finiate	finiscano

Non voglio che mi <u>parlino</u>.	I don't want them to speak to me.
Può darsi che non ti <u>creda</u>.	Maybe she doesn't believe you.
È meglio che lo <u>finisca</u> io.	It'll be best if I finish it.

➤ Some common verbs that are irregular in the ordinary present tense also have irregular present subjunctives:

Infinitive	io, tu, lui, lei	noi	voi	loro
andare *to go*	vada	andiamo	andiate	vadano
avere *to have*	abbia	abbiamo	abbiate	abbiano
dare *to give*	dia	diamo	diate	diano
dire *to say*	dica	diciamo	diciate	dicano
dovere *to have to*	debba	dobbiamo	dobbiate	debbano
essere *to be*	sia	siamo	siate	siano
fare *to do/make*	faccia	facciamo	facciate	facciano
potere *to be able*	possa	possiamo	possiate	possano
scegliere *to choose*	scelga	scegliamo	scegliate	scelgano
stare *to be*	stia	stiamo	stiate	stiano
tenere *to hold*	tenga	teniamo	teniate	tengano
tradurre *to translate*	traduca	traduciamo	traduciate	traducano
uscire *to go out*	esca	usciamo	usciate	escano
venire *to come*	venga	veniamo	veniate	vengano
volere *to want*	voglia	vogliamo	vogliate	vogliano

È meglio che tu te ne <u>vada</u>.	You'd better leave.
Vuoi che lo <u>traduca</u>?	Do you want me to translate it?
È facile che <u>scelgano</u> quelli rossi.	They'll probably choose those red ones.
Spero che tua madre <u>stia</u> meglio ora.	I hope your mother is better now.
Credi che <u>possa</u> essere vero?	Do you think it can be true?

KEY POINTS

✔ When you express a wish, hope, or belief with a verb + **che**, the verb following **che** should be in the subjunctive.

✔ **che** cannot be missed out in Italian.

Test yourself

127 Fill the gap with the correct form of the present subjunctive.

  a Vuole che la sua amica .... **(venire)**

  b Spero che Luca mi .... **(parlare)**

  c Può darsi che mia madre non ci .... **(credere)**

  d Voglio che i ragazzi .... i loro compiti. **(finire)**

  e Pensi che Maria .... contenta? **(essere)**

  f È meglio che sua moglie gli .... la verità. **(dire)**

  g Vuole che sua fratello gli .... una mano. **(dare)**

  h Penso che i miei genitori .... domani. **(arrivare)**

  i È meglio che Marta se ne .... **(andare)**

  j Vuoi che ti .... qualcosa? **(fare)**

128 Translate the following into Italian, where appropriate using *tu* for 'you'.

  a I think her decision is fair.

  ....

  b I don't want them to see me.

  ....

  c Maybe she isn't coming.

  ....

  d My brothers want us to help them.

  ....

  e Do you think she can do it?

  ....

  f I hope he is happy.

  ....

  g I'd better leave.

  ....

  h He wants Lucia to translate the letter.

  ....

  i I think they're at home.

  ....

  j She wants them to leave tomorrow.

When to use the present subjunctive

➤ Use the present subjunctive when you're saying what you think, feel or hope.

➤ The following are common verbs and expressions used to express opinions and hopes. They are used with **che** followed by the subjunctive:

- **pensare che** to think (that)
  Pensano che abbia ragione io.   They think I'm right.
  Pensi che sia giusto?   Do you think that's fair?

- **credere che** to believe/think (that)
  Crede che sia stata una macchina rossa. He thinks it was a red car.

- **supporre che** to suppose (that)
  Suppongo che quello sia il padre.   I suppose he's the father.

- **sperare che** to hope (that)
  Spero che vada bene.   I hope it'll be okay.

- **essere contento che** to be glad (that)
  Sono contento che faccia bel tempo.   I'm glad the weather's nice.

- **mi dispiace che** I'm sorry (that)
  Mi dispiace che non vengano.   I'm sorry they're not coming.

- **è facile che** it's likely (that)
  È facile che piova.   It'll probably rain.

- **può darsi che** it's possible (that)
  Può darsi che non venga.   It's possible that he won't come.

- **è un peccato che** it's a pity (that)
  È un peccato che non sia potuto venire. It's a pity he couldn't come.

> *Tip*
> It is best to learn the irregular subjunctives of common verbs such as **avere** (meaning *to have*), **essere** (meaning *to be*), **andare** (meaning *to go*) and **fare** (meaning *to make* or *do*).

➤ **che** is not always followed by the subjunctive. Use the ordinary present, future and so on, when you're saying what you know, or are sure of.
So che è tuo.   I know it's yours.
Sa che vale la pena.   She knows it's worth it.
Sono certo che verrà.   I'm sure she'll come.

KEY POINTS
✔ Use the present subjunctive + **che** to say what you think, feel or hope.
✔ Do not use the subjunctive + **che** to say what you know or are sure of.

For further explanation of grammatical terms, please see pages viii-xii.

Test yourself

129 Fill the gap with the correct form of the present subjunctive.

    a Suppongo che Luca .... il vincitore. **(essere)**

    b Pensa che Marta .... ragione. **(avere)**

    c Siamo contenti che .... bel tempo. **(fare)**

    d È un peccato che i tuoi amici se ne .... **(andare)**

    e Mi dispiace che mio marito non .... **(venire)**

    f È un peccato che Giulia non .... venire. **(potere)**

    g Credo che le scarpe blu .... le tue. **(essere)**

    h È facile che .... brutto tempo. **(fare)**

    i Suppongo che loro .... le chiavi. **(avere)**

    j È facile che mio fratello .... quello nero. **(scegliere)**

130 Translate the following into Italian, where appropriate using _tu_ for 'you'.

    a I think they can come.

    ....

    b Are you sorry she can't go?

    ....

    c They are certain she is here.

    ....

    d It's a pity it's raining.

    ....

    e I know she is French.

    ....

    f I hope your mother is well.

    ....

    g It's possible that they aren't coming.

    ....

    h It's a pity the children are ill.

    ....

    i They know she's going out this evening.

    ....

    j Are you happy they're leaving?

    ....

Grammar Extra!

Verbs and verbal expressions that express thoughts and hopes are followed by **di** + the infinitive, instead of **che** + the subjunctive if the subject of the sentence is thinking, hoping or feeling something about themselves.

Compare the following examples: in the sentences on the left side the two verbs have the same subect – I... I... and so on. These use **di** + infinitive. In the sentences on the right the two verbs have different subjects – I... they... and so on. These use **che** + subjunctive.

Infinitive construction	Subjunctive construction
Penso di <u>poter</u> venire.	**Penso che <u>possano</u> venire.**
I think I can come.	I think that <u>they</u> can come.
Credo di <u>aver sbagliato</u>.	**Credo che <u>abbiamo sbagliato</u>.**
I think I've made a mistake.	I think <u>we</u>'ve made a mistake.
È contenta di <u>esser promossa</u>.	**Sono contento che <u>sia stata promossa</u>.**
She's glad <u>she</u> passed.	I'm glad <u>she</u> passed.
Vi dispiace <u>di partire</u>?	**Ti dispiace che loro <u>partano</u>?**
Are <u>you</u> sorry <u>you</u>'re leaving?	Are <u>you</u> sorry <u>they</u>'re leaving?

Infinitive or subjunctive after volere?

➤ **volere** can be used with either the infinitive <u>or</u> the subjunctive.

➤ As in English, the <u>infinitive</u> is used in Italian to say what you want to do.

Voglio <u>essere</u> felice.	I want <u>to be</u> happy.
Vogliamo <u>aiutarla</u>.	We want <u>to help</u> her.

➤ However, when you're saying what you want someone else to do, or how you want something to be, you use **che** followed by the <u>present subjunctive</u>.

Voglio <u>che</u> tutto <u>sia</u> pronto.	I want everything to be ready.
Vuole <u>che</u> tu <u>faccia</u> il tuo meglio.	He wants you to do your best.
Vogliamo <u>che</u> loro <u>vadano</u> via.	We want them to go away.

➤ When you're saying what you wanted someone else to do in the past, or how you wanted something to be, change the present subjunctive to the <u>imperfect subjunctive</u>.

Volevo <u>che</u> tutto <u>fosse</u> pronto.	I wanted everything to be ready.
Voleva <u>che</u> loro <u>andassero</u> via.	She wanted them to go away.

⇨ *For more information on the **Imperfect subjunctive**, see page 180.*

Grammar Extra!
The subjunctive is used after certain conjunctions which include **che**:

- **prima che** before
  Vuoi parlargli <u>prima che parta</u>?   Do you want to speak to him <u>before</u>
                                               he goes?

  ⓘ Note that **prima di** and the <u>infinitive</u> is used if the two verbs have the same subject:

  Mi ha parlato <u>prima di</u> partire.   <u>He</u> spoke to me before <u>he</u> went.
  Gli ho parlato <u>prima di</u> partire.   <u>I</u> spoke to him before <u>I</u> went.

- **affinché** so that
  Ti do venti euro <u>affinché possa</u>   I'll give you twenty euros <u>so that</u> you
    comprarlo.   can buy it.

- **a meno che** unless
  Lo prendo io, <u>a meno che</u> tu lo <u>voglia</u>. I'll take it, <u>unless</u> you want it.

- **nel caso che** in case
  Ti do il mio nume___ ___ ___lefono   I'll give you my phone number <u>in case</u>
    nel caso che ven___ ___ma.   you come to Rome.

  ⇨ *For more informatio___ ___junctions, see page 244.*

How to make the perfe___ ___bjunctive

➤ To make the perfect subjun___ ___ou simply use the subjunctive of **avere** (meaning *to have*)
  or **essere** (meaning *to be*) w___ ___he past participle.

➤ For example, **fare** (meaning *to make* or *to do*) makes its ordinary perfect tense and its perfect
  subjunctive with **avere**, while **essere** makes its ordinary perfect tense and its perfect
  subjunctive with **essere**.

  ⇨ *For more information on the **Perfect tense** and **Past participles**, see pages 141-142.*

		ordinary perfect	perfect subjunctive
fare *to do/make*	io, tu, lui, lei	ho fatto, hai fatto, ha fatto	abbia fatto
	noi	abbiamo fatto	abbiamo fatto
	voi	avete fatto	abbiate fatto
	loro	hanno fatto	*a*bbiano fatto
essere *to be*	io	sono stato, sono stata	sia stato, sia stata
	tu	sei stato, sei stata	sia stato, sia stata
	lui	è stato	sia stato
	lei	è stata	sia stata
	lei/Lei	è stato, è stata	sia stato, sia stata
	noi	siamo stati, siamo state	siamo stati, siamo state
	voi	siete stati, siete state	siate stati, siate state
	loro	sono stati, sono state	*s*iano stati, *s*iano state

Non credo che l'*abbiano fatto* loro.	I don't think they did it.
È possibile che <u>sia stato</u> un errore.	It might have been a mistake.

When to use the perfect subjunctive

➤ When you want to say what you think or hope about something in the past, use a verb such as **penso che** and **spero che**, followed by the <u>perfect subjunctive</u>.

Penso che <u>sia stata</u> una buona idea.	I think it was a good idea.
Spero che non si <u>sia fatta</u> male.	I hope she didn't hurt herself.
Spero che <u>abbia detto</u> la verità?	I hope you told the truth?
È poss*i*bile che *abbiano cambiato* idea.	It's possible they've changed their minds.

Avoiding the perfect subjunctive

➤ Instead of using expressions such as **penso che** and **è possibile che** with the perfect subjunctive, you can use **secondo me** (meaning *in my opinion*) or **forse** (meaning *perhaps*) with the ordinary perfect tense to say what you think or believe.

<u>Secondo me</u> è stata una buona idea.	In my opinion it was a good idea.
<u>Forse</u> hanno cambiato idea.	Perhaps they've changed their minds.

⇨ *For more information on the* **Perfect tense***, see page* 141.

➤ You can also avoid using the perfect subjunctive by saying what you think first, and adding a verb such as **penso**, **credo** or **spero** to the end of the sentence.

Hai detto la verità, <u>spero</u>?	You told the truth, I hope?
Hanno fatto bene, <u>penso</u>.	They did the right thing, I think.

KEY POINTS

✔ When you express a wish, hope, or belief about something in the past, the verb following **che** should be in the perfect subjunctive.

✔ You can sometimes reword sentences to avoid using the perfect subjunctive.

Test yourself

131 **Translate the following into Italian, where appropriate using *tu* for 'you'.**

a I don't think she did it.

....

b I think she left at eight o'clock.

....

c It's possible it was a mistake.

....

d I hope they didn't hurt themselves.

....

e I'm sorry they didn't come.

....

f I didn't do it, I think it was him.

....

g I hope they left early this morning.

....

h Maria is pleased that her brother came to the party.

....

i I suppose she told you the truth.

....

j Do you think he went out with them?

....

132 **Match the sentences that have the same meaning.**

a Penso che sia stata giusta.	Secondo me non l'ha preso.
b Non credo che l'abbia preso.	Secondo me è stata giusta.
c Spero che tu abbia fatto del tuo meglio.	Forse se n'è andata.
d È possibile che non siano venuti.	Hai fatto del tuo meglio, spero.
e Può darsi che se ne sia andata.	Forse non sono venuti.

How to make the imperfect subjunctive

➤ The imperfect subjunctive is made by adding endings to the verb <u>stem</u>.

➤ The endings for **–are** verbs are **–assi**, **–assi**, **–asse**, **–assimo**, **–aste**, and **–assero**; the endings for **–ere** verbs are **–essi**, **–essi**, **–esse**, **–essimo**, **–este**, and **–essero**; the endings for **–ire** verbs are **–issi**, **–issi**, **–isse**, **–issimo**, **–iste** and **–issero**.

➤ The following table shows the imperfect subjunctive of three regular verbs: **parlare** (meaning *to speak*), **credere** (meaning *to believe*) and **finire** (meaning *to finish*).

	parlare	credere	finire
(io)	parlassi	credessi	finissi
(tu)	parlassi	credessi	finissi
(lui/lei) (lei/Lei)	parlasse	credesse	finisse
(noi)	parlassimo	credessimo	finissimo
(voi)	parlaste	credeste	finiste
(loro)	parlassero	credessero	finissero

Volevano che <u>parlassi</u> con l'inquilino.	They wanted me to speak to the tenant.
Anche se mi <u>credesse</u>, non farebbe niente.	Even if he believed me he wouldn't do anything.
Se solo <u>finisse</u> prima delle otto!	If only it finished before eight o'clock!

➤ The imperfect subjunctive of **essere** is as follows:

(io)	fossi
(tu)	fossi
(lui/lei)	fosse
(lei/Lei)	fosse
(noi)	fossimo
(voi)	foste
(loro)	fossero

Se <u>fossi</u> in te non lo pagherei.	If I were you I wouldn't pay it.
Se <u>fosse</u> più furba verrebbe.	If she had more sense she'd come.

➤ The imperfect subjunctive of the other important irregular verbs – **bere** (meaning *to drink*), **dare** (meaning *to give*), **dire** (meaning *to say*), **fare** (meaning *to make* or *to do*) and **stare** (meaning *to be*) – is as follows:

	(io)	(tu)	(lui/lei)	(noi)	(voi)	(loro)
bere	bevessi	bevessi	bevesse	bevessimo	beveste	bevessero
dare	dessi	dessi	desse	dessimo	deste	dessero
dire	dicessi	dicessi	dicesse	dicessimo	diceste	dicessero
fare	facessi	facessi	facesse	facessimo	faceste	facessero
stare	stessi	stessi	stesse	stessimo	steste	stessero

Se solo <u>bevesse</u> meno!	If only he drank less!
Voleva che gli <u>dessero</u> il permesso.	He wanted them to give him permission.

For further explanation of grammatical terms, please see pages viii-xii.

When to use the imperfect subjunctive

➤ The imperfect subjunctive is used to talk about what you wanted someone to do in the past, or about how you wanted things to be.

Voleva che <u>fossimo</u> pronti alle otto.	He wanted us to be ready at eight.
Volevano che tutto <u>fosse</u> in ordine.	They wanted everything to be tidy.
Volevo che <u>andasse</u> più veloce.	I wanted him to go faster.

➤ In English, when you are talking about what you would do in an imagined situation, the <u>past tense</u> is used to describe the situation, for example, *What would you do if you <u>won</u> the lottery?*

➤ In Italian the <u>imperfect subjunctive</u> is used for this kind of imagined situation, which is often introduced by **se** (meaning *if*).

Se ne <u>avessi</u> bisogno, te lo darei.	If you needed it I'd give it to you.
Se lo <u>sapesse</u> sarebbe molto deluso.	If he knew he'd be very disappointed.
Se solo <u>avessi</u> più denaro!	If only I had more money!

KEY POINTS
- ✔ The imperfect subjunctive is used when talking about what you wanted someone to do, or how you wanted things to be.
- ✔ The imperfect subjunctive is used to talk about imagined situations.

133 **Translate the following into Italian, where appropriate using *tu* for 'you'.**

a If I were you I wouldn't go.

....

b She wanted us to finish at ten o'clock.

....

c Even if she came she wouldn't be happy.

....

d I wanted her to give me the bag.

....

e If only we had money!

....

f If they knew they would be angry.

....

g She wanted me to speak to her teacher.

....

h They wanted me to finish my homework.

....

i Even if I believed you I wouldn't give it to you.

....

j If only he would tell me!

....

134 **Match subjunctive form with its infinitive.**

a dessimo   dire

b facessero   essere

c dicessi   dare

d foste   stare

e stesse   fare

135 **Match the verb to the subject.**

a credessero   io

b parlasse   voi

c finiste   loro

d dicessi   noi

e fossimo   lui

The Infinitive

> ## What is the infinitive?
> In English the **infinitive** is the basic form of the verb, for example, *walk, see, hear.*
> It is used after other verbs such as *should, must and can.* The infinitive is often used
> with *to: to speak, to eat, to live.*

Using the infinitive

➤ In English the infinitive may be one word, for example, *speak*, or two words, for example,
to speak. In Italian the infinitive is always one word, and is the verb form that ends in **–are**,
–ere, or **–ire**, for example, **parlare** (meaning *to speak*), **credere** (meaning *to believe*), **finire**
(meaning *to finish*). The final **–e** of the infinitive ending is sometimes dropped.

> *i* Note that there are a few verbs with infinitives ending in **–urre**, for example, **tradurre**
> (meaning *to translate*), **produrre** (meaning *to produce*) and **ridurre** (meaning *to reduce*).
> **–urre** verbs follow the pattern of **produrre**, which you can find in the verb tables at the
> back of the book.

➤ The infinitive is the form of the verb shown in dictionaries.

➤ In Italian the infinitive is used in the following ways:

- after adjectives and nouns that are followed by **di**
Sono <u>contento di vederti</u>.	I'm glad to see you.
Sono <u>sorpreso di vederti</u> qui.	I'm surprised to see you here.
Sono <u>stufo di studiare</u>.	I'm fed up of studying.
Ho <u>voglia di uscire</u>.	I feel like going out.
Non c'è <u>bisogno di</u> prenotare.	There's no need to book.

- after another verb
Non <u>devi andarci</u> se non vuoi.	You don't have to go if you don't want to.
<u>Posso entrare</u>?	Can I come in?
Cosa ti <u>piacerebbe fare</u>?	What would you like to do?
<u>Preferisce spendere</u> i suoi soldi in vestiti.	He prefers to spend his money on clothes.

- to give instructions and orders, particularly on signs, on forms, and in recipes and
  manuals
<u>Rallentare</u>.	Slow down.
<u>Spingere</u>.	Push.
<u>Scaldare</u> a fuoco lento per cinque minuti.	Heat gently for five minutes.

- to tell someone you call **tu** not to do something
<u>Non fare</u> sciocchezze!	Don't do anything silly!
<u>Non toccarlo</u>!	Don't touch it!

⇨ *For more information on the **Imperative**, see page 107.*

Infinitive or gerund?

➤ In English, prepositions such as *before*, *after* and *without*, are followed by the *-ing* form of the verb, for example, *before leaving*, *after eating*.

➤ In Italian prepositions are followed by the infinitive.

<u>Prima di aprire</u> il pacchetto, leggi le istruzioni.	Before opening the packet, read the instructions.
È andato via <u>senza dire</u> niente.	He went away without saying anything.
<u>Dopo aver telefonato</u> è uscita.	After making a phone call she went out.

➤ In English the *-ing* form of the verb can be used as a noun, for example, *They enjoy dancing*. In Italian the infinitive, not the gerund, is used as a noun.

<u>Ascoltare</u> la musica è rilassante.	Listening to music is relaxing.
<u>Camminare</u> fa bene.	Walking is good for you.

Tip

Remember to use the infinitive with **mi piace** when saying what activities you like:

Mi piace cavalcare.	I like riding.

Grammar Extra!

As well as the ordinary infinitive there is also the perfect infinitive. In English this is made with the infinitive *have* + the past participle, for example, *He could <u>have done</u> better; He claims <u>to have seen</u> an eagle*. In Italian the perfect infinitive is made with **avere** or **essere** + the past participle.

Può <u>aver avuto</u> un incidente.	He may have had an accident.
Dev'<u>essere successo</u> ieri.	It must have happened yesterday.

KEY POINTS

✔ In Italian the infinitive is one word.

Linking verbs together

➤ In English both the infinitive and the *–ing* form can follow after another verb, for example, *Do you <u>want to come</u>?*; *They <u>stopped working</u>*.

➤ In Italian only the infinitive can follow another verb. Verbs are generally linked to the infinitive in one of these three ways:

- directly
  Volete <u>aspettare</u>?   Do you want to wait?

- with the preposition **a**
  Hanno cominciato <u>a ridere</u>.   They started to laugh.

- with the preposition **di**
  Quando sono entrato hanno   When I came in they stopped talking.
  smesso <u>di parlare</u>.

⇨ *For more information on the **Prepositions a and di**, see pages 231 and 232.*

ⓘ Other linking prepositions are sometimes used, for example, **stare <u>per</u> far qualcosa** (meaning *to be about to do something*).

Stavo <u>per uscire</u> quando ha   I was about to go out when the phone rang.
squillato il telefono.

Verbs that are not linked to the infinitive by a preposition

➤ A number of very common verbs are followed directly by the infinitive:

- **dovere** to have to, must
  <u>È dovuto partire</u>.   He had to leave.
  <u>Dev'essere</u> tardi.   It must be late.

- **potere** can, may
  Non <u>posso aiutarti</u>.   I can't help you.
  <u>Potresti aprire</u> la finestra?   Could you open the window?
  <u>Potrebbe essere</u> vero.   It might be true.

- **sapere** to know how to, can
  <u>Sai farlo</u>?   Do you know how to do it?
  Non <u>sapeva nuotare</u>.   He couldn't swim.

- **volere** to want
  <u>Voglio comprare</u> una macchina nuova. I want to buy a new car.

Tip
voler dire (literally *to want to say*) is the Italian for to *mean*.
Non so che cosa vuol dire.   I don't know what it means.

- verbs such as **piacere**, **dispiacere** and **convenire**
  Mi <u>piace andare</u> in bici.   I like cycling.
  Ci <u>dispiace andar</u> via.   We're sorry to be leaving.
  Ti <u>conviene partire</u> presto.   You'd best set off early.

- **vedere** (meaning *to see*), **ascoltare** (meaning *to listen to*) and **sentire** (meaning *to hear*)
  Ci <u>ha visto arrivare</u>.   He saw us arriving.
  Ti <u>ho sentito cantare</u>.   I heard you singing.
  L'<u>abbiamo ascoltato parlare</u>.   We listened to him talking.

- **fare** (meaning *to make*) and **lasciare** (meaning *to let*)
  Non mi <u>far ridere</u>!   Don't make me laugh!
  <u>Lascia fare</u> a me.   Let me do it.

  [i] Note that **far fare qualcosa** and **farsi fare qualcosa** both mean *to have something done*:

  Ho <u>fatto riparare</u> la macchina.   I had the car repaired.
  Mi <u>sono fatta tagliare</u> i capelli.   I had my hair cut.

➤ The following common verbs are also followed directly by the infinitive:
bisognare	to be necessary
desiderare	to want
odiare	to hate
preferire	to prefer

  <u>Odio alzarmi</u> presto al mattino.   I hate getting up early in the morning.
  <u>Desiderava migliorare</u> il suo inglese.   He wanted to improve his English.
  <u>Bisogna prenotare</u>.   You need to book.
  <u>Preferisco</u> non <u>parlarne</u>.   I prefer not to talk about it.

Verbs followed by a and the infinitive

➤ Some very common verbs can be followed by **a** and the infinitive:
andare a fare qualcosa	to go to do something
venire a fare qualcosa	to come to do something
imparare a fare qualcosa	to learn to do something
cominciare a fare qualcosa	to start doing *or* to do something
continuare a fare qualcosa	to go on doing something
abituarsi a fare qualcosa	to get used to doing something
riuscire a fare qualcosa	to manage to do something

  Sono venuti <u>a trovarci</u>.   They came to see us.
  Siamo riusciti <u>a convincerla</u>.   We managed to persuade her.
  Dovrò abituarmi <u>ad alzarmi</u> presto.   I'll have to get used to getting up early.

➤ As in English, you can put an object between the verb and the infinitive:
aiutare <u>qualcuno</u> a fare qualcosa	to help <u>somebody</u> to do something
invitare <u>qualcuno</u> a fare qualcosa	to invite <u>somebody</u> to do something
insegnare <u>a qualcuno</u> a fare qualcosa	to teach <u>somebody</u> to do something

  [i] Note that **insegnare** takes an indirect object.

Hanno invitato Lucia a sedersi al loro tavolo.	They invited Lucia to sit at their table.
Ho aiutato mamma a lavare i piatti.	I helped mum wash up.
Ha insegnato a mio fratello a nuotare.	He taught my brother to swim.

Verbs followed by di and the infinitive

➤ The following are the most common verbs that can be followed by **di** and the infinitive:

cercare di fare qualcosa	to try to do something
decidere di fare qualcosa	to decide to do something
dimenticare di fare qualcosa	to forget to do something
smettere di fare qualcosa	to stop doing something
ricordarsi di aver fatto qualcosa	to remember having done something
negare di aver fatto qualcosa	to deny doing something

Cerca di smettere di fumare.	He's trying to stop smoking.
Ho deciso di non andarci.	I decided not to go.
Non mi ricordo di aver detto una cosa del genere.	I don't remember saying anything like that.
Ho dimenticato di prendere la chiave.	I forgot to take my key.

> *Tip*
> Learn the linking preposition that goes with important verbs.

KEY POINTS

✔ Italian verbs can be followed by the infinitive, with or without a linking preposition.
✔ Italian verbs are not followed by the gerund.

Test yourself

136 Fill the gap with *a* or *di*.

a È venuta .... trovarmi.

b Le ragazze cercavano .... fare i compiti.

c Avevano dimenticato .... chiudere la porta.

d Mi hanno invitato .... andare al cinema con loro.

e Abbiamo deciso .... stare a casa.

f Chi ti ha insegnato .... suonare la chitarra?

g Cominciavano .... mangiare.

h Mi abituo .... alzarmi presto.

i Mio padre ha smesso .... fumare.

j Il bambino ha negato .... aver rotto il bicchiere.

137 Translate the following into Italian, where appropriate using *tu* for 'you'.

a She was about to go out when they arrived.

....

b My sister can't swim. ....

c We have to leave. ....

d I like skiing. ....

e She had her hair cut. ....

f I heard him singing. ....

g They want to buy a new house. ....

h Are you glad to see her? ....

i Can I come in? ....

j We don't know what it means. ....

138 Match the two halves of the sentence.

a	Vuoi	a lavare la macchina?
b	Hanno smesso	aspettare?
c	Non sappiamo	a suonare il violino.
d	Imparavo	di ridere.
e	Potresti aiutarmi	farlo.

Prepositions after verbs

➤ English verbs are often followed by prepositions, for example, *I'm relying <u>on</u> you; They'll write <u>to</u> him; He was accused <u>of</u> murder*.

➤ The same is true of Italian verbs, which are often followed by prepositions.

- **entrare in** to go into
  Siamo entrati in aula.　　　　　　　　We went into the classroom.

➤ As in English, Italian verbs can be followed by two prepositions.
　　parlare <u>a</u> qualcuno <u>di</u> qualcosa　　　　to talk <u>to</u> someone <u>about</u> something

➤ With some verbs the Italian preposition may not be the one you would expect. For example, *to* in English is not always **a** in Italian, **di** is not always translated by *of* and so forth. The most important ones of these are shown in the examples on the following pages.

➡ For more information on **Verbs used with a preposition and the infinitive**, see page 186.

> **Tip**
> When you learn a new verb, check if there's a preposition that goes with it, and learn that too.

Verbs followed by a

➤ **a** is used with the indirect object of verbs such as **dire** (meaning *to say*) and **dare** (meaning *to give*).

dare qualcosa <u>a</u> qualcuno	to give something to someone
dire qualcosa <u>a</u> qualcuno	to say something to someone
mandare qualcosa <u>a</u> qualcuno	to send something to someone
scrivere qualcosa <u>a</u> qualcuno	to write something to someone
mostrare qualcosa <u>a</u> qualcuno	to show something to someone

➡ For more information about **Indirect objects**, see page 60.

> **Tip**
> In English you can say *to give someone something*. In Italian you <u>cannot</u> leave out the preposition – you have to use a with the person who is the indirect object.

➤ Here are some verbs taking **a** in Italian when you might not expect it, since the English equivalent either does not have the preposition *to* or has no preposition at all:

arrivare <u>a</u> (una città)	to arrive at (*a town*)
avvicinarsi <u>a</u> qualcuno	to approach someone
chiedere qualcosa <u>a</u> qualcuno	to ask someone for something
far male <u>a</u> qualcuno	to hurt someone
giocare <u>a</u> qualcosa	to play something (*game/sport*)
insegnare qualcosa <u>a</u> qualcuno	to teach somebody something
partecipare <u>a</u> qualcosa	to take part in something

rispondere <u>a</u> qualcuno	to answer someone
rivolgersi <u>a</u> qualcuno	to ask someone
somigliare <u>a</u> qualcuno	to look like someone
permettere <u>a</u> qualcuno di fare qualcosa	to allow someone to do something
proibire <u>a</u> qualcuno di fare qualcosa	to forbid someone to do something
rubare qualcosa <u>a</u> qualcuno	to steal something from someone
ubbidire <u>a</u> qualcuno	to obey someone

Chiedi <u>a</u> Lidia come si chiama il suo cane.	Ask Lidia what her dog's called.
Quandi arrivi <u>a</u> Londra?	When do you arrive in London?
Parteciperai <u>alla</u> gara?	Are you going to take part in the competition?
Non permette <u>a</u> Luca di uscire.	She doesn't allow Luca to go out.

⇨ *For verbs such as **piacere**, **mancare** and **rincrescere**, see **Verbal idioms** on page 194.*

Tip
Remember that you often have to use a preposition with an Italian verb when there is no preposition in English.

Verbs followed by di

➤ Here are some verbs taking **di** in Italian when the English verb is not followed by *of*:

accorgersi <u>di</u> qualcosa	to realize something
aver bisogno <u>di</u> qualcosa	to need something
aver voglia <u>di</u> qualcosa	to want something
discutere <u>di</u> qualcosa	to discuss something
fidarsi <u>di</u> qualcosa/qualcuno	to trust something/someone
intendersi <u>di</u> qualcosa	to know about something
interessarsi <u>di</u> qualcosa	to be interested in something
lamentarsi <u>di</u> qualcosa	to complain about something
ricordarsi <u>di</u> qualcosa/qualcuno	to remember something/someone
ridere <u>di</u> qualcosa/qualcuno	to laugh at something/someone
stufarsi <u>di</u> qualcosa/qualcuno	to get fed up with something/someone
stupirsi <u>di</u> qualcosa	to be amazed by something
trattare <u>di</u> qualcosa	to be about something
vantarsi <u>di</u> qualcosa	to boast about something

Non mi fido <u>di</u> lui.	I don't trust him.
Ho bisogno <u>di</u> soldi.	I need money.
Discutono spesso <u>di</u> politica.	They often discuss politics.
Mi sono stufato <u>di</u> loro.	I got fed up with them.

Verbs followed by da

➤ Here are some verbs taking **da** in Italian when the English verb is not followed by *from*:

dip*e*ndere <u>da</u> qualcosa/qualcuno	to depend on something/someone
giudicare <u>da</u> qualcosa	to judge by something
sc*e*ndere <u>da</u> qualcosa	to get off something (*bus, train, plane*)
sp*o*rgersi <u>da</u> qualcosa	to lean out of something
Dipende <u>dal</u> tempo.	It depends on the weather.

Verbs that are followed by a preposition in English but not in Italian

➤ Although the English verb is followed by a preposition, you <u>don't</u> use a preposition with the following Italian verbs:

guardare qualcosa/qualcuno	to look at something/someone
ascoltare qualcosa/qualcuno	to listen to something/someone
cercare qualcosa/qualcuno	to look for something/someone
chi*e*dere qualcosa	to ask for something
aspettare qualcosa/qualcuno	to wait for something/someone
pagare qualcosa	to pay for something
Guarda la sua f*a*ccia.	Look at his face.
Mi stai ascoltando?	Are you listening to me?
Sto cercando la chiave.	I'm looking for my key.
Ha chiesto qualcosa da mangiare.	He asked for something to eat.
Asp*e*ttami!	Wait for me!
Ho già pagato il biglietto.	I've already paid for my ticket.

KEY POINTS

✔ Many Italian verbs are not followed by the preposition you would expect.
✔ There can be a preposition with a verb in Italian, but not in English, and vice versa.

Test yourself

139 Fill the gap with *a*, *di* or *da*, where appropriate combining it with the article. The first one has been done for you.

a Si lamentava sempre ..... *del* ..... rumore.

b Francesca ha dato il libro .... suo fratello.

c Mi piace giocare .... calcio.

d Ho bisogno .... una macchina.

e Siamo arrivati .... Parigi la sera.

f Chiedi .... Luca se vuole venire.

g È sceso .... treno.

h Sono stufo .... questo traffico.

i Sporgevano .... finestra.

j Mia sorella somiglia .... mia madre.

140 Translate the following into Italian, where appropriate using *tu* for 'you'.

a I'm waiting for my brother.

....

b It depends on the children.

....

c I asked for something to drink.

....

d We were listening to the radio.

....

e I'm fed up with work.

....

f The children were looking at the horses.

....

g They don't allow Marco to go out in the evening.

....

h I remember that film.

....

i She has already paid for the beer.

....

j She was looking for her shoes.

....

Test yourself

141 Create a sentence in the present tense using the elements below. Don't forget to add the article for the noun and a preposition if it is required. The first one has been done for you.

a Paolo/soldi/bisogno/avere *Paolo ha bisogno di soldi.* ....

b non/loro/si fida/Gianni ....

c arrivi/Milano/quando/? ....

d spesso/far male/Elena/fratello/suo ....

e guardando/ragazzo/sta/albero ....

f come/si chiama/mi/sorella/chiedere/mia/Flavio.

....

g ragazze/ridere/film ....

h giocatori/partita/partecipare ....

i fratelli/politica/discutere ....

j ascoltare/concerto/musicisti ....

Verbal Idioms

➤ Some important Italian verbs behave differently from their English equivalent, for example:

Mi piace l'Italia.	I like Italy.
Mi piacciono i cani.	I like dogs.

➤ Both English sentences have the same verb *like*, which agrees with the subject, *I*.

➤ The Italian sentences have different verbs, one singular (**piace**) and the other plural (**piacciono**). This is because the verb **piacere** literally means *to be pleasing*, and in one sentence what's pleasing is singular (**l'Italia**) and in the other it's plural (**i cani**).

➤ If you use this wording in English you also get two different verbs: Italy <u>is</u> pleasing to me; Dogs <u>are</u> pleasing to me.

> *Tip*
> Remember to turn the sentence around in this way when talking about what you like in Italian.

Present tense of piacere

➤ When talking about likes and dislikes in the present use **piace** if the subject of the verb is singular, and **piacciono** if it is plural.

➤ Use the appropriate indirect pronoun: **mi**, **ti**, **gli**, **le**, **ci**, or **vi**.

> ⒤ Note that **gli** means both *to him* and *to them*, so it is used to say what he likes, and what they like.

Questo colore non mi <u>piace</u>.	I don't like this colour. (*literally: this colour <u>is</u> not pleasing to me*)
Ti <u>piacciono</u> le mie scarpe?	Do you like my shoes? (*literally: <u>are</u> my shoes pleasing to you?*)
Non gli <u>piacciono</u> i dolci.	He doesn't like desserts. (*literally: desserts <u>are</u> not pleasing to him*)
Le piace l'Italia, signora?	Do you like Italy, madam? (*literally: <u>is</u> Italy pleasing to you?*)
Ci <u>piace</u> il mare.	We like the sea. (*literally: the sea <u>is</u> pleasing to us*)
Vi <u>piacciono</u> le montagne?	Do you like the mountains? (*literally: <u>are</u> the mountains pleasing to you?*)
Sono vecchi, non gli <u>piace</u> questa musica.	They're old, they don't like this music. (*literally: this music <u>isn't</u> pleasing to them*)

➪ *For more information on **Indirect object pronouns**, see page 60.*

> **Tip**
> Use the infinitive, not the gerund, when talking about the activities you like:
> **Mi piace cucinare.**   I like cooking.
> **Ci piace camminare.**   We like walking.

➤ If it is not used with the pronouns **mi**, **ti**, **gli**, **le**, **ci**, or **vi**, **piacere** is followed by the preposition **a**.

> **Il giardinaggio piace <u>a</u> mia sorella.**   My sister likes gardening.
> (*literally: gardening is pleasing to my sister*)
>
> **I suoi film non pi<u>a</u>cciono <u>a</u> tutti.**   Not everyone likes his films.
> (*literally: his films are not pleasing to everyone*)
>
> **L'It<u>a</u>lia piace <u>ai</u> tuoi?**   Do your parents like Italy?
> (*literally: Is Italy pleasing to your parents?*)

Other tenses of piacere

➤ You can use **piacere** in any tense.

> **Credi che la casa <u>piacerà</u> a Sara?**   Do you think Sara will like the house?
> **Questo libro ti <u>piacerebbe</u>.**   You'd like this book.
> **Da giovane gli <u>piaceva</u> nuotare.**   When he was young he liked swimming.
> **Il concerto <u>è piaciuto</u> a tutti.**   Everyone liked the concert.
> **Non credo che il *calcio* pi<u>a</u>ccia**   I don't think the teacher likes football.
>   **al professore.**

> **Tip**
> **Mi dispiace** means *I'm sorry*. Change the pronoun to **gli**, **le**, **ci** and so on if you want to say *He's sorry*, *She's sorry* or *We're sorry*.

Other verbs like piacere

➤ There are a number of other important verbs that are used with an indirect pronoun, or are followed by the preposition **a**.

➤ As with **piacere**, the person who is the subject of the verb in English is the indirect object in Italian.

- **convenire** (*literally*) to be advisable
  <u>Ti</u> conviene partir presto.   You'd better set off early.
  Non conviene <u>a</u> nessuno fare così.   Nobody should behave like that.

- **mancare** (*literally*) to be missing
  Fammi sapere se <u>ti</u> manca qualcosa.   Let me know if you need anything.
  Mi manchi.   I miss you.

- **interessare** to be of interest
  Se <u>ti</u> interessa puoi venire   If you're interested you can come.
  Pensi che interesserebbe <u>a</u> Luigi?   Do you think Luigi would be interested?

- **importare** to be important
  Non mi importa!   I don't care!
  Non importa a mio marito.   My husband doesn't care.

- **rincrescere** (*literally*) to make sorry
  Ci rincresce di non poterlo fare.   We're sorry we can't do it.
  Se non ti rincresce vorrei pensarci su.   If you don't mind I'd like to think it over.

- **restare** to be left
  Mi restano cinquanta euro.   I've got fifty euros left.
  A Maria restano solo ricordi.   Maria only has memories left.

KEY POINTS

✔ Turn the sentence around when using verbs like **piacere**.
✔ Use the preposition **a**, or an indirect object pronoun.

Test yourself

142 Translate the following into Italian, where appropriate using *tu* for 'you'.

a Does your sister like Paris?

....

b I like these shoes.

....

c They don't like dogs.

....

d We like swimming.

....

e You'd like that film.

....

f Did she like the book?

....

g I've got two apples left.

....

h I miss them.

....

i Not everyone likes that music.

....

j Do you think the boys would be interested?

....

143 Complete the following sentences with the correct form of the present tense.

a Ti .... qualcosa? (**mancare**)

b Non mi .... molti soldi. (**restare**)

c Gli .... sciare. (**piacere**)

d Ci .... i gatti. (**piacere**)

e Il mare .... a Giulia. (**piacere**)

f Non gli .... il prezzo. (**importare**)

g Mi .... i film francesi. (**interessare**)

h I suoi figli gli .... molto. (**mancare**)

i Il giardinaggio .... a tuo fratello? (**piacere**)

j Ti .... i dolci? (**piacere**)

Negatives

<u>non</u>

➤ The Italian word **non** (meaning *not*) is the one you need to make a statement or a question negative:

Non posso venire.	I can't come.
Non hai la chiave?	Haven't you got the key?
Giuliana <u>non</u> abita qui.	Giuliana doesn't live here.

➤ In English *not* or *n't* comes <u>after</u> verbs. In Italian **non** comes <u>in front of</u> verbs.

Non è qui.	It's not here.
Non è venuta.	She didn't come.
I miei <u>non</u> hanno la macchina.	My parents haven't got a car.
Lei <u>non</u> è molto alta.	She's not very tall.

➤ In English we sometimes make sentences negative by adding *don't*, *doesn't* or *didn't* before the main verb, but in Italian you always just add **non** to the verb.

Positive		**Negative**	
Lavorano.	They work.	**Non lavorano.**	They don't work.
Lo vuole.	He wants it.	**Non lo vuole.**	He doesn't want it.

> *Tip*
> NEVER use the verb **fare** to translate *don't*, *doesn't* or *didn't* in negatives.

➤ If there are words such as **mi**, **ti**, **lo**, **la**, **ci**, **vi**, **li** or **le** in front of the verb, **non** goes immediately <u>in front of</u> them.

Non l'ho visto.	I didn't see it.
Non mi piace il calcio.	I don't like football.

➤ If you have a phrase consisting of *not* with another word or phrase, such as *not now*, or *not yet*, use **non** before the other word.

<u>non</u> adesso	not now
<u>non</u> ancora	not yet
<u>non</u> sempre	not always
<u>non</u> dopo sabato	not after Saturday

➤ BUT, if you want to be more emphatic, or to make a contrast, use **no** instead of **non**, and put it <u>after</u> the other word.

Sempre <u>no</u>, ma qualche volta.	Not ALWAYS, but sometimes.

For further explanation of grammatical terms, please see pages viii-xii.

➤ You use **no** instead of **non** in certain phrases:

- In the phrase **o no** (meaning *or not*)

Vieni <u>o no</u>?	Are you coming or not?
che gli piaccia <u>o no</u>	whether he likes it or not

- In the phrase **di no** after some verbs

Credo <u>di no</u>.	I don't think so.
Spero <u>di no</u>.	I hope not.
Ha detto <u>di no</u>.	He said not.

Other negative phrases

➤ In English you only use one negative word in a sentence: *I haven't ever seen him*. In Italian you use **non** followed by another negative word such as **niente** (meaning *nothing*), or **mai** (meaning *never*).

<u>Non</u> succede <u>mai</u>.	It never happens.
<u>Non</u> ha detto niente.	She didn't say anything.

➤ The following are the most common phrases of this kind.

- **non ... mai**

<u>Non</u> la vedo <u>mai</u>.	never *or* not ever
	I never see her.

> ### Tip
> You put **mai** between the two parts of the perfect tense.
>
> | | |
> |---|---|
> | **Non <u>l'ho mai vista</u>.** | I've never seen her. |
> | **Non ci <u>siamo mai stati</u>.** | We've never been there. |

- **non ... niente**

<u>Non</u> hanno fatto <u>niente</u>.	nothing *or* not ...anything
	They didn't do anything.

- **non ... nessuno**

<u>Non</u> ho visto <u>nessuno</u>.	nobody *or* not ... anybody
	I didn't see anybody.

- **non ... da nessuna parte**

<u>Non</u> riuscivo a trovarlo <u>da nessuna parte</u>.	nowhere *or* not ... anywhere
	I couldn't find it anywhere.

- **non ... nessuno/nessuna** + *noun*

<u>Non</u> c'è <u>nessun</u> bisogno di andare.	no *or* not ... any
	There's no need to go. *or*
	There isn't any need to go.

- **non ... più**

<u>Non</u> escono <u>più</u> insieme.	no longer *or* not ... any more
	They're not going out together any more.

- **non ...né ... né ...**

<u>Non</u> verranno <u>né</u> Chiara né Donatella.	neither ... nor Neither
	Chiara nor Donatella are coming.

➤ If you <u>begin</u> a sentence with a negative word such as **nessuno** or **niente**, do not use **non** with the verb that comes after it.

Nessuno è venuto.	Nobody came.
Niente è cambiato.	Nothing has changed.
BUT	
Non è venuto nessuno.	
Non è cambiato niente.	

➤ In Italian you can have more than one negative word following a negative verb.

<u>Non</u> fanno <u>mai niente</u>.	They never do anything.
<u>Non</u> si confida <u>mai</u> con <u>nessuno</u>.	He never confides in anyone.

➤ As in English, negative words can be used on their own to answer a question.

Cos'hai comprato? – <u>Niente</u>.	What did you buy? – Nothing.
Chi ti accompagna? – <u>Nessuno</u>.	Who's going with you? – Nobody.

KEY POINTS

✔ To make a verb negative put **non** in front of it.

✔ Unlike English, in Italian it is good grammar to follow **non** with another negative word.

Test yourself

144 **Create a negative sentence in the present tense using the elements below. Remember to add the article for the noun where appropriate.**

   a non/conoscere/strada/Maria ....

   b essere/qui/non/Lucia ....

   c mai/non/venire/Mario. ....

   d incontrarsi/ragazzi/più/non ....

   e Chiara/vedere/mi/non ....

   f piacere/non/ci/tennis ....

   g non/qui/abitare/Teresa ....

   h nessuno/venire/non ....

   i andare/né/Francesca/non/sorella/né/sua

    ....

   j nessuna/trovare/lo/non/parte/Paolo/da

    ....

145 **Translate the following into Italian, where appropriate using *tu* for 'you'.**

   a She never does anything on a Sunday. ....

   b We didn't see anybody. ....

   c The don't want anything. ....

   d My parents have never been there.

    ....

   e We don't see each other any more in the evenings.

    ....

   f They couldn't find him anywhere. ....

   g Is he coming or not? ....

   h You didn't eat anything. ....

   i Who did you see at the party? — Nobody. ....

   j I said no. ....

Test yourself

146 Change the following sentences into the negative.

a Le chiavi sono qui.

....

b Pietro l'ha mangiato.

....

c Lavorano il sabato sera.

....

d Luca viene? — Credo di sì.

....

e Mi piace il caldo.

....

f Claudio è molto alto.

....

g Hai i biglietti?

....

h Hanno detto di sì.

....

i I bambini guardavano la televisione.

....

j Ci siete mai stati?

....

Questions

> **What is a question?**
> A **question** is a sentence which is used to ask someone about something and which often has the verb in front of the subject.

Different types of questions

➤ Some questions can be answered by <u>yes</u> or <u>no</u>. They are sometimes called <u>yes/no questions</u>. When you ask this type of question your voice goes up at the end of the sentence.

Is it raining?
Do you like olives?
You're leaving tomorrow?

➤ Other questions begin with <u>question words</u> such as *why*, *where* and *when* and have to be answered with specific information.

Why are you late?
Where have you been?
When did they leave?

How to ask yes/no questions in Italian

➤ If you are expecting the answer *yes* or *no*, make your voice go up at the end of the question.

> *Tip*
> In Italian you can turn an adjective or a verb into a question simply by making your voice go up on the last syllable.
>
> | | |
> |---|---|
> | **Basta?** | Is that enough? |
> | **Piove?** | Is it raining? |
> | **Chiaro?** | Is that clear? |
> | **Buono?** | Is it nice? |

➤ If you are asking about a person, place or thing using a noun, put the noun at the <u>end</u> of the question.

È partita <u>tua sorella</u>?	Has your sister gone?
È bella <u>la Calabria</u>?	Is Calabria beautiful?
Sono <u>buoni gli spaghetti</u>?	Is the spaghetti nice?

➤ If the English question has a pronoun such as *you*, *they* or *he* in it, you:

- keep to normal word order

- don't translate the pronoun into Italian unless you want to stress it

Parlano italiano?	Do they speak Italian?
Ha francobolli?	Have you got stamps?
È caro?	Is it expensive?
C'è tempo?	Is there time?

Fa l'avvocato?	Is he a lawyer?
Va bene?	Is that okay?

➤ If you do want to stress *you*, *he*, *they* and so on, use a pronoun in Italian, and put it at the end of the sentence.

Parla italiano <u>lei</u>?	Do <u>you</u> speak Italian?
Viene anche <u>lui</u>?	Is <u>he</u> coming too?
L'hanno fatto <u>loro</u>?	Did <u>they</u> do it?

➪ *For more information on* **Pronouns**, *see page* 53.

How to answer yes/no questions

➤ In English you can answer questions simply by saying *yes* or *no*. If this doesn't seem quite enough you add a short phrase, using the verb that starts the question.

<u>Do</u> you speak Italian?	Yes, I <u>do</u>.
<u>Can</u> he swim?	Yes, he <u>can</u>.
<u>Have</u> you been to Rome?	No, I <u>haven</u>'t.
<u>Are</u> they leaving now?	No, they'<u>re</u> not.

➤ In Italian you can very often answer just with **sì** or **no**.

Stai bene? – <u>Sì</u>.	Are you okay? – Yes.
Ti piace? – <u>No</u>.	Do you like it? – No.

➤ If you don't want to answer this sort of question with a definite *yes* or *no* you can use phrases such as:

Penso di sì.	I think so.
Spero di sì.	I hope so.
Credo di no.	I don't think so.
Spero di no.	I hope not.

➤ If you want to answer more fully you have to repeat the verb that's in the Italian question.

<u>Sai</u> nuotare? – Sì, <u>so</u> nuotare.	Can you swim? – Yes, I can (swim).
<u>Piove</u>? – Sì, <u>piove</u>.	Is it raining? – Yes, it's raining OR Yes, it is.
<u>Capisci</u>? – No, non <u>capisco</u>.	Do you understand? – No, I don't (understand).

ℹ️ Note that there is no Italian equivalent for answers using short phrases such as *Yes, I do; No, I don't; No, they haven't*.

KEY POINTS

✔ Make your voice go up at the end of questions.
✔ Put nouns and stressed pronouns at the end of the question.
✔ If you want to answer more fully, repeat the verb that is used in the question.

Test yourself

147 **Make these statements into questions by adding question marks and changing the word order where necessary. The first one has been done for you.**

a Tuo fratello viene. *Viene tuo fratello?*

b Quelle scarpe sono care. ....

c Tuo fratello è dottore. ....

d I ragazzi sono stati bravi. ....

e Va bene. ....

f Ti piace la macchina. ....

g Tuo nipote voleva andare al cinema. ....

h Hanno soldi. ....

i I fiori sono belli. ....

j C'è tempo per mangiare. ....

148 **Translate the following into Italian, where appropriate using *tu* for 'you'.**

a Was it raining?

....

b Is she coming? — I hope not.

....

c Did he like the film? — I don't think so.

....

d Do they understand? — Yes.

....

e Is your mother better? — Yes, she is.

....

f Can you play the guitar? — No, I can't.

....

g Will she buy that car? — I hope so.

....

h Have you ever been to Madrid? — No, I haven't.

....

i Is she a dentist?

....

j Has your brother arrived?

Question words

How to ask questions using question words

➤ The following are common question words which never change their form:

- **dove?** where?
  Dove abiti?   <u>Where</u> do you live?

- **come?** how?
  Come si fa?   <u>How</u> do you do it?

ⓘ Note that **come** can be translated by *what?* when it is used to mean *pardon?*

  Scusi, <u>come</u> ha detto?   Sorry, <u>what</u> did you say?

- **quando?** when
  Quando parti?   <u>When</u> are you leaving?

- **perché?** why
  Perché non vieni?   <u>Why</u> don't you come?

ⓘ Note that **perché** also means *because*.

  Lo mangio <u>perché</u> ho fame.   I'm eating it because I'm hungry.

- **chi?** who?
  Chi è?   <u>Who</u> is it?
  Chi sono?   <u>Who</u> are they?

- **che?** what?
  Che giorno è oggi?   <u>What</u> day is it today?

- **cosa?** what?
  Cosa vuoi?   <u>What</u> do you want?

- **che cosa?** what?
  Che cosa fanno?   <u>What</u> are they doing?

⇨ *For more information on* **Conjunctions**, *see page 244.*

Tip
Remember to shorten **che cosa** (meaning *what*) and **come** (meaning *how*, *what*) to **che cos'** and **com'** when they are followed by a vowel.
Che <u>cos'è</u>?   What is it?
<u>Com'è</u> successo?   How did it happen?

For further explanation of grammatical terms, please see pages viii-xii.

➤ Some question words do sometimes change their form.

➤ You can use **quale** to ask for precise information about people or things. It has a plural form **quali**, and a singular form **qual** which is used in front of a vowel:

- Use **quale** with a singular noun when you want to ask *which* or *what*.
  Per quale motivo?   For what reason?
  Quale stanza preferisci?   Which room do you prefer?

- Use the singular form **qual** when the next word starts with a vowel.
  Qual è il tuo colore preferito?   What's your favourite colour?
  Qual è la tua camera?   Which is your room?

- Use **quali** with plural nouns.
  Quali programmi hai?   What plans have you got?
  Quali sono i tuoi sport preferiti?   Which are your favourite sports?

- Use **quale** by itself when you want to ask *which one*.
  Quale vuoi?   Which one would you like?

- Use **quali** by itself when you want to ask *which ones*.
  Quali sono i migliori?   Which ones are the best?

➤ You can use **quanto** or the feminine form **quanta** to ask *how much*:

- Use **quanto** by itself to ask *how much?*
  Quanto costa?   How much does it cost?
  Quanta ne vuoi?   How much do you want?

- Use **quanto** as an adjective with masculine nouns and **quanta** with feminine nouns.
  Quanto tempo hai?   How much time have you got?
  Quanta stoffa ti serve?   How much material do you need?

➤ Use **quanti** to ask *how many*. Use **quanti** as an adjective with masculine nouns and **quante** with feminine nouns.
  Quanti ne vuoi?   How many do you want?
  Quanti giorni?   How many days?
  Quante notti?   How many nights?

⇨ For more information on **Adjectives**, see page 24.

ⓘ Note that some very common questions do not start with the Italian question word you might expect.

  Quanti anni hai?   How old are you?
  Come si chiama?   What's he called?
  Com'è?   What's it like?

How to answer questions which use question words

➤ If someone asks you a question such as **Chi è?** or **Quanto costa?**, you answer using the same verb.

Chi è? – È Giulia.	Who's that? – That's Giulia.
Quanto costa? – Costa molto.	How much does it cost? – It costs a lot.

➤ When you don't know the answer you say **Non lo so**, or **Non so** followed by the original question.

Chi è? – Non lo so.	Who's that? – I don't know.
Non so chi è.	I don't know who it is.
Quanto costa? – Non lo so.	How much does it cost? – I don't know.
Non so quanto costa.	I don't know how much it costs.

Grammar Extra!

The question word *what* can be either a <u>pronoun</u> or an <u>adjective</u>. In the sentence *What do you want?* it's a <u>pronoun</u> and you can use **che**, **cosa**, or **che cosa** to translate it.

When *what* is an <u>adjective</u>, and is used with a noun, for example, *What day is it today?* you translate it by **che**, and <u>NOT</u> by **cosa**, or **che cosa**.

Che giorno è?   What day is it?

[*i*] Note that when *what?* means *pardon?* it is translated by **come**?

⇨ *For more information on **Adjectives** and **Pronouns**, see pages 24 and 53.*

Where does the question word come in the sentence?

➤ In English, question words like *who*, *what*, *where* and *when* nearly always come at the beginning of the sentence.

<u>Who</u> are you?
<u>Who</u> does it belong to?
<u>Where</u> do you come from?
<u>What</u> do you think?

➤ Italian question words often come first in the sentence, but this is by no means always the case. Here are some exceptions:

● If you want to emphasize the person or thing you are asking about, you can put a noun or pronoun first.

Tu chi sei?	Who are <u>you</u>?
Lei cosa dice?	What do <u>you</u> think?
La mia borsa dov'è?	Where's <u>my bag</u>?

● If there is a preposition such as *with*, *for*, *from* or *to* at the end of the English question, you <u>MUST</u> put the Italian preposition at the start of the question.

<u>**Di**</u> **dove sei?**	Where do you come <u>from</u>?
Con chi parlavi?	Who were you talking <u>to</u>?
<u>**A**</u> **che cosa serve?**	What's it <u>for</u>?

7 Note that when you ask someone what time they do something, the question starts with **a che ora**.

<u>A che ora</u> ti alzi? What time do you get up?

⇨ *For more information on **Prepositions**, see page 238.*

- When you are asking about the colour, make, or type of something you must start the question with **di**.
  <u>Di</u> che colore è? What colour is it?
  <u>Di</u> che marca è? What make is it?

- When you are asking who owns something start the question in Italian with **di**.

  <u>Di</u> chi è questa borsa? Whose bag is this?
  <u>Di</u> chi sono quelle scarpe rosse? Who do those red shoes belong to?

KEY POINTS
✔ Most question words don't change their form.
✔ Question words do not always come first in Italian questions.
✔ If there is a preposition in the Italian question you MUST put it first.

Test yourself

149 Complete the following sentences by adding a question word.

a .... non mangi?

b .... andate?

c .... costa?

d .... partono?

e .... fai?

f .... è quel ragazzo?

g .... si chiama?

h .... anni ha tuo figlio?

i .... sciarpa preferisci?

j .... giorno è oggi?

150 Fill the gap with the correct form of *quale* or *quanto*. The first one has been done for you.

a ...*Quali*... sono i migliori?

b .... è la sua macchina?

c .... cani ci sono?

d .... costano le fragole?

e .... sono i tuoi film preferiti?

f .... programmi ti servono?

g .... stoffa vuoi?

h Per .... motivo?

i .... anni hai?

j .... tempo abbiamo?

Test yourself

151 **Translate the following into Italian, where appropriate using *tu* for 'you'.**

a Who's she? — I don't know.

....

b Where are you from?

....

c Whose hat is this?

....

d What time do you get up in the morning?

....

e Who was she talking to?

....

f What make is the car?

....

g She hasn't gone, has she?

....

h What's this cup for?

....

i Who do these gloves belong to?

....

j How much do they cost? — They cost a lot.

....

Questions which end with question phrases

➤ In English you add a question phrase (like <u>aren't you</u>?, <u>isn't it</u>?, <u>didn't I</u> and so on) to the end of a sentence to check that an idea you have is true. You expect the person you're speaking to will agree by saying *yes* (or *no*, if your idea is negative).

> This is the house, isn't it?
> You won't tell anyone, will you?

➤ In Italian, when you expect someone to say *yes* to your idea, you put either **no**, or **vero** at the end of the sentence and make your voice go up as you say the word.

Mi scriverai, <u>no</u>?	You'll write to me, won't you?
Vieni anche tu, <u>no</u>?	You're coming too, aren't you?
Hai finito, <u>no</u>?	You've finished, haven't you?
Questa è la tua macchina, <u>vero</u>?	This is your car, isn't it?
Ti piace la cioccolata, <u>vero</u>?	You like chocolate, don't you?

➤ When you expect someone to agree with you by saying *no*, use **vero** only.

Non sono partiti, <u>vero</u>?	They haven't gone, have they?
Non fa molto male, <u>vero</u>?	It doesn't hurt much, does it?

Grammar Extra!

Questions such as *Where are you going?* and *Why did he do that?* are <u>direct questions</u>.

Sometimes this type of question is phrased in a more roundabout way, for example:
Tell me where you are going.
Would you mind telling me where you are going?
Can you tell me why he did that?
I'd like to know why he did that.
I wonder why he did that.

This type of question is called an <u>indirect question</u>. It is very simple to ask indirect questions in Italian: you simply add a phrase to the beginning of the direct question, for example, you could add **Può dirmi** (meaning *Can you tell me*) to the question **Dove va?** (meaning *where are you going?*).

Può dirmi dove va?	Can you tell me where you're going?

The following are other phrases that introduce an indirect question:

Dimmi...	Tell me...
Vorrei sapere...	I'd like to know...
Mi domando...	I wonder...
Non capisco...	I don't understand...

<u>**Dimmi**</u> **perché l'hai fatto.**	Tell me why you did it.
<u>**Vorrei sapere**</u> **quanto costa.**	I'd like to know how much it costs.
<u>**Mi domando**</u> **cosa pensano.**	I wonder what they think.
<u>**Non capisco**</u> **che vuol dire.**	I don't understand what it means.

Adverbs

What is an adverb?

An **adverb** is a word used with verbs to give information on where, when or how an action takes place, for example, *here*, *today*, *quickly*. An adverb can also add information to adjectives and other adverbs, for example, *extremely quick*, *very quickly*.

How adverbs are used

➤ You use adverbs:

- with verbs: *He's never there*; *She smiled happily*.

- with adjectives: *She's rather ill*; *I feel a lot happier*.

- with other adverbs: *He drives really slowly*; *I'm very well*.

➤ Adverbs are also used at the start of a sentence to give an idea of what the speaker is thinking or feeling.
> Luckily, nobody was hurt.
> Surprisingly, he made no objection.

How to form adverbs

The basics

➤ In English you can make an adverb from the adjective *slow* by adding *–ly*. You can do a similar kind of thing in Italian.

➤ Here are some guidelines:

- if the adjective ends in **–o** in the masculine, take the feminine form, ending in **–a**, and add **–mente**

Masculine adjective	Feminine adjective	Adverb	Meaning
lento	lenta	lentamente	slowly
fortunato	fortunata	fortunatamente	luckily

Cammina molto lentamente.	He walks very slowly.
Fortunatamente non ha piovuto.	Luckily, it didn't rain.

- if the adjective ends in **–e** for both masculine and feminine, just add **–mente**

Adjective	Adverb	Meaning
veloce	velocemente	quickly, fast
corrente	correntemente	fluently

Parla corrent<u>emente</u> l'italiano.   She speaks Italian fluently.

- if the adjective ends in **–le**, or **–re**, you drop the final **e** before adding **–mente**

Adjective	Adverb	Meaning
facile	facilmente	easily
particolare	particolarmente	particularly

Puoi farlo <u>facilmente</u>.   You can easily do it.
Non è <u>particolarmente</u> buono.   It's not particularly nice.

> *Tip*
> Don't try to make adverbs agree with anything – they always keep the
> same form.

Irregular adverbs

➤ In Italian there are two kinds of adverbs which do not behave in the way just described. They are:

- adverbs which are completely different from the adjective

- adverbs which are exactly the same as the masculine adjective

➤ The adverb related to **buono** (meaning *good*) is **bene** (meaning *well*). The adverb related to **cattivo** (meaning *bad*) is **male** (meaning *badly*).
     Parlano <u>bene</u> l'italiano.   They speak Italian well.
     Ho giocato <u>male</u>.   I played badly.

➤ Words such as *fast* and *hard* can be both adjectives and adverbs:
     a <u>fast</u> car
     You're driving too <u>fast</u>.
     a <u>hard</u> question
     He works very <u>hard</u>.

➤ The same kind of thing happens in Italian: some adverbs are the same as the masculine adjective. The following are the most common ones:

- **chiaro** (adjective: *clear*; adverb: *clearly*)
     Il significato è <u>chiaro</u>.   The meaning is clear.
     Giulia parla <u>chiaro</u>.   Giulia speaks clearly.

- **giusto** (adjective: *right, correct*; adverb: *correctly, right*)
  il momento <u>giusto</u>.   the right moment.
  Marco ha risposto <u>giusto</u>.   Marco answered correctly.

- **vicino** (adjective: *near, close*; adverb: *nearby, near here*)
  È molto <u>vicino</u>.   He's very close.
  I miei amici *a*bitano <u>vicino</u>.   My friends live nearby.
  C'è una piscina <u>vicino</u>?   Is there a swimming pool near here?

- **diritto** (adjective: *straight*; adverb: *straight on*)
  Il bordo non è <u>diritto</u>.   The edge is not straight.
  Siamo andati sempre <u>diritto</u>.   We kept straight on.

- **certo** (adjective: *sure, certain*; adverb: *of course*)
  Non ne sono certo.   I'm not sure.
  Vieni stasera? – <u>Certo</u>!   Are you coming this evening? – Of course!

- **solo** (adjective: *alone, lonely*; adverb: *only*)
  Si sente solo.   He feels lonely.
  L'ho incontrata <u>solo</u> due volte.   I've only met her twice.

- **forte** (adjective: *strong, hard*; adverb: *fast, hard*)
  È più forte di me.   He's stronger than me.
  Correva <u>forte</u>.   He was running fast.

- **molto** (adjective: *a lot of*; adverb: *a lot, very, very much*)
  Non hanno molto denaro.   They haven't got a lot of money.
  Quel quadro mi piace <u>molto</u>.   I like that picture a lot.

- **poco** (adjective: *little, not very much*; adverb *not very much, not very*)
  Hai mangiato poco riso.   You haven't eaten very much rice.
  Viene in ufficio <u>poco</u> spesso.   She doesn't come to the office very often.

i Note that although these adverbs look like adjectives, they NEVER change their form.

KEY POINTS
✔ You generally make adverbs by adding **–mente** to adjectives.
✔ Adverbs never agree with anything.
✔ Some adverbs have the same form as the masculine adjective.

Test yourself

152 **Replace the English highlighted adverb with the Italian equivalent.**

   a Guida molto **slowly**. ....

   b **Luckily** non si è fatta male. ....

   c Abbiamo mangiato **quickly**. ....

   d Nono sono **particularly** amichevole. ....

   e Possono andarci **easily**. ....

   f Mi piacciono **a lot** quelle scarpe. ....

   g La piscina è **nearby**. ....

   h Devi andare sempre **straight on**. ....

   i Camminava **fast**. ....

   j Va al mare **not very** spesso. ....

153 **Translate the following into Italian, where appropriate using *tu* for 'you'.**

   a She speaks German well.

   ....

   b He's not particularly good.

   ....

   c Do you want to come to the cinema? — Of course!

   ....

   d I only saw it once.

   ....

   e Is there a bank nearby?

   ....

   f The student replied correctly.

   ....

   g She was speaking English fluently.

   ....

   h I had to drive quickly.

   ....

   i He could easily do the exercise.

   ....

   j The teacher speaks clearly.

   ....

Test yourself

154 Give the adverb that relates to each of the following adjectives.

a corretto ....

b semplice ....

c buono ....

d poco ....

e veloce ....

f cattivo ....

g ovvio ....

h regolare ....

i felice ....

j molto ....

Making comparisons using adverbs

➤ In English, there are two major ways of comparing things using an adverb.

- To express the idea of 'more' or 'less' you either put **–er** on the end of the adverb, or *more* or *less* in front of it: *earlier, sooner, more/less* often. This way of comparing things is called the comparative.

- To express the idea of 'the most' or 'the least' you either put **–est** on the end, or *most* or *least* in front of it: *earliest, soonest, most/least* often. This way of comparing things is called the superlative.

Comparatives and superlatives of adverbs

➤ In Italian you make comparisons expressing the idea of 'more' or 'less' by putting **più** (meaning *more*) and **meno** (meaning *less*) in front of the adverb.

più spesso	more often
più lentamente	more slowly
meno velocemente	less quickly

➤ You use **di** to say *than*.

Correva più forte di me.	He was running faster than me.
Viene meno spesso di lui.	She comes less often than he does.
Luca parla più correttamente l'inglese di me.	Luca speaks English more correctly than I do.
Ha agito più prudentemente di me.	She's acted more sensibly than I have.
Loro lavorano più sodo di prima.	They work harder than before.

➤ In Italian you can make comparisons expressing the idea of 'the most' or 'the least' by putting **più** (meaning *more*) or **meno** (meaning *less*) in front of the adverb and by putting **di tutti** (meaning *of all*) after it.

Cammina più piano di tutti.	She walks the slowest (of all).
L'ha fatto meno volentieri di tutti.	He did it the least willingly.
Mia madre ci veniva più spesso di tutti.	My mother came most often.

➡ *For more information on* **Adjectives** *see page* 24.

Irregular comparatives and superlatives of adverbs

➤ Some very common Italian adverbs have irregular comparatives and superlatives. Here are the commonest ones.

Adverb	Meaning	Comparative	Meaning	Superlative	Meaning
bene	well	**meglio**	better	**meglio di tutti**	best (of all)
male	badly	**peggio**	worse	**peggio di tutti**	worst (of all)
molto	a lot	**più**	more	**più di tutti**	most (of all)
poco	not much	**meno**	less	**meno di tutti**	least (of all)

Loro hanno giocato <u>meglio</u> di noi.	They played better than us.
Si sono comportati <u>peggio</u> del solito.	They behaved worse than usual.
Ho speso <u>più</u> di dieci sterline.	I spent more than ten pounds.
Andrea ha giocato <u>meglio di tutti</u>.	Andrea played best of all.

più di..., meno di...; di più, di meno

➤ These are very common phrases, meaning *more* and *less*, which are used in rather different ways.

- You use **più di** and **meno di** to say *more than* and *less than* when comparing things where you would use *than* in English.

Paolo le piace <u>più di</u> Marco.	She likes Paolo more than Marco.
Leggo <u>meno di</u> te.	I read less than you.
Non guadagna <u>più di</u> me.	He doesn't earn more than I do.
Pesa <u>meno di</u> Luca.	He weighs less than Luca.

- If there is no *than* in the sentence in English use **di più** and **di meno**.

Costa <u>di più</u>.	It costs more.
Quello mi piace <u>di meno</u>.	I like that one less.
Ho speso <u>di meno</u>.	I spent less.

- **di più** and **di meno** are also used to mean *most* and *least*.

la cosa che temeva <u>di più</u>	the thing she feared most
quello che mi piace <u>di meno</u>	the one I like least
Sono quelli che guadagnano <u>di meno</u>.	They're the ones who earn least.

Grammar Extra!

To say that something is getting *better and better*, *worse and worse*, *slower and slower*, and so on, use **sempre** with the comparative adverb.

Le cose vanno sempre meglio.	Things are going better and better.
Mio nonno sta sempre peggio.	My grandfather's getting worse and worse.
Cammina sempre più lento.	He's walking slower and slower.

KEY POINTS

✔ To express the idea of 'more' and 'most' with adverbs use **più**.
✔ To express the idea of 'less' and 'least' use **meno**.
✔ Use **di** to mean 'than'.

Test yourself

155 **Create a sentence using the elements below. The first one has been done for you.**

a Luca/camminavo/forte/+ ... *Camminavo più forte di Luca.* ....

b guidare/velocemente/dovresti/- ....

c parlare/potresti/lentamente/+? ....

d squadra/noi/l'altra/è/forte/+ ....

e il/francese/Pietro/correntemente/parla/me/+

....

f spesso/tutti/viene/- ....

g ha risposto/Giulia/volentieri/tutti/+ ....

h te/piano/lavoravo/+ ....

i correttamente/ho risposto/Giovanni/+

....

j velocemente/correvano/noi/- ....

156 **Translate the following into Italian, where appropriate using *tu* for 'you'.**

a They earn more than us. ....

b We like that one more. ....

c She goes to the cinema less often than me. ....

d Last week we spent less. ....

e Last month they went out more. ....

f I weigh more than him. ....

g My brother is getting better and better. ....

h She likes Mario more than Chiara. ....

i Things are getting worse and worse. ....

j These apples cost more. ....

157 **Match the adverb with its superlative form.**

a **poco**	peggio di tutti
b **bene**	meno di tutti
c **piano**	più di tutti più
d **molto**	più piano di tutti
e **male**	meglio di tutti

Some common adverbs

Adverbs to use in everyday conversation

➤ Just as in English, you can often answer a question simply by using an adverb.

Vieni alla festa? – <u>Forse</u>.	Are you coming to the party? – Maybe.
Deve proprio partire? –	Do you really have to go? –
Sì, <u>purtroppo</u>.	Yes, unfortunately.

➤ The following are particularly useful adverbs:

- **ecco** here
  <u>Ecco</u> l'autobus!   Here's the bus!
  <u>Ecco</u> la sua birra!   Here's your beer!

  ⓘ Note that you can say **ecco** (meaning *here you are*) when you hand somebody
  something. **Ecco** combines with the pronouns **lo**, **la**, **li** and **le** to mean *Here she is*,
  Here they are and so forth:

Dov'è Carla? – <u>Eccola</u>!	Where's Carla? – Here she is!
Non vedo i libri – Ah, <u>*eccoli*</u>!	I can't see the books – Oh, here they are!
<u>Eccolo</u>!	Here he is!

- **anche** too
  È venuta <u>anche</u> mia sorella.   My sister came too.

- **certo** certainly; of course
  <u>Certo</u> che puoi.   Of course you can.
  <u>Certo</u> che sì.   Certainly.

- **così** so, like this, like that
  È <u>così</u> simp*a*tica!   She's so nice!
  Si apre <u>così</u>.   It opens like this.
  Non si fa <u>così</u>.   You don't do it like that.

- **davvero** really
  È successo <u>davvero</u>.   It really happened.

- **forse** perhaps, maybe
  <u>Forse</u> hanno ragione.   Maybe they're right.

- **proprio** really
  Sono <u>proprio</u> stanca.   I'm really tired.

- **purtroppo** unfortunately
  <u>Purtroppo</u> non posso venire.   Unfortunately I can't come.

> *Tip*
> These adverbs are such common words that it's a good idea to learn as
> many as possible.

Adverbs that tell you HOW MUCH

➤ **molto**, **poco**, **troppo** and **tanto** are used with adjectives, verbs and other adverbs;

- Use **molto** to mean *very* or *very much*.
Sono <u>molto</u> stanca.	I'm very tired.
Ti piace? – Sì, <u>molto</u>.	Do you like it? – Yes, very much.
Ora mi sento <u>molto</u> meglio.	I feel much better now.

- Use **poco** to mean *not very* or *not very much*.
Questa mela è <u>poco</u> buona.	This apple isn't very nice.
Mi piacciono <u>poco</u>.	I don't like them very much.
Ci vado <u>poco</u> spesso.	I don't go there very often.

- Use **tanto** to mean *so* or *so much*.
Questo libro è <u>tanto</u> noioso.	This book is so boring.
Tu mi manchi <u>tanto</u>.	I miss you so much.
Mi sento <u>tanto</u> meglio.	I feel so much better.

- Use **troppo** to mean *too* or *too much*.
È <u>troppo</u> caro.	It's too expensive.
Parlano <u>troppo</u>.	They talk too much.
Le sei? È <u>troppo</u> presto.	Six o'clock? That's too early.

☑ Note that **molto**, **poco**, **troppo** and **tanto** can also be used as adjectives. When you use them as adverbs they do NOT agree with anything.

Adverbs that tell you TO WHAT EXTENT

- **abbastanza** quite, enough
È <u>abbastanza</u> alta.	She's quite tall.
Non studia <u>abbastanza</u>.	He doesn't study enough.

- **appena** just, only just
L'ho <u>appena</u> fatto.	I've just done it.
L'indirizzo ere <u>appena</u> leggibile.	The address was only just legible.

- **piuttosto** quite, rather
Fa <u>piuttosto</u> caldo oggi.	It's quite warm today.
È <u>piuttosto</u> lontano.	It's rather a long way.

- **quasi** nearly
Sono <u>quasi</u> pronta.	I'm nearly ready.
Hanno <u>quasi</u> finito.	They've nearly finished.

For further explanation of grammatical terms, please see pages viii-xii.

Adverbs that tell you WHEN

- **adesso** now
  Non posso farlo <u>adesso</u>.   I can't do it now.

- **ancora** still, yet
  Sei <u>ancora</u> a letto?   Are you still in bed?
  Silvia non è <u>ancora</u> arrivata.   Silvia's not here yet.

- **domani** tomorrow
  Ci vediamo <u>domani</u>.   See you tomorrow.

- **dopo** after, later
  Ci vediamo <u>dopo</u>.   See you later.

- **già** already
  Te l'ho <u>già</u> detto.   I've already told you.

- **ieri** yesterday
  <u>Ieri</u> ha piovuto molto.   It rained a lot yesterday.

- **mai** never, ever
  Non sono <u>mai</u> stato in America.   I've never been to America.
  Sei <u>mai</u> stato in America?   Have you ever been to America?

- **oggi** today
  <u>Oggi</u> andiamo al mare.   We're going to the seaside today.

- **ora** now
  <u>Ora</u> cosa facciamo?   What are we going to do now?

- **poi** then
  E <u>poi</u> che cos'è successo?   And then what happened?

- **presto** soon, early
  Arriverà <u>presto</u>.   He'll be here soon.
  Mi alzo sempre <u>presto</u>.   I always get up early.

- **prima** before
  <u>Prima</u> non lo sapevo.   I didn't know that before.

- **spesso** often
  Vanno <u>spesso</u> in centro.   They often go into town.

- **subito** at once
  Fallo <u>subito</u>!   Do it at once.

- **tardi** late
  Oggi mi sono alzata <u>tardi</u>.   I got up late today.

Adverbs that tell you WHERE

- **là** there
  Vieni via di là.

  Come away from there.

- **laggiù** down there, over there
  È laggiù da qualche parte.
  È apparso laggiù in lontananza.

  It's down there somewhere.
  It appeared over there in the distance.

- **lassù** up there
  un paesino lassù in montagna

  a little village up there in the mountains

- **lì** there
  Mettilo lì.

  Put it there.

- **qua** here
  Eccomi qua!

  I'm here!

- **qui** here
  Vieni qui.

  Come here.

ⓘ Note that **lì** has an accent to distinguish it from the pronoun **li** (meaning *them*) and **là** has an accent to distinguish it from **la** (meaning *the, her* or *it*).

⇨ *For more information on* **Articles** *and* **Pronouns**, *see pages 14 and 53.*

- **ci** there
  Ci sei mai stato?

  Have you ever been there?

- **dappertutto** everywhere
  Ho cercato dappertutto.

  I looked everywhere.

- **lontano** a long way away
  Abita lontano.

  He lives a long way away.

- **sotto** underneath, downstairs
  Porta una giacca con una
  maglietta sotto.
  Il bagno è sotto.

  He's wearing a jacket with a t-shirt
  underneath.
  The bathroom is downstairs.

- **sopra** up, on top
  qui sopra
  Il dizionario è sopra quella pila
  di libri.

  up here
  The dictionary is on top of that pile of books.

- **fuori** outside
  Ti aspetto fuori.

  I'll wait for you outside.

- **dentro** inside
  Vai dentro.

  Go inside.

- **indietro** back
  Torniamo indietro.　　　　　　　　Let's turn back.

- **davanti** at the front
  Voglio sedermi davanti.　　　　　　I want to sit at the front.

Adverbs consisting of more than one word

➤ In English you sometimes use a phrase instead of a single word to give information about time, place and so on, and the same is true in Italian.

- **una volta** once
  una volta la settimana　　　　　　once a week

- **due volte** twice
  Ho provato due volte.　　　　　　　I tried twice.

- **molte volte** many times
  L'ho fatto molte volte.　　　　　　I've done it many times.

- **da qualche parte** somewhere
  **Ho lasciato le chiavi da qualche
  parte.**　　　　　　　　　　　　　I've left my keys somewhere.

- **qualche volta** sometimes
  Qualche volta arriva in ritardo.　　She sometimes arrives late.

- **di solito** usually
  Di solito arrivo prima.　　　　　　I usually get here earlier.

Where to put adverbs

Adverbs with verbs

➤ You normally put adverbs immediately after the verb.
  Non posso farlo adesso.　　　　　　I can't do it now.
  Parli bene l'italiano.　　　　　　　You speak Italian well.
  Non torno più.　　　　　　　　　　I'm not coming back.

➤ If you want to emphasize the adverb you can put it at the beginning of the sentence.
  Ora non posso.　　　　　　　　　　I can't do it just now.
  Prima non lo sapevo.　　　　　　　I didn't know that before.

> **Tip**
> In English adverbs can come between the subject and the verb: *It often changes.* Adverbs can NEVER come in this position in Italian.
> **Marco viene sempre.**　　　　　　Marco always comes.
> **Di solito vince Jessica.**　　　　　Jessica usually wins.

➤ When you are using adverbs such as **mai** (meaning *never*), **sempre** (meaning *always*), **già** (meaning *already*), **più** (meaning *again*) and **appena** (meaning *just*) with verbs in the perfect tense, you put the adverb between the two parts of the verb: **Non sono mai stata a Milano.**   I've never been to Milan.
    È sempre venuto con me.   He always came with me.
    L'ho già letto.   I've already read it.

⇨ *For more information on the **Perfect tense**, see page 141.*

Adverbs with adjectives and adverbs

➤ Put the adverb in front of the adjective or other adverb, as you do in English.
    Fa troppo freddo.   It's too cold.
    Vai più piano.   Go more slowly.

> ### KEY POINTS
> ✔ Some adverbs are very common in Italian, and it's a good idea to learn as many as possible.
> ✔ You usually put adverbs after the verb.
> ✔ If you want to emphasize the adverb, you put it at the beginning of the sentence.
> ✔ Adverbs go before adjectives or other adverbs.

158 **Create a sentence using the elements below, remembering to insert the article for the noun where appropriate.**

a studiano/troppo/ragazzi ....

b film/noioso/era/tanto ....

c pasta/pronta/è/quasi ....

d mai/siamo/in/non/Francia/stati ....

e gabinetto/sotto/è ....

f macchina/indietro/tornata/è ....

g tardi/si alza/sempre ....

h piscina/lontano/è/piuttosto..

i arrivati/presto/sono/troppo/ospiti

....

j scarpe/poco/piacciono/mi ....

159 **Translate the following into Italian, where appropriate using *tu* for 'you'.**

a I usually get here late. ....

b She can't do it just now. ....

c Here's the train! ....

d My husband went too. ....

e They don't eat enough. ....

f We were looking for the dog everywhere.

....

g She waited outside. ....

h The newspapers are at the front. ....

i I used to run twice a week. ....

j Are they coming to the theatre? — Maybe. ....

160 **Match the words on the left with their translations on the right.**

a	**proprio**	once
b	**qualche volta**	really
c	**una volta**	unfortunately
d	**da qualche parte**	sometimes
e	**purtroppo**	somewhere

Prepositions

What is a preposition?

A **preposition** is one word such as *at, for, with, into* or *from*, or words such as *in front of* or *near to*, which are usually followed by a noun or a pronoun.
Prepositions show how people and things relate to the rest of the sentence,
for example, *She's at home; It's for you; You'll get into trouble; It's in front of you.*

Using prepositions

Where they go

➤ Prepositions are used in front of nouns and pronouns to show the relationship between the noun or pronoun and the rest of the sentence.

Andiamo a Roma.	We're going to Rome.
Vieni con me.	Come with me.

➤ In English you can separate a preposition from its noun or pronoun and put it at the end of a question, or at the end of part of a sentence, for example, *Who were you talking to?; the people I came with*.

➤ In Italian prepositions <u>always</u> go in front of another word and <u>never</u> at the end of a question or part of a sentence:

Con chi sei venuto?	Who did you come with?
la ragazza alla quale ho dato la chiave	the girl I gave the key to

Which preposition to use

➤ In English certain adjectives and verbs are always followed by particular prepositions, for example, *happy with, afraid of, talk to, smile at*. The same is true in Italian.

Sono deluso del voto che ho preso.	I'm disappointed with the mark I got.
Andiamo in Italia.	We're going to Italy.

🔁 Note that when a preposition is used in front of the *–ing* form in English, a preposition is used in front of the <u>infinitive</u> (the **–re** form of the verb) in Italian.

È andato via senza salutarci.	He went away without saying goodbye to us.
Sono stufo di studiare.	I'm fed up of studying.

➤ The prepositions used in Italian may not be what you expect, for example, the Italian preposition **in** is used for both the following:

I miei sono in Italia.	My parents are *in* Italy.
I miei vanno in Italia.	My parents are going *to* Italy.

For further explanation of grammatical terms, please see pages viii-xii.

➤ You sometimes need to use a preposition in Italian when there is no preposition in English.

Hai bisogno <u>di</u> qualcosa?	Do you need anything?
Chiedi <u>a</u> Lidia cosa vuole.	Ask Lidia what she wants.

⇨ *For more information on **Prepositions after verbs**, see page 189.*

> *Tip*
> When you look up a verb in the dictionary, take note of any preposition that is shown with the translation.
> | | |
> |---|---|
> | **congratularsi <u>con</u>** | to congratulate |
> | **dire qualcosa <u>a</u> qualcuno** | to tell someone something |

Prepositions that combine with the definite article

➤ When the prepositions **a**, **di**, **da**, **in** and **su** are followed by the <u>definite article</u> – **il**, **la**, **i**, **le** and so on, they combine with it to make one word.

	+ il	+ lo	+ la	+ l'	+ i	+ gli	+ le
a	al	allo	alla	all'	ai	agli	alle
di	del	dello	della	dell'	dei	degli	delle
da	dal	dallo	dalla	dall'	dai	dagli	dalle
in	nel	nello	nella	nell'	nei	negli	nelle
su	sul	sullo	sulla	sull'	sui	sugli	sulle

⇨ *For more information on **Articles**, see page 14.*

Si guardava <u>allo</u> specchio.	He was looking at himself <u>in the</u> mirror.
la cima <u>del</u> monte	the top <u>of the</u> mountain
Sto <u>dai</u> miei.	I live <u>with</u> my parents.
Cos'hai <u>nella</u> tasca?	What have you got <u>in</u> your pocket?
I soldi sono <u>sul</u> tavolo.	The money's <u>on the</u> table.

> **KEY POINTS**
> ✔ Italian prepositions are always used in front of another word.
> ✔ The preposition used in Italian may not be what you expect.
> ✔ Italian prepositions combine with the definite article to make one word.

Test yourself

161 **Fill the gap with a preposition or with a preposition combined with an article. The first one has been done for you.**

a Il libro è ....*sul*.... tavolo.

b .... chi parlavi?

c Vanno .... Palermo.

d Erano stufi .... lavorare.

e Le chiavi sono .... mia borsa.

f Mi piacerebbe andare .... Spagna.

g Ha detto la verità .... sua madre.

h Avete bisogno .... macchina?

i Hanno chiesto .... professore.

j Vuoi venire .... noi?

162 **Translate the following into Italian, where appropriate using *tu* for 'you'.**

a She lives in London. ....

b We have to be at the station at six. ....

c They got off at the stop. ....

d We live in Spain. ....

e Who did he come with? ....

f She was speaking to her husband. ....

g I went for a shower. ....

h Have you ever been to Bologna? ....

i What did she have in her suitcase? ....

j He told the teacher his name. ....

a, di, da, in, su and per

a

➤ **a** is used with nouns to tell you <u>where</u>.

alla porta	<u>at</u> the door
al sole	<u>in</u> the sun
all'ombra	<u>in</u> the shade
Vivo **al terzo piano**	I live <u>on</u> the third floor
È **a letto**	He's <u>in</u> bed
alla radio	<u>on</u> the radio
alla tivù	<u>on</u> TV

➤ Use **a** to mean *to* when you're talking about <u>going to a place</u>.

Andiamo al cinema?	Shall we go <u>to</u> the cinema?
Sei mai stato a New York?	Have you ever been <u>to</u> New York?

[i] Note that if the place is a country, use **in** in Italian.

Andrò in Germania quest'estate.	I'm going <u>to</u> Germany this summer.

➤ Use **a** to mean *at* when you're talking about <u>being at a place</u>.

Devo *essere* all'aeroporto alle dieci.	I've got to be <u>at</u> the airport at ten.
Scendo alla prossima fermata.	I'm getting off <u>at</u> the next stop.
Luigi è a casa.	Luigi is <u>at</u> home.

➤ Use **a** to mean *in* when you're talking about being <u>in a town</u>.

Abitano a Bologna.	They live <u>in</u> Bologna.

[i] Note that if the place is a country, use **in** in Italian.

Vivo in Scozia.	I live <u>in</u> Scotland.
Vive in Canada.	He lives <u>in</u> Canada.

➤ Use **a** to mean *away* when you're talking about distances.

a tre chilometri da qui	three kilometres <u>away</u> from here
a due ore di distanza in macchina	two hours <u>away</u> by car

[i] Note that *away* can be left out of this kind of phrase, but **a** has to be used in Italian.

L'albergo è ad un chilometro dalla spiaggia.	The hotel is a kilometre from the beach.

➤ **a** is used with nouns to tell you <u>when</u>.

a volte	<u>at</u> times
a tempo	<u>on</u> time
alla fine	<u>in</u> the end

➤ Use **a** to mean *at* with <u>times and festivals</u>.

alle cinque	<u>at</u> five o'clock
a mezzogiorno	<u>at</u> midday
al fine settimana	<u>at</u> the weekend
a Pasqua	<u>at</u> Easter
a Natale	at Christmas

> *Tip*
> Remember that questions beginning *What time ...* must start with the preposition **a** in Italian.
>
> **A che ora parti?**   What time are you leaving?
>
> • Use **a** with <u>months</u> to mean *in*.
>   **Sono nata a maggio.**   I was born <u>in</u> May.

➤ **a** is used with nouns to tell you <u>how</u>.
    a piedi   <u>on</u> foot
    a mano   <u>by</u> hand
    a poco a poco   little <u>by</u> little

➤ Use **a** with <u>flavours</u>.
    un gelato alla fragola   a strawberry ice cream
    una torta al cioccolato   a chocolate cake
    gli spaghetti al pomodoro   spaghetti with tomato sauce

➤ **a** is used with <u>nouns and pronouns</u> after some verbs.
    L'ho dato a Selene.   I gave it to Selene.
    Piace a me, ma a mia sorella no.   I like it, but my sister doesn't.
    A che cosa stai pensando?   What are you thinking about?

⇨ *For more information on **Prepositions after verbs**, see page 189.*

ⓘ Note that the unstressed pronouns **mi**, **ti**, **gli**, **le**, **ci** and **vi** come in front of the verb and are not used with **a**.

    Ti ha parlato?   Did she speak to you?
    Gliel'ho dato.   I gave it to her.
    Mi piace.   I like it.

⇨ *For more information on **Indirect pronouns**, see page 60.*

➤ **a** is used with the <u>infinitive</u> (the **–re** form of the verb) to say what your purpose is.
    Sono uscita a fare due passi.   I went out for a little walk.
    Sono andati a fare il bagno.   They've gone to have a swim.

<u>di</u>

➤ **di** is used to talk about who or what something belongs to.
    il nome del ristorante   the name of the restaurant
    il capitano della squadra   the captain of the team
    È di Marco.   It belongs to Marco.
    Di chi è?   Whose is it?

➤ Use **di** to refer to the person who made something.
    un quadro di Picasso   a picture <u>by</u> Picasso
    una commedia di Shakespeare   a play <u>by</u> Shakespeare
    un film di Fellini   a Fellini film

➤ In English, ownership can be shown by using a noun with 's, or s' added to it, for example the *child's* name, *the boys'* teacher. In Italian you change the word order and use **di** to translate this sort of phrase.

la macchina di mia madre	my mother's car
	(*literally: the car of my mother*)
la casa dei miei amici	my friends' house
l'Otello di Verdi	Verdi's Othello

⇨ *For more information on **Possessive adjectives** and **Possessive pronouns**, see pages 34 and 52.*

➤ In English, when there is a connection between two things, one noun can be used in front of another, for example *the car* keys, *the bathroom* window. In Italian you change the word order and use **di** to translate this sort of phrase.

il tavolo della cucina	the kitchen table
il periodo delle vacanze	the holiday season
il professore di inglese	the English teacher
il campione del mondo	the world champion

➤ When a noun such as *cotton, silver, paper* is used as an adjective, use **di** in Italian.

una maglietta di cotone	a cotton T-shirt
una collana d'argento	a silver necklace
dei tovaglioli di carta	paper napkins

➤ **di** sometimes means *from*.

È di Firenze.	He's from Florence.
Di dove sei?	Where are you from?

➤ **di** is used to say what something contains or what it is made of.

un gruppo di studenti	a group of students
un bicchiere di vino	a glass of wine
È fatto di plastica.	It's made of plastic.

➤ **di** is used after **milione** (meaning *million*), and words for approximate numbers, such as **un migliaio** (meaning *about a thousand*) and **una ventina** (meaning *about twenty*).

un milione di dollari	a million dollars
un migliaio di persone	about a thousand people
una ventina di macchine	about twenty cars

➤ **di** is used after certain verbs and adjectives.

Ti ricordi di Laura?	Do you remember Laura?
Sto tentando di concentrarmi.	I'm trying to concentrate.
Le arance sono ricche di vitamina C.	Oranges are rich in vitamin C.
Era pieno di gente.	It was full of people.

⇨ *For more information on **Prepositions after verbs** and **Adjectives**, see pages 189 and 24.*

Tip
Remember that some verbs are single words in English, but in Italian they are phrases ending with **di**, for example, **aver bisogno di** (meaning *to need*) and **aver voglia di** (meaning *to want*).

Non ho bisogno di niente.	I don't need anything.
Non ho voglia di andare a letto.	I don't want to go to bed.

➤ **di** is used with nouns to say <u>when</u>.

di domenica	<u>on</u> Sundays
di notte	<u>at</u> night
di giorno	<u>during</u> the day

➤ Use **di** to mean *in* with seasons and parts of the day.

d'estate	<u>in</u> summer
d'inverno	<u>in</u> winter

> 🔢 Note that **in** can also be used with seasons, for example, **in estate** (meaning *in summer*).

di mattina	<u>in</u> the morning
di sera	<u>in</u> the evening

➤ **di** is used in comparisons to mean *than*.

È più alto <u>di</u> me.	He's taller <u>than</u> me.
È più brava <u>di</u> lui.	She's better <u>than</u> him.

➤ Use **di** to mean *in* after a superlative.

il più grande <u>del</u> mondo	the biggest <u>in</u> the world
la più brava <u>della</u> classe	the best <u>in</u> the class
il migliore <u>d'</u>Italia	the best <u>in</u> Italy

⇨ *For more information on* **Superlatives***, see page* 33.

> *Tip*
> **È più bravo di tutti** and **è più brava di tutti** are ways of saying *He's the best* and *She's the best*.

➤ **del**, **della**, **dei**, **delle** and so on (**di** combined with the definite article) are used to mean *some*.

C'era <u>della</u> gente che aspettava.	There were <u>some</u> people waiting.
Vuoi <u>dei</u> biscotti?	Would you like <u>some</u> biscuits?

➤ **di** is used with the <u>infinitive</u> (the **–re** form of the verb) when it is used as a noun.

Ho paura <u>di</u> volare.	I'm afraid of flying.
Non ho voglia <u>di</u> mangiare.	I don't feel like eating.

da

➤ **da** is used with places to mean *from*.

a tre chilometri <u>da</u> qui	three kilometres from here.
Viene <u>da</u> Roma.	He comes from Rome.

➤ Use **da** to talk about getting, jumping or falling <u>off</u> something, or getting or falling <u>out of</u> something.

Isobel è scesa <u>dal</u> treno.	Isobel got <u>off</u> the train.
Il vaso è cascato <u>dal</u> terrazzo.	The plant pot fell <u>off</u> the balcony.
Il gatto è saltato <u>dal</u> muro.	The cat jumped <u>off</u> the wall.
È scesa <u>dalla</u> macchina.	She got <u>out of</u> the car.
Sono cascato <u>dal</u> letto.	I fell <u>out of</u> bed.

For further explanation of grammatical terms, please see pages viii-xii.

ⓘ Note that **da ... a ...** means *from ... to ...*

<u>da</u> cima <u>a</u> fondo	<u>from</u> top <u>to</u> bottom
<u>dalle</u> otto <u>alle</u> dieci	<u>from</u> eight <u>to</u> ten

➤ Use **da** with **andare** to say you're going <u>to</u> a shop, or <u>to</u> someone's house or workplace.

Vado <u>dal</u> giornalaio.	I'm going <u>to</u> the paper shop.
È <u>andato dal</u> dentista.	He's gone <u>to</u> the dentist's.
Andiamo <u>da</u> Gabriele?	Shall we go <u>to</u> Gabriele's house?

➤ Use **da** with *essere* to say you're <u>at</u> a shop, or <u>at</u> someone's house or workplace.

Laura è <u>dal</u> parucchiere.	Laura's <u>at</u> the hairdresser's.
Sono <u>da</u> Anna.	I'm <u>at</u> Anna's house.

➤ **da** is used to talk about <u>how long</u> something has been happening.

● Use **da** with periods of time to mean *for*.

Vivo qui <u>da</u> un anno.	I've been living here <u>for</u> a year.

● Use **da** with points in time to mean *since*.

<u>da</u> allora	<u>since</u> then
Ti aspetto <u>dalle</u> tre.	I've been waiting for you <u>since</u> three o'clock.

ⓘ Note that the present tense is used in Italian to talk about what has been happening for a period, or since a certain time.

È a Londra <u>da</u> martedì.	He's been in London <u>since</u> Tuesday.

⇨ *For more information on the **Present tense**, see page 87.*

➤ **da** is used with passive verbs to mean *by*.

dipinto <u>da</u> un grande artista	painted <u>by</u> a great artist
I ladri sono stati catturati <u>dalla</u> polizia.	The thieves were caught <u>by</u> the police.

⇨ *For more information on the **Passive**, see page 159.*

➤ **da** is used with the <u>infinitive</u> (the **–re** form of the verb) when you're talking about things to do.

C'è molto <u>da</u> fare.	There's lots to do.
È un film <u>da</u> vedere.	It's a film that you've got to see.
Non c'è niente <u>da</u> mangiare.	There's nothing to eat.
E, da bere?	And what would you like to drink?

➤ In English you can say what something is used for by putting one noun in front of another, for example *a racing car, an evening dress*. In Italian change the word order and use **da**.

un nuovo paio di scarpe <u>da</u> corsa	a new pair of running shoes
Paolo non ha il costume <u>da</u> bagno.	Paolo hasn't got his swimming trunks.

➤ **da** is used when describing someone or something.

una ragazza <u>dagli</u> occhi azzurri	a girl with blue eyes
un vestito <u>da</u> cento euro	a dress costing a hundred euros

➤ **da** is used with nouns to mean *as*.

    <u>Da</u> bambino avevo paura del buio.   <u>As</u> a child I was afraid of the dark.

in

➤ Use **in** with **essere** to mean *in* when you are talking about where someone or something is – except in the case of towns.

    Vive <u>in</u> Canada.   He lives <u>in</u> Canada.
    È <u>nel</u> cassetto.   It's <u>in</u> the drawer.

(i) Note that in the case of towns you use **a** in Italian.

    Abitano <u>a</u> Bologna.   They live <u>in</u> Bologna.

> *Tip*
> You don't use **in** with adverbs such as **qui** (meaning *here*) and **lì** (meaning *there*).
> **qui dentro**   in here
> **lì dentro**   in there

➤ Use **in** with **andare** to mean *to* when you're talking about where someone or something is going *to*, except in the case of towns.

    Andrò <u>in</u> Germania quest'estate.   I'm going <u>to</u> Germany this summer.
    È andato <u>in</u> ufficio.   He's gone <u>to</u> the office.

(i) Note that in the case of towns you use **a** in Italian.

    Sei mai stato <u>a</u> New York?   Have you ever been <u>to</u> New York?

> *Tip*
> **essere in vacanza** means *to be on holiday*, **andare in vacanza** means *to go on holiday*.

➤ Use **in** to mean *into* when you're talking about getting <u>into</u> something, or putting something <u>into</u> something.

    Su, sali <u>in</u> macchina.   Come on, get <u>into</u> the car.
    Come sono penetrati <u>in</u> banca?   How did they get <u>into</u> the bank?
    L'ha gettato <u>in</u> acqua.   He threw it <u>into</u> the water.

(i) Note that **in** is also used with verbs such as **dividere** (meaning *to divide*) and **tagliare** (meaning *to cut*).

    L'ha tagliato <u>in</u> due.   She cut it <u>into</u> two.

⇨ *For more information on **Prepositions after verbs**, see page 189.*

➤ Use **in** to mean *in* with years, seasons and months.

nel duemilasei	<u>in</u> two thousand and six
in estate	<u>in</u> summer
in ottobre	<u>in</u> October

ℹ Note that you can also use **di** with seasons (**d'estate**) and **a** with months (**ad ottobre**).

➤ **in** is used with periods of time to mean *in*.

L'ha fatto <u>in</u> sei mesi.	He did it <u>in</u> six months.
Puoi finirlo <u>in</u> trenta minuti.	You can finish it <u>in</u> thirty minutes.

➤ **in** is used with modes of transport to mean *by*.

Siamo andati <u>in</u> treno.	We went <u>by</u> train.
È meglio andare <u>in</u> bici.	It's better to go <u>by</u> bike.

➤ **in** is used to say <u>how</u> something is done.

Camminavano <u>in</u> silenzio.	They walked in silence.
È scritto <u>in</u> tedesco.	It's written in German.

su

➤ Use **su** to mean *on*.

Il tuo cellulare è <u>sul</u> pavimento.	Your mobile phone is <u>on</u> the floor.
Mettilo <u>sulla</u> sedia.	Put it <u>on</u> the chair.
È <u>sulla</u> sinistra.	It's <u>on</u> the left.

ℹ Note that **sul giornale** means *in the paper*.

L'ho letto <u>sul</u> giornale.	I read it in the paper.

> *Tip*
> **qui su** and **qua su** mean *up here*. **là** combines with **su** to make one word
> with a double s: **lassù** (meaning *up there*).
>
> | | |
> |---|---|
> | **Siamo <u>qui su</u>.** | We're <u>up here</u>. |
> | **Eccoli <u>lassù</u>.** | They're <u>up there</u>. |

➤ **su** is used with topics to mean *about*.

un libro <u>sugli</u> animali	a book about animals

➤ **su** is used with numbers:

- to talk about ratios

in tre casi <u>su</u> dieci	in three cases <u>out of</u> ten
due giorni <u>su</u> tre	two days <u>out of</u> three

- with an article and a number to indicate an approximate amount

È costato <u>sui</u> cinquecento euro.	It cost <u>around</u> five hundred euros.
È <u>sulla</u> trentina.	She's <u>about</u> thirty.

per

➤ **per** often means *for*.

Questo è per te.	This is for you.
È troppo difficile per lui.	It's too difficult for him.
L'ho comprato per trenta centesimi.	I bought it for thirty cents.
Ho guidato pertrecento chilometri.	I drove for three hundred kilometres.

[*i*] Note that when you are talking about how long you <u>have been doing</u> something you use **da**.

Aspetto da un pezzo.	I've been waiting for a while.

➤ **per** is used with destinations.

il volo per Londra	the flight to London
il treno per Roma	the train to Rome

➤ **per** is used with verbs of movement to mean *through*.

I ladri sono entrati per la finestra.	The burglars got in through the window.
Siamo passati per Birmingham.	We went through Birmingham.

➤ **per** is used to indicate how something is transported or communicated.

per posta	by post
per via aerea	by airmail
per posta elettronica	by email
per ferrovia	by rail
per telefono	by or on the phone

[*i*] Note that **per** is NOT used when referring to means of transport for people, **in** is used instead.

in macchina	by car

➤ **per** is used to explain the reason for something.

L'ho fatto per aiutarti.	I did it to help you.
L'abbiamo fatto per ridere.	We did it for a laugh.
Ci sono andato per abitudine.	I went out of habit.
Non l'ho fatto per pigrizia.	I didn't do it out of laziness.
È successo per errore.	It happened by mistake.

➤ **per** is used in some very common phrases.

uno per uno	one by one
giorno per giorno	day by day
una per volta	one at a time
due per tre	two times three

Some other common prepositions

One-word and two-word prepositions

➤ As in English, Italian prepositions can be one word or consist of more than one word, for example **vicino a** (meaning *near*) and **prima di** (meaning *before*).

The following are some of the commonest prepositions in Italian:

- **prima di** before, until
prima di me	before me
prima delle sette	before seven o'clock
Non sarà pronto prima delle otto.	It won't be ready until eight o'clock.

> **Tip**
> When a preposition includes **a** or **di** remember to combine these words with definite articles such as **il**, **la** and **le**.

🔟 Note that **prima di**, like many other Italian prepositions, can be used in front of an infinitive (the **–re** form of the verb).

Dobbiamo informarci prima di cominciare.	We need to find out before starting *or* before we start.

- **dopo** after
Ci vediamo dopo le vacanze.	See you after the holidays.
Dopo aver mandato l'sms ha spento il telefonino.	After sending or after she'd sent the text she switched off the phone.

🔟 Note that **dopo di** is used with pronouns.

Loro sono arrivati dopo di noi.	They arrived after us.

⇨ *For more information on **Pronouns**, see page 53.*

- **fino a** until, as far as
Resto fino a venerdì.	I'm staying until Friday.
Vengo con te fino alla posta.	I'll come with you as far as the post office.

🔟 Note that **Fino a quando?** (meaning literally *until when*) is used to ask *How long?*

Fino a quando puoi rimanere?	How long can you stay?

> **Tip**
> When a preposition includes **a** or **di** remember to combine these words with definite articles such as **il**, **la** and **le**.

- **fra** in, between, among
  Torno fra un'ora. — I'll be back <u>in</u> an hour.
  Era seduto fra il padre e lo zio. — He was sitting <u>between</u> his father and his uncle.

  Fra i sopravvissuti c'era anche il pilota. — The pilot was <u>among</u> the survivors.

🛈 Note that **fra di** is used with pronouns.

    Fra di noi ci sono alcuni mancini. — There are some left-handers <u>among us</u>.

⇨ *For more information on* **Pronouns**, *see page* 53.

> *Tip*
> **fra poco** means in *a short time*, or *soon*.
> **Lo sapremo fra poco.** — We'll <u>soon</u> know.

- **tra** is an alternative form of **fra**, and can be used in exactly the same way

  tra un'ora — <u>in</u> an hour
  tra poco — soon
  tra il padre e lo zio — <u>between</u> his father and his uncle
  tra i feriti — <u>among</u> the injured

- **durante** during
  durante la notte — <u>during</u> the night

- **con** with, to
  Ci andrò con lei. — I'll go <u>with</u> her.
  Hai parlato con lui? — Have you spoken <u>to</u> him?

- **senza** without
  Esci senza cappotto? — Are you going out <u>without</u> a coat?

🛈 Note that **senza di** is used with pronouns.

    Non posso vivere senza di lui. — I can't live <u>without him</u>.

⇨ *For more information on* **Pronouns**, *see page* 53.

- **contro** against
  Sono contro la caccia. — I'm <u>against</u> hunting.

🛈 Note that **contro di** is used with pronouns.

    Non ho niente contro di lui. — I've got nothing <u>against him</u>.

- **davanti a** in front of, opposite
  Era seduta davanti a me nell'aereo. — She was sitting <u>in front of</u> me in the plane.
  la casa davanti alla mia — the house <u>opposite</u> mine

> *Tip*
> When a preposition includes **a** or **di** remember to combine these words
> with definite articles such as **il**, **la** and **le**.

- **dietro** behind
  dietro la porta   behind the door

[i] Note that **dietro di** is used with pronouns.

  Sono seduti dietro di me.   They're sitting behind me.

⇨ *For more information on **Pronouns**, see page 53.*

- **sotto** under, below
  Il gatto si è nascosto sotto il letto.   The cat hid under the bed.
  cinque gradi sotto zero   five degrees below zero

- **sopra** over, above, on top of
  le donne sopra i sessant'anni   women over sixty
  cento metri sopra il livello del mare   a hundred metres above sea level
  sopra l'armadio   on top of the cupboard

- **accanto a** next to
  Siediti accanto a me.   Sit next to me.

> *Tip*
> When a preposition includes **a** or **di** remember to combine these words
> with definite articles such as **il**, **la** and **le**.

- **verso** towards, around
  Correva verso l'uscita.   He was running towards the exit.
  Arriverò verso le sette.   I'll arrive around seven.

[i] Note that **verso di** is used with pronouns.

  Correvano verso di lui.   They were running towards him.

⇨ *For more information on **Pronouns**, see page 53.*

- **a causa di** because of
  L'aeroporto è chiuso a causa della   The airport is closed because of fog.
  nebbia.

> *Tip*
> When a preposition includes **a** or **di** remember to combine these words
> with definite articles such as **il**, **la** and **le**.

- **maigrado** in spite of
  Malgrado tutto siamo ancora amici.   We're still friends <u>in spite of</u> everything.

Preposition or adverb?

➤ In English some words can be used both as <u>adverbs</u>, which describe verbs, and as <u>prepositions</u>, which go in front of nouns and pronouns.

➤ The word *before* is an <u>adverb</u> in the sentence *We've met before* and a <u>preposition</u> in the phrase *before dinner*.

⇨ *For more information on **Adverbs**, see page 213.*

➤ In Italian you <u>don't</u> usually use exactly the same word as both an adverb and a preposition:

- **prima** and **davanti** are <u>adverbs</u>
  Perché non me l'hai detto prima?   Why didn't you tell me <u>before</u>?
  la casa davanti   the house <u>opposite</u>.

- **prima di** and **davanti a** are <u>prepositions</u>
  Ne ho bisogno prima di giovedì.   I need it <u>before</u> Thursday.
  Ero seduto davanti a lui a cena.   I was sitting <u>opposite</u> him at dinner.

KEY POINTS

✔ **dopo**, **senza**, **fra**, **dietro**, **contro**, **verso** are used without **di**, except when followed by a pronoun.

✔ Italian prepositions often have **di** or **a** as their second element; Italian adverbs are not followed by **di** or **a**.

Test yourself

163 **Fill the gap with a prepostion or with a preposition combined with an article. The first one has been done for you.**

a È il più bravo ..*della*.. classe.

b Mia madre è .... dottore.

c C'è qualcosa .... mangiare?

d Questo esercizio è troppo difficile .... lui.

e Di solito non vado .... ufficio il sabato.

f Il ristorante è .... destra.

g Ho tagliato la torta .... due.

h L'ha mandato .... via aerea.

i Aspettavano .... tre ore.

j Vado a scuola .... piedi.

164 **Match the two columns.**

a a causa di   until

b prima di   because of

c accanto a   before

d fino a   opposite

e davanti a   next to

165 **Translate the following into Italian, where appropriate using *tu* for 'you'.**

a She was sitting between the trees. ....

b Did you go out without shoes on? ....

c We have nothing against them. ....

d They should get there around eight. ....

e After finishing the book I went to bed. ....

f She was awake during the night. ....

g We put the suitcase on top of the wardrobe

....

h You were sitting next to me. ....

i She doesn't want to go without him. ....

j He's around forty. ....

Conjunctions

What is a conjunction?
A **conjunction** is a word such as *and, but, or, so, if* and *because*, that links two words or phrases, or two parts of a sentence, for example, *Diane <u>and</u> I have been friends for years; I left <u>because</u> I was bored.*

---

e, ma, anche, o, perché, che and se

➤ These common Italian conjunctions correspond to common English conjunctions, such as *and* and *but*. However they are sometimes used differently from their English counterparts, for example, **Ma no!** (literally, *But no!*) means *No!*, or *Of course not!*

➤ Shown below are the common Italian conjunctions **e**, **anche**, **o**, **ma**, **perché**, **che** and **se** and how they are used:

- **e** and, but, what about
io <u>e</u> Davide	David <u>and</u> I
tu <u>ed</u> io	you <u>and</u> me
Lo credevo simpatico <u>e</u> non lo è.	I thought he was nice, <u>but</u> he isn't.
Io non ci vado, <u>e</u> tu?	I'm not going, <u>what about</u> you?

  ⓘ Note that you use **di** or **a**, not the conjunction **e**, to translate *try <u>and</u>, go <u>and</u>* and so on.

Cerca <u>di</u> capire!	Try and understand!
Vado <u>a</u> vedere.	I'll go and see.

  ⇨ *For more information on **di** and **a**, see page 231.*

- **ma** but
strano <u>ma</u> vero	strange <u>but</u> true
Dice così, <u>ma</u> non ci credo.	That's what he says, <u>but</u> I don't believe it.

  ⓘ Note that **ma** is used for emphasis with **sì** and **no**.

Ti dispiace? – <u>Ma</u> no!	Do you mind? – <u>Of course</u> not.
Non ti piace? – <u>Ma</u> sì!	Don't you like it? – Yes <u>of course</u> I do.

- **anche** also, too, even
Parla tedesco e <u>anche</u> francese.	She speaks German and <u>also</u> French.
Ho fame. – <u>Anch'io!</u>	I'm hungry. – Me <u>too</u>!
Lo saprebbe fare <u>anche</u> un bambino.	<u>Even</u> a child could do it.

- **o** or
due <u>o</u> tre volte	two <u>or</u> three times

> *Tip*
> **oppure** is another word for *or*. It is used to join two parts of a sentence when you're talking about alternatives.
>
> | | |
> |---|---|
> | **Possiamo guardare la TV <u>oppure</u> ascoltare musica.** | We can watch TV <u>or</u> listen to music. |

For further explanation of grammatical terms, please see pages viii-xii.

- **perché** because
  Non posso uscire perché ho molto da fare.
  I can't go out <u>because</u> I've got a lot to do.

ⓘ Note that **perché** also means *why*.

Perché vai via? – Perché è tardi.
<u>Why</u> are you going? – Because it's late.

- **che** that
  Ha detto che farà tardi.
  He said <u>that</u> he'll be late.
  Penso che sia il migliore.
  I think <u>that</u> it's the best.

⇨ *For more information on* **che** *followed by the* **Subjunctive**, *see page 171.*

> *Tip*
> In English you can say either *He says he loves me* or *He says <u>that</u> he loves me*.
> In Italian che is <u>NOT</u> optional in this way.
> **So che le piace la cioccolata.**   I know (that) she likes chocolate.

- **se** if, whether
  Fammi sapere se c'è qualche problema.
  Let me know <u>if</u> there are any problems.
  Se fosse più furbo verrebbe.
  <u>If</u> he had more sense he'd come.
  Non so se dirglielo o no.
  I don't know <u>whether</u> to tell him or not.

⇨ *For more information on* **se** *followed by the* **Subjunctive**, *see page 171.*

Some other common conjunctions

➤ The following conjunctions are used a lot in colloquial Italian:

- **allora** so, right then
  Allora, cosa pensi?
  <u>So</u>, what do you think?
  Allora, cosa facciamo stasera?
  <u>Right then</u>, what shall we do this evening?

- **dunque** so, well
  Ha sbagliato lui, dunque è giusto che paghi.
  It was his mistake, <u>so</u> it's right he should pay.
  Dunque, come dicevo...
  <u>Well</u>, as I was saying...

- **quindi** so
  L'ho già visto, quindi non vado.
  I've already seen it, <u>so</u> I'm not going.

- **però** but, however, though
  Mi piace, però è troppo caro.
  I like it – <u>but</u> it's too expensive.
  Non è l'ideale, però può andare.
  It's not ideal, <u>however</u> it'll do.
  Sì, lo so – strano però.
  Yes, I know – it's odd <u>though</u>.

- **invece** actually
  Ero un po' pessimista, ma invece è andato tutto bene.
  I wasn't too hopeful, but <u>actually</u> it all went fine.

> *Tip*
> **invece** is often used for emphasis in Italian – it isn't always translated in English.
>
> | | |
> |---|---|
> | **Ho pensato che fosse lui, ma <u>invece</u> no.** | I thought it was him but it wasn't. |

- **anzi** in fact
Non mi dispiace, <u>anzi</u> sono contento.	I don't mind, <u>in fact</u> I'm glad.

- **quando** when
Giocano fuori <u>quando</u> fa bel tempo.	They play outside <u>when</u> the weather's nice.

[i] Note that in sentences referring to the future, the future tense is used after **quando**.

Lo farò <u>quando avrò</u> tempo.	I'll do it <u>when</u> I <u>have</u> time.

⇨ *For more information on the **Future tense**, see page 124.*

- **mentre** while
È successo <u>mentre</u> eri fuori.	It happened <u>while</u> you were out.

- **come** as
Ho fatto <u>come</u> hai detto tu.	I did <u>as</u> you told me.

[i] Note that **quando** and **mentre** tell you <u>WHEN</u> something happens; **come** tells you <u>HOW</u> something happens.

Split conjunctions

➤ English split conjunctions such as *either ... or* and *both ... and* are translated by split conjunctions in Italian.

- **o ... o** either ... or
o oggi o domani	<u>either</u> today <u>or</u> tomorrow
Ti accompagneranno o Carlo o Marco.	<u>Either</u> Carlo <u>or</u> Marco will go with you.

- **né ... né** neither ... nor, either ... or
Non mi hanno chiamato <u>né</u> Claudio <u>né</u> Luca.	<u>Neither</u> Claudio <u>nor</u> Luca has phoned me.
Non avevo <u>né</u> guanti <u>né</u> scarponi.	I didn't have <u>either</u> gloves <u>or</u> boots.

- **sia ... che** both ... and
Verrano <u>sia</u> Luigi <u>che</u> suo fratello.	<u>Both</u> Luigi <u>and</u> his brother are coming.

[i] Note that in English a <u>singular</u> verb is used in sentences that have split conjunctions. In Italian a <u>plural</u> verb is used in sentences with split conjunctions if the two people or things involved are both the subject of the verb.

Non <u>vengono</u> né lui né sua moglie.	Neither he nor his wife <u>is</u> coming.

Spelling

How to spell words that have a hard k or g sound

➤ In Italian the [k] sound you have in the English words *kite* and *car* is spelled in two different ways, depending on the following vowel:

- **c** before **a**, **o** and **u**

- **ch** before **e** and **i**

➤ This means that the Italian word for *singer* is spelled **cantante** (pronounced [*kan-tan-tay*]; the word for *necklace* is spelled **collana** (pronounced [*kol-la-na*]), and the word for *cure* is spelled **cura** (pronounced [*koo-ra*]).

➤ However, the Italian word for *that* is spelled **che** (pronounced [*kay*]) and the word for *chemistry* is spelled **chimica** (pronounced [*kee-mee-ka*].

> *Tip*
> Remember that the Italian words for *kilo* and *kilometre* are spelled with **ch**:
> **due chili**   two kilos
> **cento chilometri**   a hundred kilometres

➤ In the same way, the hard [g] sound that you have in the English word *gas* is also spelled two ways in Italian:

- **g** before **a**, **o** and **u**

- **gh** before **e** and **i**

➤ This means that the Italian word for *cat* is spelled **gatto** (pronounced [*ga-toe*]; the word for *elbow* is spelled **gomito** (pronounced [*go-mee-toe*]), and the word for *taste* is spelled **gusto** (pronounced [*goos-toe*]).

➤ However, the Italian word for *leagues* is spelled **leghe** (pronounced [*lay-gay*]) and the word for *lakes* is spelled **laghi** (pronounced [*lah-ghee*].

How to pronounce c + a vowel

➤ As we have seen, the Italian letter **c** is pronounced like a [k] when it's followed by **a**, **o**, or **u**.

➤ When **c** is followed by **e** or **i** it is pronounced like the [ch] in *children*. This means that **centro** (meaning *centre*) is pronounced [*chen-tro*] and **città** (meaning *city*) is pronounced [*chee-tah*].

How to pronounce g + a vowel

➤ The Italian letter **g** is pronounced like the [g] in *gas* when it's followed by **a**, **o**, or **u**. When an Italian **g** is followed by **e** or **i**, however, it's pronounced like the [j] in *jet*. This means that **gente** (meaning *people*) is pronounced [*jen-tay*] and **giorno** (meaning *day*) is pronounced [*jor-no*].

How to spell verb endings which have c or g + vowel

➤ When an Italian verb has a hard [k] or [g] sound before the infinitive ending, for example **cercare** (meaning *to look for*) and **pagare** (meaning *to pay*), you have to change the spelling to **ch** and **gh** in forms of the verb that have endings starting with **e** or **i**.

➤ Here are the present and future tenses of **cercare** and **pagare**, showing how the spelling changes.

Vowel that follows c/g	Present of cercare	Meaning	Present of pagare	Meaning
o	cerco	I look for	pago	I pay
i	cerchi	you look for	paghi	you pay
a	cerca	he/she looks for	paga	he/she pays
i	cerchiamo	we look for	paghiamo	we pay
a	cercate	you look for	pagate	you pay
a	cercano	they look for	pagano	they pay

Vowel that follows c/g	Present of cercare	Meaning	Present of pagare	Meaning
e	cercherò	I'll look for	pagherò	I'll pay
e	cercherai	you'll look for	pagherai	you'll pay
e	cercherà	he/she will look for	pagherà	he/she will pay
e	cercheremo	we'll look for	pagheremo	we'll pay
e	cercherete	you'll look for	pagherete	you'll pay
e	cercheranno	they'll look for	pagheranno	they'll pay

Cosa cerchi? – Cerco le chiavi.	What are you looking for? – I'm looking for my keys.
Pago io. – No, paghiamo noi.	I'll pay. – No, we'll pay.

➤ When an Italian verb has a [sh] or [j] sound before the infinitive ending, for example **lasciare** (meaning *to leave*) and **mangiare** (meaning *to eat*), you drop the **i** of the stem before endings starting with **e** or **i**.

➤ This means that you spell the **tu** form of the present tense of these verbs **lasci** and **mangi**.

Lasci la finestra aperta?	Are you leaving the window open?
Cosa mangi?	What are you eating?

For further explanation of grammatical terms, please see pages viii-xii.

➤ The futures of the two verbs are spelled **lascerò**, **lascerai**, **lascerà**, **lasceremo**, **lascerete**, lasceranno and **mangerò**, **mangerai**, **mangerà**, **mangeremo**,

> **Fa caldo, la<u>sc</u>erò a casa il maglione.**   It's hot, I'll leave my jumper at home.
> **Domani man<u>g</u>eremo meno.**   We'll eat less tomorrow.

> *Tip*
> Although the spelling of some verb endings changes, the pronunciation stays the same.

How to spell plurals of nouns and adjectives ending in –ca or –ga

➤ When a feminine noun or adjective has a hard [k] or [g] sound before the singular ending **–a**, you add an **h** to the plural ending.

Singular	Meaning	Plural	Meaning
amica	friend	amiche	friends
riga	line	righe	lines
ricca	rich	ricche	rich
lunga	long	lunghe	long

> **una sua amica ricca**   a rich friend of hers
> **le sue ami<u>ch</u>e ric<u>ch</u>e**   her rich friends
> **una riga sotto le parole**   a line under the words
> **Ne ho letto solo poche rig<u>h</u>e.**   I just read a few lines of it.

> *Tip*
> Feminine nouns and adjectives always keep their hard [k] and [g] sounds in the plural.

How to spell plurals of nouns and adjectives ending in –co or –go

➤ There is not a fixed rule for the sound of the consonants **c** and **g** in the plural of masculine nouns and adjectives ending in **–co** and **–go**.

➤ Some words keep the hard sound of their **c** or **g** in the plural, and add an **h** to the spelling.

Singular	Meaning	Plural	Meaning
fuoco	fire	fuochi	fires
albergo	hotel	alberghi	hotels
ricco	rich	ricchi	rich
lungo	long	lunghi	long

> **È un albergo per ric<u>ch</u>i.**   It's a hotel for rich people.
> **Ho i capelli lung<u>h</u>i.**   I've got long hair.

➤ The plurals of many other words, however, change from the hard [k] sound to the [ch] sound, or from the hard [g] to [j]. This means their plurals are not spelled with an added **h**.

Singular	Meaning	Plural	Meaning
amico	friend	amici	friends
astrologo	astrologer	astrologi	astrologers
greco	Greek	greci	Greek
psicologico	psychological	psicologici	psychological

un astrologo greco	a Greek astrologer
i miei amici e i loro problemi psicologici	my friends and their psychological problems

How to spell plurals of nouns ending in –io

➤ When the **i** of the **–io** ending is stressed, as it is in **zio** (meaning *uncle*) and **invio** (meaning *dispatch*), the plural is spelled with double **i**: **zii, invii**.
   Ho sei zii e sette zie.   I've got six uncles and seven aunts.

➤ If the **i** of the **–io** ending is not stressed you spell the plural ending with only one **i**, for example **figlio → figli**; **occhio → occhi**.
   Ha gli occhi azzurri.   He's got blue eyes.

How to spell plurals of nouns ending in –cia and –gia

➤ The spelling of the plurals of these words also depends on whether the **i** of the ending is stressed.

➤ In some words, such words as **farmacia** (meaning *chemist's*) and **bugia** (meaning *lie*), the stress is on the **i**, and the plurals keep the **i**: **farmacie**; **bugie**.
   Non dire bugie.   Don't tell lies.

➤ In others, such as **faccia** (meaning *face*) and **spiaggia** (meaning *beach*) the **i** of the singular ending is not stressed, and the plural is not spelled with **i**: **facce**; **spiagge**.
   le nostre spiagge preferite   our favourite beaches

How to use accents

➤ Accents have two main uses: one is to show that a word is stressed on the last syllable, which is not normal in Italian, for example **città** (meaning *city*), **università** (meaning *university*), **perché** (meaning *why/because*), **cercherò** (meaning *I will look for*).

⇨ *For more information on **Stress**, see page 253.*

➤ The second use of accents is to distinguish between words that have identical pronunciations and spellings.

Without an accent		With an accent	
da	from	dà	he/she gives
e	and	è	is
la	the/it	là	there
li	them	lì	there
ne	of it/them	né	neither
se	if	sé	himself
si	himself/herself/one	sì	yes
te	you	tè	tea

Mettila là.   Put it there.
Non so se l'ha fatto da sé.   I don't know if he made it himself.

> *Tip*
> The words **può**, **già**, **ciò**, **più** and **giù** are spelled with an accent.

KEY POINTS

✔ Spelling changes are sometimes necessary to keep the consonants **c** and **g** hard.
✔ Accents show that the last syllable of a word is stressed.

Test yourself

166 **Replace the following with the plural form.**

a lo zio .... *gli zii* ....

b la spiaggia ....

c la mia amica ricca ....

d il vestito lungo ....

e il greco ....

f la farmacia ....

g l'albergo ....

h la riga ....

i poco ....

j il figlio ....

167 **Replace the highlighted words with an accented form if required.**

a Mio fratello **e** mia sorella. ....

b Vuole fare tutto da **se**. ....

c Vorrei un **te**, per favore. ....

d La porta **e** aperta. ....

e Se fossi in **te** non andrei. ....

f **Se** solo avessi più soldi! ....

g L'ho messo **li** sul tavolo. ....

h Come **si** fa? ....

i Non **li** conosciamo. ....

j Credo di **si**. ....

Stress

Which syllable to stress

➤ Most Italian words have two or more <u>syllables</u>, (units containing a vowel sound). In this section syllables are shown divided by | and the stressed vowel is in italic.

➤ Most words are stressed on the next to the last syllable, for example, **fi|ne|stra**.

➤ Some words are stressed on the last vowel, and this is always shown by an accent, for example, **u|ni|ver|si|tà**.

➤ Some words have their stress on an unexpected vowel, but are not spelled with an accent, for example, **mac|chi|na** (meaning *car*).

➤ If a word has the stress on a vowel you wouldn't expect, the stressed vowel is in italics, for example, **vogliono** (meaning *they want*), **vendere** (meaning *to sell*), **quindici** (meaning *fifteen*), **medico** (meaning *doctor*).

➤ This book also marks the stress in words in which **i** before another vowel is pronounced like **y**, for example **Lidia**.

Words that are stressed on the next to last syllable

➤ Two-syllable words <u>always</u> stress the first vowel, unless the final vowel has an accent: **ca|sa** house **gior|no** day

bel|la	beautiful	**du|e**	two
so|no	I am	**spes|so**	often
lu|i	he	**og|gi**	today

➤ Words with three or more syllables <u>generally</u> have the stress on the next to the last vowel: **in|gle|se** English **par|la|vo** I was speaking

gen|ti|le	nice	**an|dreb|be**	he'd go
set|ti|ma|na	week	**par|le|re|mo**	we'll speak
sta|zio|ne	station	**su|per|mer|ca|to**	supermarket
stra|or|di|na|ria|men|te	extraordinarily		

Words that stress the last syllable

➤ There are a number of nouns in Italian that have the stress on the final syllable and are spelled with an accent. They sometimes correspond to English nouns that end with *ty*, such as *university* and *faculty*.

re|al|tà	reality	**u|ni|ver|si|tà**	university
fe|li|ci|tà	happiness, felicity	**fe|del|tà**	fidelity
cu|rio|si|tà	curiosity	**fa|col|tà**	faculty
bon|tà	goodness	**cit|tà**	city
cru|del|tà	cruelty	**e|tà**	age
ti|vù	TV	**me|tà**	half

➤ There are some common adverbs and conjunctions that have the stress on the final syllable and are spelled with an accent, for example, **per|ché**, **co|sì**, and **pe|rò**.

➪ *For more information about Spelling, see page 247.*

Words that stress an unexpected syllable

➤ Some words have the stress on a syllable which is neither the last, nor the next to the last.

u|ti|le	useful	por|*ta*|ti|le	portable
dif|*fi*|ci|le	difficult	*su*|bi|to	suddenly
nu|me|ro	number	pen|*to*|la	saucepan
ca|me|ra	bedroom	com|*pi*|to	homework
mo|du|lo	form		

ⓘ Note that <u>past participles</u> such as **fi|ni|to** (meaning *finished*) and **par|ti|to** (meaning *left*) <u>always</u> have the stress on the next to last syllable, but there are similar-looking words, such as **su|bi|to** (meaning *immediately*) and **com|pi|to** (meaning *homework*), that are not past participles, and that have the stress on a syllable you wouldn't expect.

> *Tip*
> When learning new vocabulary, check in the dictionary where the stress goes.

Stress in verb forms

➤ In the present tense, the **loro** form <u>always</u> has the stress on the same vowel as the **io** form:

io form		**loro form**	
par|lo	I speak	*par*|la|no	they speak
con|*si*|de|ro	I consider	con|*si*|de|ra|no	they consider
mi al|*le*|no	I'm training	si al|*le*|na|no	they're training

➤ In the future tense of all verbs the stress is on the last syllable of the **io** form and the **lui/lei** form. These two verb forms are spelled with an accent on the stressed vowel.

Future	
sa|*rò*	I will be
la|vo|re|*rò*	I will work
fi|ni|*rà*	it will finish
as|pet|te|*rà*	she'll wait

➤ The infinitive of **–are** verbs <u>always</u> has the stress on the **a** of the ending, for example **in|vi|*ta*|re** (meaning *to invite*) and **cam|mi|*na*|re** (meaning *to walk*). The infinitive of **–ire** verbs always has the stress on the **i** of the ending, for example **par|*ti*|re** (meaning *to leave*) and **fi|*ni*|re** (meaning *to finish*).

➤ The infinitive of **–ere** verbs <u>sometimes</u> has the stress on the first **e** of the ending, for example, **ve|*de*|re** (meaning *to see*) and **av|*e*|re** (meaning *to have*). However, these verbs <u>often</u> stress a syllable before the **–ere** ending, for example **ven|*de*|re** (meaning *to sell*), **di|*vi*|de|re** (meaning *to divide*) and **es|*se*|re** (meaning *to be*).

> *Tip*
> Remember that **–ere** verbs do not always stress the **e** of the ending, and take note of the stress when learning a new verb.

Different stress for different meanings

➤ In a few cases one word has two pronunciations, depending on its meaning. The following are some examples:

Normal stress	Meaning	Unusual stress	Meaning
an|co|ra	again	*an*|co|ra	anchor
ca|pi|ta|no	captain	ca|*pi*|ta|no	they happen
me|tro	meter	me|trò	metro

KEY POINTS

✔ Two-syllable words are stesssed on the first syllable, unless there's an accent.
✔ Longer words are usually stressed on the next to the last syllable.
✔ If the stress is on an unexpected vowel you need to learn it.

Test yourself

168 In each of the words below, identify which syllable is stressed.

    a in|gle|se...............

    b u|ni|ver|si|tà...............

    c nu|me|ro...............

    d par|la|no...............

    e dif|fi|ci|le...............

    f cit|tà...............

    g set|ti|ma|na...............

    h an|dreb|be|ro...............

    i pen|to|la...............

    j por|ta|ti|le...............

169 Match the Italian word with its translation, being careful of where the stress lies. The stressed vowel is in italics.

    a s*u*bito   again

    b anc*o*ra   immediately

    c m*e*tro   homework

    d *a*ncora   meter

    e c*o*mpito   anchor

Numbers

1	uno (un, una)	31	trentuno
2	due	40	quaranta
3	tre	41	quarantuno
4	quattro	50	cinquanta
5	cinque	58	cinquantotto
6	sei	60	sessanta
7	sette	63	sessantatré
8	otto	70	settanta
9	nove	75	settantacinque
10	dieci	80	ottanta
11	undici	81	ottantuno
12	dodici	90	novanta
13	tredici	99	novantanove
14	quattordici	100	cento
15	quindici	101	centouno
16	sedici	200	duecento
17	diciassette	203	duecentotré
18	diciotto	300	trecento
19	diciannove	400	quattrocento
20	venti	500	cinquecento
21	ventuno	600	seicento
22	ventidue	700	settecento
23	ventitré	800	ottocento
24	ventiquattro	900	novecento
25	venticinque	1000	mille
26	ventisei	1001	milleuno
27	ventisette	2000	duemila
28	ventotto	2500	duemilacinquecento
29	ventinove	1.000.000	un milione
30	trenta		(in English 1,000,000)

a pagina diciannove	on page nineteen
nel capitolo sette	in chapter seven
dieci per cento	ten per cent
seicento euro	six hundred euros
tremila persone	three thousand people

ⓘ Note that in the numbers 21, 31, 41 and so on, the final vowel of **venti**, **trenta** and **quaranta** is lost: **ventuno**, **trentuno**, **quarantuno**. The same thing happens with the numbers 28, 38, 48 and so on: **ventotto**, **trentotto**, **quarantotto**. When **tre** is combined with another number it takes an accent: **trentatré** (33), **centotré** (103), **milletré** (1003).

uno, un or una?

➤ In Italian the same word – **uno** – is used for the number *one* and the indefinite article *a*.

➤ When using **uno** as a number in front of a noun, follow the same rules as for the indefinite article.

un uomo	one man
uno scienzato	one scientist
una ragazza	one girl
un'*a*natra	one duck

⇨ *For more information on the* **Indefinite article**, *see page 21.*

➤ When replying to a question, use **uno** if what's referred to is masculine, and **una** if it's feminine.

Quanti giorni? – Uno.	How many days? – One.
Quante notti? – Una.	How many nights? – One.

➤ Use **uno** when counting, unless referring to something or someone feminine.

➤ Do NOT use **un** to translate *one hundred*, or *one thousand*.

cento metri	one hundred metres
mille euro	one thousand euros

➤ You do use **un** with **milione** (meaning *million*) and **miliardo** (meaning *thousand million*).

Quante persone? – Un milione.	How many people? – One million.
un milione di d*o*llari	one million dollars
un miliardo di euro	one thousand million euros

🛈 Note that when **un milione** and **un miliardo** are followed by a noun, **di** is added.

Which numbers have plurals?

➤ The only numbers which have plurals are **mille**, **milione**, and **miliardo**. **Due**, **tre**, **quattro** and so on are added to **mila** to make **duemila** (meaning *two thousand*), **tremila** (meaning *three thousand*) and **quattromila** (meaning *four thousand*).

mille euro	one thousand euros
diecimila euro	ten thousand euros
un milione di d*o*llari	one million dollars
venti milioni di d*o*llari	twenty million dollars
un miliardo di sterline	one thousand million pounds
due miliardi di sterline	two thousand million pounds

Full stop or comma?

➤ Use a full stop, not a comma, to separate thousands and millions in figures.

700.000 (settecentomila)	700,000 (seven hundred thousand)
5.000.000 (cinque milioni)	5,000,000 (five million)

➤ Use a comma instead of a decimal point to show decimals in Italian.

0,5 (zero virgola cinque)	0.5 (nought point five)
3,4 (tre virgola quattro)	3.4 (three point four)

1st	**primo (1°)**	
2nd	**secondo (2°)**	
3rd	**terzo (3°)**	
4th	**quarto (4°)**	
5th	**quinto (5°)**	
6th	**sesto (6°)**	
7th	**settimo (7°)**	
8th	**ottavo (8°)**	
9th	**nono (9°)**	
10th	**decimo (10°)**	
11th	**undicesimo (11°)**	
18th	**diciottesimo (18°)**	
21st	**ventunesimo (21°)**	
33rd	**trentatreesimo (33°)**	
100th	**centesimo (100°)**	
101st	**centunesimo (101°)**	
1000th	**millesimo (1000°)**	

Tip
Learn the first ten of these numbers.

➤ To make the others, take numbers such as **venti** and **trentotto**, drop the final vowel and add **–esimo**. If the number ends in **tre**, DON'T drop the final **e** before adding **–esimo**.

la ventesima settimana	the twentieth week
il trentottesimo anno	the thirty-eighth year
il loro trentatreesimo anniversario di matrimonio	their thirty-third wedding anniversary

➤ These numbers are adjectives and can be made masculine or feminine, singular or plural.

il quindicesimo piano	he fifteenth floor
la terza lezione	the third lesson
i primi piatti	the first courses
le loro seconde scelte	their second choices

[i] Note that when writing these numbers in figures you should use a little °, or ª, depending on whether what's referred to is masculine or feminine.

il 15° piano	the 15th floor
la 24ª giornata	the 24th day

➤ Roman numerals are often used for centuries, popes and monarchs.

il XIV secolo	the 14th century
Paolo VI	Paul VI
Enrico III	Henry III

⇨ *For more information on **Numbers used in dates**, see page 261.*

L'ora	**The time**
Che ora è? *or* **Che ore sono?**	What time is it?
È l'una meno venti.	It's twenty to one.
È l'una meno un quarto.	It's a quarter to one.
È l'una.	It's one o'clock.
È l'una e dieci.	It's ten past one.
È l'una e un quarto.	It's a quarter past one.
È l'una e mezza.	It's half past one.
Sono le due meno venticinque.	It's twenty-five to two.
Sono le due meno un quarto.	It's a quarter to two.
Sono le due.	It's two o'clock.
Sono le due e dieci.	It's ten past two.
Sono le due e un quarto.	It's a quarter past two.
Sono le due e mezza.	It's half past two.
Sono le tre.	It's three o'clock.

> *Tip*
> Use **sono le** for all times not involving **una** (meaning *one*).

A che ora?	**(At) what time?**
Arrivano oggi. – A che ora?	They're arriving today. – What time?

ⓘ Note that *at* is optional in English when asking what time something happens, but **a** must always be used in Italian.

a mezzanotte	at midnight
a mezzogiorno	at midday
all'una (del pomeriggio)	at one o'clock (in the afternoon)
alle otto (di sera)	at eight o'clock (in the evening)
alle 9:25 *or* **alle nove e venticinque**	at twenty-five past nine
alle 16:50 *or* **alle sedici e cinquanta**	at 16:50 *or* sixteen fifty

ⓘ Note that the twenty-four hour clock is often used in Italy.

La data	**The date**
I giorni della settimana	**The days of the week**
lunedì	Monday
martedì	Tuesday
mercoledì	Wednesday
giovedì	Thursday
venerdì	Friday
sabato	Saturday
domenica	Sunday

Quando?	**When?**
lunedì	on Monday
di lunedì	on Mondays
tutti i lunedì	every Monday
martedì scorso	last Tuesday
venerdì prossimo	next Friday

For further explanation of grammatical terms, please see pages viii–xii.

sabato della settimana prossima	a week on Saturday
sabato tra due settimane	two weeks on Saturday

ⓘ Note that days of the week <u>DON'T</u> have a capital letter in Italian.

I mesi dell'anno — The months of the year

gennaio	January
febbraio	February
marzo	March
aprile	April
maggio	May
giugno	June
luglio	July
agosto	August
settembre	September
ottobre	October
novembre	November
dicembre	December

Quando?	When?
in *or* **a febbraio**	in February
il primo dicembre	on December 1st
il due dicembre	on December 2nd
nel 1999 (millenovecento-novantanove)	in 1999 (in nineteen ninety-nine)
il primo dicembre 2000	on December 1st 2000
nel duemilasei	in two thousand and six

ⓘ Note that months of the year <u>DON'T</u> have a capital letter in Italian.

> *Tip*
> In Italian you use **il primo** for the first day of the month. For all the other days you use the equivalent of *two*, *three*, *four* and so on.
> **il tre maggio**   the third of May

Frasi utili — Useful phrases

Quando?	When?
oggi	today
stamattina	this morning
stasera	this evening

Ogni quanto?	How often?
ogni giorno	every day
ogni due giorni	every other day
una volta alla settimana	once a week
due volte alla settimana	twice a week
una volta al mese	once a month

Quando è successo?	**When did it happen?**
di mattina	in the morning
di sera	in the evening
ieri	yesterday
ieri mattina	yesterday morning
ieri sera	yesterday evening/last night
ieri notte	last night
l'altro ieri	the day before yesterday
una settimana fa	a week ago
due settimane fa	two weeks ago
la settimana scorsa	last week
l'anno scorso	last year
Quando succederà?	**When is it going to happen?**
domani	tomorrow
domani mattina	tomorrow morning
domani sera	tomorrow evening/night
dopodomani	the day after tomorrow
fra *or* **tra due giorni**	in two days' time
fra *or* **tra una settimana**	in a week's time
fra *or* **tra quindici giorni**	in two weeks' time
il mese prossimo	next month
l'anno prossimo	next year

Solutions

1
a una mela **a fruit; feminine noun**
b la notte **opposite of day; feminine noun**
c un armadio **a piece of furniture; masculine noun**
d un delfino **a marine mammal; masculine noun**
e l'acqua **a liquid; feminine noun**

2
a una
b un
c una
d un
e un
f una
g un
h una
i una
j un

3
a una gatta
b un'attrice
c una cuoca
d una fotografa
e una ragazza
f una scrittrice
g un'italiana
h una professoressa
i una pittrice
j una leonessa

4
a la nipote
b un'italiana
c una leonessa
d la giornalista
e la professoressa
f una gatta
g una collega
h la dentista
i una turista
j una ragazza

5
a la fine **the end**
b il programma **the programme**
c la mano **the hand**
d l'occasione **the opportunity**
e il mare **the sea**

6
a mesi
b ragazzi
c gatti
d donne
e francesi
f settimane
g regole
h treni
i mele
j giorni

7
a luogo
b italiani
c ciclisti
d pittore
e topo
f moto
g dita
h mobile
i amiche
j problemi

8
a 2
b 2
c 1
d 1
e 2
f 2
g 1
h 2
i 2
j 1

9
a i capelli **hair**
b i mobili **furniture**
c un consiglio **a piece of advice**
d le notizie **the news**
e le uova **the eggs**

10
a l'
b i
c lo
d le
e gli
f la
g il
h l'
i gli
j le

11
a nell'albergo
b alla stazione
c sul pavimento
d dal concerto
e agli stadi
f sulle strade
g del ragazzo
h al cinema
i dall'aeroporto
j sulla spiaggia

12
a della
b delle
c dello
d del
e dei
f dell'
g degli
h del
i dei
j delle

13
a le
b il
c all'
d la
e il
f le
g la
h i
i alle
j nel

14
a una
b uno
c un
d un'
e un
f un
g uno
h una
i un'
j un

15
a Che lavoro fa tuo fratello? **Fa l'avvocato.**
b Hai fratelli? **Ho un fratello e una sorella.**
c Perché non vieni al cinema? **Non ho soldi.**
d Quanto costa il divano? **Costa mille sterline.**
e Tuo padre è professore? **No, è medico.**

16
a Non ho macchina.
b C'è pane?
c È ingeniere./Fa l'ingeniere.
d Non ha computer.
e Vendono gelati, uova e frutta.
f Che sorpresa!
g Mio fratello ha molti soldi.
h Che bello!
i Ci sono cento bambini nella scuola.
j Non ci sono posti liberi.

17
a italiana
b simpatico
c bianche
d blu
e veloci

Solutions

f francese
g nera
h interessanti
i pop
j alte

18 a strade pericolose
b siti interessanti
c computer nuovi
d ragazzi alti
e magliette rosa
f fiori rossi
g macchine veloci
h persone snob
i scrittori italiani
j case nuove

19 a bei fiori
b un grande pittore/una grande pittrice
c un buon uomo
d un bell'albero
e buon viaggio!
f una bella donna
g un buon strumento
h un bel vestito
i buoni studenti
j una gran torre/una grande torre

20 a Povera Maria!
b una macchina cara
c bambini poveri
d il suo nuovo lavoro
e questo ragazzo
f una città molto bella
g una bella borsa
h mio fratello
i capelli biondi
j quello studente

21 a interessanti
b pronta
c tristi
d bianco
e bei
f buona
g bianchi
h vecchie
i buona
j inglesi

22 a delle storie **interessanti**
b i ragazzi **alti**
c una casa **molto bella**
d le città **italiane**
e un bambino **molto bravo**

23 a Carlo è più alto di Luca.
b Luca è meno alto di Carlo.

c Roma è più grande di Siena.
d Maria è intelligente come Paola.
e Il nero è più bello del verde.
f Giovanni è meno ambizioso di suo fratello.
g Il negozio è vicino come il ristorante.
h L'aereo è meno economico del treno.
i Lucia è più simpatica di Silvia.
j Silvia è meno simpatica di Lucia.

24 a la più alta
b il più caro
c il più intelligente
d la più interessante
e le meno comode
f i migliori
g il più economico
h il più cattivo/il peggiore
i la più alta
j il meno ambizioso

25 a bellissimo
b educatissimi
c carissime
d stanchissimo
e elegantissima
f altissima
g grandissima
h lunghissimo
i buonissima
j piccolissime

26 a questo
b questa
c questi
d queste
e questa
f questi
g questo
h questa
i questi
j queste

27 a Quei ragazzi sono intelligenti.
b Quel giardino è bello.
c Quell'albero è grande.
d Quelle donne sono inglesi.
e Mi piace quella gonna.
f Quelle macchine sono vecchie.
g Quello zaino è pesante.

h Quegli studenti sono maleducati.
i Quella ragazza è molto simpatica.
j Quei pantaloni sono cari.

28 a quella
b questi
c queste/quelle
d quegli
e questa
f questo/quel
g questa/quella
h quelle
i questa
j questi/quei

29 a Che giorno è oggi? **È mercoledì.**
b Quante mele ci sono? **Ce ne sono quattro.**
c Quale gusto preferisci? **Il cioccolato.**
d A che ora si alza la mattina? **Alle otto.**
e Quanti biscotti vuoi? **Due, per favore.**

30 a Quale/Che vestito preferisci?
b A che ora dobbiamo partire?
c Quanta pasta vuoi?
d Quante macchine ci sono?
e Quali voli sono i più economici?
f Quale/Che film hai visto?
g Quali/Che programmi hanno?
h Quanto zucchero ci vuole?
i Quanti alberi vedi?
j Quali studenti sono i più educati?

31 a le mie scarpe
b la sua valigia
c la loro macchina
d la vostra scuola
e il mio portafoglio
f il suo indirizzo
g i loro biglietti
h la sua camera
i i suoi amici
j le tue chiavi

32 a il mio
b il suo

Solutions

c i tuoi
d le mie
e il nostro
f i loro
g le vostre
h i nostri
i i tuoi
j la mia

33
a suo
b i miei
c la sua
d nostro
e la sua
f mio
g i loro
h tua
i il suo
j nostro

34
a padre
b fratello maggiore
c mani
d madre
e amico
f sorelle
g indirizzo
h gonna
i famiglia
j portafoglio

35
a ogni
b molti
c pochi
d tanta
e qualche volta
f troppi
g molti
h parecchio
i altro
j qualsiasi

36
a Non abbiamo visto **nessun treno.**
b Ciascuno studente **ha comprato il libro.**
c Vado a Parigi **fra qualche mese.**
d Guarda la televisione **tutta la giornata.**
e Ha avuto **tanti problemi.**

37
a io
b lui/lei
c noi
d loro
e voi
f io
g tu

h noi
i lui
j lui

38
a your best friend **tu**
b a group of teachers **voi**
c your doctor **lei**
d your grandmother **tu**
e your manager **lei**

39
a Vado al cinema.
b Non mi piace nuotare. — Neanche a me.
c Chi è? — È lei!
d Che ore sono? — Sono le due.
e Lui viene alla festa, tu fai come vuoi.
f Vanno anche loro.
g Lei va a letto, ma lui no.
h Fa freddo oggi.
i Ci pensano loro.
j Maria, tu cosa pensi?

40
a le
b lo
c la
d l'
e li
f li
g le
h la
i lo
j l'

41
a Lo guarda.
b Non li vediamo.
c Ci cerca.
d La borsa è bellissima. La compro.
e Giulia, ho un panino, lo vuoi?
f Li conosce.
g La conosco.
h Il cane? L'abbiamo preso con noi.
i Vi invita tutti alla festa.
j Mi ama.

42
a Gli chiedo permesso.
b Le scrive.
c Gli abbiamo dato le chiavi.
d Gli hanno detto la verità.
e Le telefono.
f Gli danno i soldi.
g Gli scrivo una lettera.
h Le chiedono di venire.
i Gli hai dato le notizie?
j Claudio le ha dato il suo numero di telefono.

43
a Le piacciono i cani.
b Non mi importa il prezzo.
c Gli interessa il cinema francese.
d Marta, ti piace questa borsa?
e Mi ha chiesto di venire.
f Ci chiedono il permesso.
g Daniele e Mario, vi telefono domani.
h Non gli interessano i libri.
i Non mi piace la pioggia.
j Ci hanno dato un regalo.

44
a io/tu
b ti/gli
c io/tu
d le/gli
e me/tu
f io/vi
g ci/io
h tu/ci
i gli/io
j io/ci

45
a Vuole venire **con me.**
b Lei è più intelligente **di lui.**
c Questi pantaloni **piacciono a lei.**
d Il film non interessa **a loro**
e Ama solo **te.**

46
a Mi aiuti?
b Mi dai un bicchiere d'acqua?
c Ci aspetti?
d Gli dai la palla?
e Lo finisci?
f Lo chiami domani?
g Le dici la verità?
h Ci dai una mano?
i Lo fai subito?
j Mi guardi?

47
a Me lo dai?
b Ve la mando domani.
c Te li portiamo.
d Gliela dico.
e Ce li spedisce.
f Gliele dai?
g Te le do.
h Me le comprano.
i Ve la facciamo vedere
j Gliel'ha promesso

48
a Puoi mandarmelo? **Can you send me it?**

Solutions

b Puoi darglieli? **Can you give them to her?**

c Puoi comprarceli? **Can you buy them for us?**

d Puoi prenderglielo? **Can you take it for them?**

e Puoi dirglielo? **Can you tell her it?**

49 a la mia
b il suo
c i suoi
d le sue
e il mio
f la sua
g i suoi
h la sua
i i miei
j il loro

50 a Questo cappello è il suo, signore?
b La borsa nera è la mia.
c La nostra casa è più grande della loro.
d Quale macchina è la sua?
e Quel gatto è il nostro.
f I suoi genitori e i miei vengono a cena.
g Non è il mio amico, è il tuo.
h Quelle scarpe sono le sue.
i Non è il tuo portafoglio, è il mio.
j I bambini sono i loro.

51 a Quante ne vuoi?
b Ne prendo la metà.
c Ne volete?
d Ne ha paura.
e Ne ho scritto.
f Ne sono stufi.
g Ne è contenta.
h Ne sei sicura?
i Ne hai bisogno?
j Ne è conscia.

52 a Parliamo del film. **Sì, parliamone.**
b Quanti fiori vuole, signora? **Ne voglio dieci, per favore.**
c Hai bisogno della matita? **No, no ne ho più bisogno.**
d Perchè non hai finito il libro? **Ne ero stufo.**
e Vuoi del vino? **Ne ho, grazie.**

53 a Vuole parlarne.
b Ne hanno paura.
c Ne prende un po'.
d Cani? Ne ha quattro.
e Ne abbiamo sentito parlare.
f Dagliene una nera.
g C'è la torta? Ne voglio!
h Ne siamo molto contenti.
i Non se ne accorgono.
j Ne ho, grazie.

54 a Maria ha rotto la finestra? **No, lei non c'entra.**
b Credi la sua storia? **Non ci credo per niente.**
c Prepariamo noi il pranzo? **No, ci pensano loro.**
d Parli inglese? **No, non ci capisco niente.**
e Vuoi venire al cinema? **Ci penserò.**

55 a Non ci crede.
b Cosa c'entra?
c Cosa c'entra il tempo?
d Non sanno che farci.
e Loro non c'entrano.
f Viene alla festa? — Ci penserà.
g Non vogliamo pensarci.
h Ha preso la macchina? — Non ci ho fatto caso.
i Quel film? Non ci ho capito niente.
j Non ci pensa più.

56 a niente
b nessuno
c nessuna
d nessuno
e niente
f nessuno
g niente
h nessuna
i nessuno
j nessuno

57 a Vengono tutti stasera?
b L'ha mangiato tutto.
c Molti di loro vanno al cinema.
d Mi piace questa sciarpa, ma preferisco l'altra.
e Ci sono turisti? — Sì, alcuni.
f Ci sono delle torte — Sì,

parecchie.
g C'è un libro per ognuno di voi.
h I biglietti costano dodici euro ciascuno.
i Signore, desidera altro?
j Guarda le macchine! Sono così tante.

58 a che
b chi
c che
d che
e cui
f cui
g cui
h che
i chi
j che

59 a The woman I know. **La signora che conosco.**
b The person I was talking about. **La persona di cui parlavo.**
c Someone I admire. **Qualcuno che ammiro.**
d The family we go on holiday with. **La famiglia con cui andiamo in vacanza.**
e The boy that you saw. **Il ragazzo che hai visto.**

60 a quello che/quelli che
b quelli che/quella che
c quelle che/quello che
d quella che/quelle che
e quelli che/quella che
f quello che/quella che
g quella che/quelli che
h quelle che/quello che
i quello che/quelle che
j quelli che/quella che

61 a quanti/quali
b chi
c quanto
d quanto
e che/che cosa
f chi
g quale
h quante/quali
i quanto
j che/che cosa

62 a Quali sono le stagioni dell'anno? **Sono la primavera, l'estate, l'autunno e l'inverno.**

Solutions

b Che cos'è questo? **È un giocattolo.**

c Qual è il tuo film preferito? **È 'La Strada'.**

d Che cosa sono quelle? **Sono zucche.**

e Qual'è il suo nome? **È Luca.**

63 a Di chi è quella macchina?

b Chi te l'ha detto?

c Con chi parlava?

d Di chi sono queste scarpe?

e Quale squadra ha vinto la partita?

f Cosa vuole da bere?

g Zucchero? Quanto ce ne vuole?

h Quante di quelle donne parlano inglese?

i A chi l'ha dato?

j Quale sciarpa preferisci?

64 a questa

b questi

c questo

d questa

e questa

f queste

g questo

h questi

i questi

j questa

65 a Quella è mia sorella. **That's my sister.**

b Quanto costano quelli? **How much do those cost?**

c Questo è il mio cane. **This is my dog.**

d Questi sono i miei occhiali. **These are my glasses.**

e Quella donna è attrice. **That woman is an actor.**

66 a giocano

b parla

c arriva

d studio

e mangiate

f abitano

g compri

h guardiamo

i entra

j ascolto

67 a Mangiamo **tutti insieme.**

b Non **parlo inglese.**

c Valentina studia **all'università di Bologna.**

d I miei **arrivano domani.**

e Guardate **la televisione?**

68 a Studia molto.

b Lui ascolta la musica, ma lei no.

c Fumano troppo.

d Lavoro in un ufficio.

e Abitate tutti in quella casa?

f Compri queste scarpe?

g Quella borsa costa troppo.

h Mio figlio gioca in giardino.

i Mi passa quel libro, per favore?

j Prepariamo il pranzo.

69 a piove

b vende

c ripetiamo

d credi

e perde

f vedono

g permette

h prendo

i splende

j dividete

70 a Paolo non crede ai fantasmi.

b Le ragazze ricevono una buona notizia.

c Non prendi mai il treno?

d Mia madre vende la sua casa.

e Non vedo una soluzione.

f Perdiamo tempo con questo problema.

g Quando riceve Lei lo stipendio?

h Dipende dal tempo.

i Quale strada prendete?

j La mia amica non ci crede.

71 a Non hanno una macchina. **Prendono sempre il treno.**

b Perde spesso le chiavi. **Bisogna comprare un portachiavi.**

c Sono povera! **Spendi troppi soldi.**

d Che tempo fa oggi? **Fa caldo e splende il sole.**

e Dove sono le mie scarpe? **Non le vedo.**

72 a puliscono

b capisce

c dormite

d soffre

e serviamo

f preferisci

g parte

h aprono

i sento

j finisce

73 a (Lei) capisce tutto.

b Preferiamo l'altro.

c Il film finisce alle nove.

d Partite tutti stasera?

e I cani dormono sotto il tavolo.

f A che cosa serve?

g Fortunatamente non sentiamo il traffico da casa nostra.

h Giorgio pulisce la sua macchina ogni giorno.

i Mi apri la bottiglia?

j I gatti soffrono il caldo.

74 a Mio fratello dorme sempre fino a tardi.

b Paola finisce il lavoro.

c A che cosa serve il coltello?

d Puliamo la casa domani.

e Lui preferisce quello nero.

f Sentite gli uccelli la mattina?

g Molte persone soffrono la fame.

h Mia sorella apre la porta.

i A che ora parti?

j Le lezioni finiscono alle cinque.

75 a pone

b traduco

c andiamo

d propongono.

e avete

f conduce

g fai

h vanno

i ha

j faccio

Solutions

76
a Da quanto tempo abiti in Francia? **Da tre anni.**
b Parla bene l'inglese? **Sì, lo studia da cinque anni.**
c Claudia, dove sei? **Arrivo!**
d È rotta la finestra. **Ci penso io.**
e Conosci Londra? **Sì, ci vado spesso.**

77
a Aspetto da venti minuti.
b Non mangia niente?
c I legumi fanno bene.
d Il concerto comincia fra un'ora.
e Se lei chiama, lui viene.
f I miei genitori abitano a Roma.
g Quale gonna preferisci?
h Studio l'italiano da tre anni.
i Cosa facciamo più tardi?
j I bambini hanno i capelli biondi.

78
a è
b sta
c sta
d sono
e sono
f stiamo
g è
h sono
i siete
j sei

79
a Dove sei? **Sono nel soggiorno.**
b Come sta tuo padre? **Sta meglio, grazie.**
c Quanti sono i bambini alla festa? **Sono dieci.**
d Perché non viene? **Vuole stare solo.**
e Chi è? **Sono io.**

80
a sta
b sono
c è
d sono
e sta
f è
g stanno
h è
i sono
j sta

81
a mangiando
b cercando
c arrivando

d scrivendo
e tornando
f dormendo
g cercando
h parlando
i finendo
j guardando

82
a sta mangiando
b stanno dormendo
c sta arrivando
d sta parlando
e stai leggendo
f sta studiando
g stiamo lavorando
h stai cercando
i stanno pulendo
j sta ascoltando

83
a È tardi. **Perché stanno dormendo?**
b Una biografia politica. **Cosa stai leggendo?**
c No, ho finito. **Stai mangiando?**
d Sta comprando il pane. **Cosa fa la mamma?**
e No, stanno arrivando. **Flavio e Dora sono alla festa?**

84
a Finisci i compiti, Riccardo!
b Aspettiamo qui!
c State bravi, ragazzi!
d Prenda questo, signore!
e Aspettate un attimo, signori!
f Dormi, Giuseppe!
g Andiamo alla festa!
h Di' la verità, Mario!
i Faccia pure, signora!
j Finite tutto, ragazze!

85
a Ho sonno. **Dormi!**
b Non sappiamo quali scarpe prendere. **Prendete quelle!**
c Vieni, mamma! **Aspetta un attimo!**
d Ho bisogno di un ombrello **Prenda questo, signore.**
e C'è il sole. **Andiamo al mare!**

86
a Aspettami, Claudia!
b Daglielo!
c Fallo subito!
d Aspettateci!
e Prendiamolo!

f Diteglielo!
g Ci passi il sale signore!
h Guardami, papà!
i Mi dia la chiave, signora!
j Mandatemi una cartolina!

87
a la tua borsa
b le ragazze
c lo zucchero
d il tuo indirizzo
e signora
f i guanti
g le lettere
h le mele
i il tuo nome
j le fragole

88
a La torta? **Mangiala!**
b Le scarpe? **Daglięle!**
c I soldi? **Prendeteli!**
d Il regalo? **Mandiamoglielo!**
e L'autobus? **Lo aspetti, signore!**

89
a Non mangiare tutto!
b Non darmi la borsa!/Non mi dare la borsa!
c Non guardate, ragazzi!
d Non prenderlo!/Non lo prendere!
e Non mi lasciate da sola!/ Non lasciatemi da sola!
f Non toccare il disegno!
g Non li guardino, signori!
h Non mangiamola!/Non la mangiamo!
c Non parlare con i tuoi amici!
d Non partire senza di loro!

90
a Non toccarlo!
b Fallo subito!
c Non mi parlare!/Non parlarmi!
d Andiamo al cinema!
e Non mangiare la torta!
f Daglielo!
g Non aspettiamoli!/Non li aspettiamo!
h Non metterlo lì!/Non lo mettere lì!
i Non guardino, signori!
j Non dirlo!/Non lo dire!

91
a È caldo! **Non toccarlo!**
b Ho sonno! **Vai a dormire!**
c Ho fame! **Mangi un panino!**

Solutions

d Abbiamo freddo!
Mettete le giacche!
e Abbiamo paura! **Non vi preoccupate!**

92
a ti
b mi
c si
d si
e vi
f ti
g si
h ti
i ci
j mi

93
a annoia
b ricordo
c svegliate
d vestono
e chiede
f laviamo
g arrabbia
h chiami
i fa
j fermano

94
a A che ora si sveglia tua figlia?
b Come si chiama tua sorella?
c Dobbiamo alzarci./Ci dobbiamo alzare.
d Si stanno annoiando?
e Non ti bruciare!/Non bruciarti!
f Ci incontriamo spesso al mercato.
g Vi divertite, ragazzi?
h Siediti!
i Laura si sta vestendo per la festa.
j Ci amiamo.

95
a sono alzati
b è addormentata
c siete lavate
d siamo incontrati
e sono pettinate
f sei svegliato
g sono fatto
h è arrabbiata
i sono fermati
j sono abbronzati.

96
a Si è lavata i capelli ieri mattina.
b Mio fratello si è rotto la gamba.
c Come si dice 'dog' in italiano?
d I bambini si sono addormentati in macchina.
e Mi sono messo il cappotto.
f Non si fa così.
g I nostri vicini si odiano.
h Si è bruciato la mano.
i Vi conoscete?
j Ci siamo incontrati al parco.

97
a finirò
b partiremo
c cominicerà
d mangerai
e diranno
f andrò
g vorrete
h vedremo
i sapranno
j farà

98
a verranno
b andranno
c comprerà
d vedremo
e potrò
f dovrete
g farà
h viaggeranno
i parlerà
j finirete

99
a Farà freddo domani.
b Andrò dal medico la settimana prossima.
c Non potranno aiutarci.
d Verrete tutti al cinema?
e Lo saprà stasera.
f Ce lo diranno fra qualche giorno.
g Gliene parlerai?
h Non ti crederà.
i Mangerò più tardi.
j Signore, quando manderà il libro?

100
a sarebbe
b vorrei
c dovremmo
d potrebbe
e avreste
f comincerebbero
g mangeresti
h daresti
i verrei
j sapreste

101
a Quando comincerebbe il lavoro? **Probabilmente fra due giorni.**
b Vorresti mangiare con noi? **No, grazie. Ho già mangiato.**
c A che ora arriva Domenico? **Dovrebbe arrivare verso le dieci.**
d Non hanno soldi. **Potrebbero vendere la macchina.**
e Ti piacerebbe vivere in Islanda? **No, non vivrei mai in un paese freddo.**

102
a Sarebbe bello vederti.
b Quei bambini guarderebbero la televisione tutto il giorno.
c Non mangerei questi funghi.
d Quanto pagherebbero per la casa?
e Non sa se sarebbe capace di farlo.
f Dovresti telefonare a tua madre.
g Saremmo contenti di aiutarli.
h Mio figlio avrebbe paura del cane.
i Non potrebbe finire il lavoro.
j Vorreste venire tutti con noi?

103
a cominciava
b giocavano
c eravamo
d faceva
e bevevano
f diceva
g parlavo
h avevano
i stavi
j aspettavate

104
a si divertivano
b lavorava
c giocavamo
d faceva
e sapeva
f eravate
g dicevano
h parlavano
i aveva
j credevano

Solutions

105
a Mentre parlavi l'ho visto arrivare.
b Cosa guardava?/Cosa stava guardando?
c Gli ho dato un bacio mentre dormiva.
d Aspettavo da due ore.
e Faceva tanto caldo che non potevamo neanche uscire.
f Da quanto tempo studiavi l'inglese?
g Traducevo il libro quando Giulia mi ha chiamato.
h Era un uomo molto simpatico.
i Da studente lavorava in un bar.
j Ci vedevamo ogni sabato.

106
a chiuso
b comprato
c letto
d voluto
e detto
f messa
g fatto
h viste
i finito
j offerto

107
a ha parlato
b ho visto
c hanno scritto
d ha aperto
e è finito
f ho creduto
g abbiamo speso
h hanno risposto
i ha fatto
j avete preso

108
a Le tue scarpe? Non le ho viste.
b Quale squadra ha vinto?
c Chi te l'ha detto?
d Abbiamo deciso di comprare la macchina blu.
e Dove ho messo quel libro?
f Hai chiamato tua madre? — No, non l'ho chiamata.
g Ha comprato delle fragole al mercato.
h Non gli hanno ancora scritto.
i Abbiamo preso il treno per andare in montagna.
j Ha prenotato, signore?

109
a arrivati
b andata
c alzato
d rimaste
e uscita
f diventati
g piaciuta
h divertiti
i venuti
j successo

110
a Conosci Londra? **No, non ci sono mai stato.**
b Cosa avete fatto ieri? **Niente, siamo rimasti a casa tutto il giorno.**
c Viene Maria alla festa? **Sì, sono riuscita a convincerla.**
d Hai dormito da tua sorella? **No, sono tornata a casa mia.**
e È andato anche Luca? **Sì, è venuto con noi.**

111
a Le foto mi sono piaciute molto.
b Il regalo è arrivato ieri.
c I bambini si sono lavati le mani prima di mangiare.
d Mio fratello è uscito con degli amici ieri sera.
e Siamo andati a teatro la settimana scorsa.
f Sei mai stata a Palermo, Giovanna?
g Sei andato a scuola stamattina?
h Mi sono alzato alle otto.
i Quante persone sono venute?
j È diventato molto maleducato.

112
a fu
b parlò
c partirono
d ebbero
e credetti
f parlammo
g furono
h partì
i parlai
j avesti

113
a Partimmo la mattina.
b Ci fu un problema.
c Non lo credette.
d Ebbe la febbre.
e Parlasti con la ragazza.
f Le case furono costruite

nel 1920.
g Partirono in fretta.
h Gli credetti.
i Mia madre fu malata.
j Non ebbe speranza.

114
a mangiato
b dimenticato
c dormito
d vista
e lavorato
f parlato
g letto
h scritte
i prenotato
j sbagliato.

115
a aveva parlato
b avevo visto
c avevano scritto
d aveva aperto
e era finito
f avevo creduto
g avevamo speso
h avevano risposto
i aveva fatto
j aveva preso

116
a Le tue scarpe? Non le avevo viste.
b Mi ha detto quale squadra aveva vinto.
c Chi te l'aveva detto?
d Avevamo deciso di comprare la macchina blu.
e Dove avevo messo quel libro?
f Avevi chiamato tua madre? — No, non l'avevo chiamata.
g Aveva comprato delle fragole al mercato.
h Non gli avevano mai scritto.
i Avevamo preso il treno per andare in montagna.
j Lei aveva letto il libro, signore?

117
a venuti
b divertita
c addormentato
d rimasto
e arrivata
f diventato
g piaciuto
h andati
i venuta
j successo

Solutions

118
a I fiori mi erano piaciuti molto.
b Il regalo era arrivato prima.
c I bambini si erano lavati le mani prima di mangiare.
d Mio marito era uscito con degli amici quella sera.
e Eravamo andati al cinema.
f Eri mai stata a Londra, Marta?
g Tua figlia era andata a scuola quel giorno?
h Mi ero alzato alle dieci.
i Quante persone erano venute alla festa?
j Era diventato molto maleducato.

119
a costruita
b invitati
c guardata
d cambiata
e rimasti
f scritte
g fatti
h conosciuta
i festeggiato
j comprato

120
a Ha mandato la lettera stamattina. **È stata già mandata.**
b Mi hanno rubato la borsa ieri. **È stata rubata ieri.**
c Si invitano tutti alla festa. **Tutti sono invitati.**
d Hanno cambiato l'indirizzo. **È stato cambiato.**
e Si mangia il prosciutto col melone. **È mangiato col melone.**

121
a La festa è stata rinviata.
b I biglietti saranno controllati più tardi.
c Erano stati feriti dall'esplosione.
d La casa è stata venduta il mese scorso.
e Queste uova sono state comprate ieri.
f Saranno criticati dalla loro famiglia.
g È stato ucciso dal suo amico.

h L'inglese è parlato in molti paesi.
i Sei stato invitato?
j Saremo costretti a tornare a casa.

122
a entrando
b credendo
c dicendo
d vedendo
e parlando
f facendo
g essendo
h andando
i cominciando
j spendendo

123
a cercando
b entrando
c cantando
d parlando
e piangendo
f dicendo
g ascoltando
h finendo
i dormendo
j vedendo

124
a Sentendosi male, **è andato a letto.**
b Stavo leggendo il giornale, **quando mi ha chiamato.**
c Volendo, **potrebbe vendere la casa.**
d Vedendomi piangere, **è venuto ad abbracciarmi.**
e Incontrandoci alla stazione, **siamo andati a bere un caffè.**

125
a Pioveva da una settimana.
b Stava piovendo?
c Fa sempre brutto tempo a gennaio.
d È vero che è arrabbiata.
e Bisogna/É necessario prenotare?
f Vengono? — Pare di no.
g Sarebbe bello vederli.
h Era Natale.
i É tardi.
j Ho dimenticato il libro. — Non importa.

126
a Basta? **Sì, grazie.**
b Che tempo faceva? **Nevicava da due giorni quando siamo arrivati.**

c Perché vuoi andare a letto? **È tardi.**
d Fa notte. **Bisogna accendere la luce.**
e Vendono la casa? **Pare di sì.**

127
a venga
b parli
c creda
d finiscano
e sia
f dica
g dia
h arrivino
i vada
j faccia

128
a Penso/Credo che la sua decisione sia giusto.
b Non voglio che mi vedano.
c Può darsi che non venga.
d I miei fratelli vogliono che li aiutiamo.
e Pensi/Credi che possa farlo?
f Spero che sia contento.
g È meglio che me ne vada.
h Vuole che Lucia traduca la lettera.
i Penso/Credo che siano a casa.
j Vuole che partino domani.

129
a sia
b abbia
c faccia
d vadano
e venga
f possa
g siano
h faccia
i abbiano
j scelga

130
a Penso/Credo che possano venire.
b Ti dispiace che lei non possa andare?
c Sono certi che è qui.
d È un peccato che piova.
e So che è francese.
f Spero che tua madre stia bene.
g Può darsi che non vengano.
h È un peccato che i bambini siano malati.

Solutions

i Sanno che esce stasera.
j Sei contenta che partano?

131 a Non credo/penso che l'abbia fatto.
b Penso/Credo che sia partita alle otto.
c È possibile che sia stato un errore.
d Spero che non si siano fatto male.
e Mi dispiace che non siano venuti.
f Non l'ho fatto io, penso che sia stato lui.
g Spero che siano partiti presto stamattina.
h Maria è contenta che suo fratello sia venuto alla festa.
i Suppongo che ti abbia detto la verità.
j Pensi/Credi che sia uscito con loro?

132 a Penso che sia stata giusta. **Secondo me è stata giusta.**
b Non credo che l'abbia preso. **Secondo me non l'ha preso.**
c Spero che tu abbia fatto del tuo meglio. **Hai fatto del tuo meglio, spero.**
d È possibile che non siano venuti. **Forse non sono venuti.**
e Può darsi che se ne sia andata. **Forse se n'è andata.**

133 a Se fossi in te, non andrei.
b Voleva che finissimo alle dieci.
c Anche se venisse, non sarebbe contenta.
d Volevo che me desse la borsa.
e Se solo avessimo dei soldi!
f Se sapessero, si sarebbero arrabbiati.
g Voleva che parlassi con il suo professore.
h Volevano che finissi i miei compiti.
i Anche se ti credessi, non telo darei.
j Se solo me lo dicesse!

134 a dessimo **dare**
b facessero **fare**
c dicessi **dire**
d foste **essere**
e stesse **stare**

135 a credessero **loro**
b parlasse **lui**
c finiste **voi**
d dicessi **io**
e fossimo **noi**

136 a a
b di
c di
d ad
e di
f a
g a
h ad
i di
j di

137 a Stava per uscire quando sono arrivati.
b Mia sorella non sa nuotare.
c Dobbiamo partire.
d Mi piace sciare.
e Si è tagliata i capelli.
f L'ho sentito cantare.
g Vogliono comprare una casa nuova.
h Sei contento di vederla?
i Posso entrare?
j Non sappiamo cosa vuol dire.

138 a Vuoi **aspettare?**
b Hanno smesso **di ridere.**
c Non sappiamo **farlo.**
d Imparavo **a suonare il violino.**
e Potresti aiutarmi **a lavare la macchina?**

139 a del
b a
c a
d di
e a
f a
g dal
h di
i dalla
j a

140 a Aspetto mio fratello.
b Dipende dai bambini.
c Ho chiesto qualcosa da bere.
d Ascoltavamo la radio.
e Sono stufo del lavoro.
f I bambini guardavano i cavalli.
g Non permettono a Marco di uscire la sera.
h Mi ricordo di quel film.
i Ha già pagato la birra.
j Stava cercando le sue scarpe.

141 a Paolo ha bisogno di soldi.
b Gianni non si fida di loro.
c Quando arrivi a Milano?
d Elena fa male spesso a suo fratello.
e Il ragazzo sta guardando l'albero.
f Flavio mi chiede come si chiama mia sorella
g Le ragazze ridono del film.
h I giocatori partecipano alla partita.
i I fratelli discutono di politica.
j I musicisti ascoltano il concerto.

142 a A tua sorella piace Parigi?
b Mi piacciono queste scarpe.
c Non gli piacciono i cani.
d Ci piace nuotare.
e Ti piacerebbe quel film.
f Le è piaciuto il libro?
g Mi restano due mele.
h Mi mancano.
i Quella musica non piace a tutti.
j Pensi che interesserebbe ai ragazzi?

143 a manca
b restano
c piace
d piacciono
e piace
f importa
g interessano
h mancano
i piace
j piacciono

144 a Maria non conosce la strada.
b Lucia non è qui.
c Mario non viene mai.
d I ragazzi non si incontrano più.

Solutions

e Chiara non mi vede.
f Non ci piace il tennis.
g Teresa non abita qui.
h Non viene nessuno.
i Non vanno né Francesca né sua sorella.
j Paolo non lo trova da nessuna parte.

145 a Non fa mai niente la domenica.
b Non abbiamo visto nessuno.
c Non vogliono niente.
d I miei genitori non ci sono mai stati.
e Non ci vediamo più la sera.
f Non riuscivano a trovarlo da nessuna parte.
g Viene o no?
h Non hai mangiato niente.
i Chi hai visto alla festa? — Nessuno.
j Ho detto di no.

146 a Le chiavi non sono qui.
b Pietro non l'ha mangiato.
c Non lavorano il sabato sera.
d Luca viene? — Credo di no.
e Non mi piace il caldo.
f Claudio non è molto alto.
g Non hai i biglietti?
h Hanno detto di no.
i I bambini non guardavano la televisione.
j Non ci siete mai stati?

147 a Viene tuo fratello?
b Sono care quelle scarpe?
c È dottore tuo fratello?
d Sono stati bravi i ragazzi?
e Va bene?
f Ti piace la macchina?
g Voleva andare al cinema tuo nipote?
h Hanno soldi?
i Sono belli i fiori?
j C'è tempo per mangiare?

148 a Pioveva?
b Viene? — Spero di no.
c Gli è piaciuto il film? — Credo di no.
d Capiscono? — Sì.

e Sta meglio tua madre? — Sì.
f Sai suonare la chitarra? — No.
g Comprerà quella macchina? — Spero di sì.
h Sei mai stato a Madrid? — No.
i È dentista?
j È arrivato tuo fratello?

149 a perché
b dove
c quanto
d quando
e che/cosa/che cosa
f chi
g come
h quanti
i quale
j che

150 a quali
b qual
c quanti
d quanto
e quali
f quali
g quanta
h quale
i quanti
j quanto

151 a Chi è lei? — Non lo so.
b Di dove sei?
c Di chi è questo cappello?
d A che ora ti alzi la mattina?
e Con chi parlava?
f Di che marca è la macchina?
g Non è partita, vero?
h A che cosa serve questa tazza?
i Di chi sono questi guanti?
j Quanto costano? — Costano molto.

152 a lentamente
b fortunatamente
c velocemente
d particolarmente
e facilmente
f molto
g qui vicino
h diritto
i velocemente
j non molto

153 a Parla bene il tedesco.
b Non è particolarmente bravo.
c Vuoi venire al cinema? — Certo!
d L'ho visto solo una volta.
e C'è una banca qui vicino?
f Lo studente ha risposto giusto.
g Parlava correntemente l'inglese.
h Ho dovuto guidare velocemente.
i Potrebbe fare l'esercizio facilmente.
j Il professore parla chiaramente.

154 a correttamente
b semplicemente
c bene
d poco
e velocemente
f male
g ovviamente
h regolarmente
i felicemente
j molto

155 a Camminavo più forte di Luca.
b Dovresti guidare meno velocemente.
c Potresti parlare più lentamente?
d L'altra squadra è più forte di noi.
e Pietro parla il francese più correntemente di me.
f Viene meno spesso di tutti.
g Giulia ha risposto meno volentieri di tutti.
h Lavoravo più piano di te.
i Ho risposto più correttamente di Giovanni.
j Correvano meno velocemente di noi.

156 a Guadagnano più di noi.
b Quello ci piace di più.
c Va al cinema meno spesso di me.
d La settimana scorsa abbiamo speso di meno.
e Il mese scorso sono usciti di più.
f Peso più di lui.

Solutions

g Mio fratello sta sempre meglio.
h Mario le piace più di Chiara.
i Le cose vanno sempre peggio.
j Queste mele costano di più.

157 a poco **meno di tutti**
b bene **meglio di tutti**
c piano **più piano di tutti**
d molto **più di tutti**
e male **peggio di tutti**

158 a I ragazzi studiano troppo.
b Il film era tanto noioso.
c La pasta è quasi pronta.
d Non siamo mai stati in Francia.
e Il gabinetto è sotto.
f La macchina è tornata indietro.
g Si alza sempre tardi.
h La piscina è piuttosto lontano.
i Gli ospiti sono arrivati troppo presto.
j Le scarpe mi piacciono poco.

159 a Di solito arrivo in ritardo.
b Ora non può.
c Ecco il treno!
d È andato anche mio marito.
e Non mangiano abbastanza.
f Cercavamo il cane dappertutto.
g Ha aspettato fuori.
h I giornali sono davanti.
i Correvo due volta la settimana.
j Vengono a teatro? — Forse.

160 a proprio **really**
b qualche volta **sometimes**
c una volta **once**

d da qualche parte **somewhere**
e purtroppo **unfortunately**

161 a sul
b con
c a
d di
e nella
f in
g a
h della
i al
j con

162 a Abita a Londra.
b Dobbiamo essere alla stazione alle sei.
c Sono scesi alla fermata.
d Viviamo in Spagna.
e Con chi è venuto?
f Parlava con suo marito.
g Sono andato a fare la doccia.
h Sei mai stato a Bologna?
i Cosa aveva nella valigia?
j Ha detto al professore il suo nome.

163 a della
b dal
c da
d per
e in
f sulla
g in
h per
i da
j a

164 a a causa di **because of**
b prima di **before**
c accanto a **next to**
d fino a **until**
e davanti a **opposite**

165 a Era seduta fra gli alberi.
b Sei uscito senza scarpe?
c Non abbiamo niente contro di loro.

d Dovrebbero arrivare verso le otto.
e Dopo aver finito il libro sono andato a letto.
f Era sveglia durante la notte.
g Abbiamo messo la valigia sopra l'armadio.
h Eri seduto accanto a me.
i Non vuole andare senza di lui.
j È sulla quarantina.

166 a gli zii
b le spiagge
c le mie amiche ricche
d i vestiti lunghi
e i greci
f le farmacie
g gli alberghi
h le righe
i pochi
j i figli

167 a e
b sé
c tè
d è
e te
f se
g lì
h si
i li
j sì

168 a gle
b tà
c nu
d par
e fi
f tà
g ma
h dreb
i pen
j ta

169 a subito **immediately**
b ancora **again**
c metro **meter**
d ancora **anchor**
e compito **homework**

Index

a 62, **231–232**, 260
a: after verbs 189, 190, 194, 195, 196, 232
a 1, 14, 21, 22
a + article 16, 21
a + infinitive 185, 186, 187, 232
a causa di 241
a meno che 177
abbastanza 222
about 69, 70
accanto a 241
accents 125, 250, 253, 254, 257
active verbs 159, 161
acute accent 250
adjectives 24–51, 168
adjectives: agreement 1, 24, 25, 26, 27, 44
adjectives: comparative and superlative 33, 34
adjectives: demonstrative 38, 39
adjectives: endings 24, 25, 26, 27, 35
adjectives: feminine 25, 26
adjectives: followed by **di** 69, 183, 233
adjectives: followed by infinitive 183
adjectives: indefinite 50, 51
adjectives: in exclamations 44
adjectives: participles used as 144
adjectives: plural 26, 27, 249, 250
adjectives: position 24, 30, 31
adjectives: possessive 18, 30, **45–48**
adjectives: shortened forms 27
adjectives: word order 30, 31
adverbs 213–226
adverbs: comparative and superlative 218, 219
adverbs: word order 225
adverbs: vs prepositions 242
affinché 177
after 223, 239
against 238
agreement: of adjectives 24, 25, 26, 27
agreement: of articles 1, 14, 15, 21, 33
agreement: of past participle 58, 121, 144, 147, 153, 154, 157, 160

agreement: of possessive adjectives 46
agreement: of possessive pronouns 67
agreement of verbs 85, 86
agli 16, 229
ai 16, 229
al 16, 229
alcuni 74
all 50, 75
all' 16, 229
alla 16, 229
alle 16, 229
allo 16, 229
allora 245
alto 34
altro 50, 51, 75
among 240
an 14, 21, 22
anche 54, 221, 244
ancora 223
and 30, 244
andare 86, 99, 100, 108, 126, 133, 143, 147, 157, 172 see **verb table 6**
andarsene 116
answers 204, 208
any 22, 50
anybody 74
anything 74
anzi 246
appena 222, 226
aprire 95, 108, 142
-are verbs 85
-are verbs: conditional 130
-are verbs: future 124, 125
-are verbs: gerund 105, 164
-are verbs: imperative 107
-are verbs: imperfect 137
-are verbs: imperfect subjunctive 180
-are verbs: past historic 150
-are verbs: past participle 141
-are verbs: present continuous 105
-are verbs: present simple 88, 89
-are verbs: present subjunctive 171, 172
arrivare 147
articles 14–22
as 236

as ... as 35
aspettare 107
at 16, 228, 231, 235
avere 99, 127, 134, 141, 150, 153, 172 see verb table 12
away 231
basso 34
bastare 168
be 102
bello 27, 168
bene 214
bisognare 168, 186
buono 27, 34, 214
but 244
by 159, 232, 235, 237, 238
c' see ci
cadere 99, 126, 133
caro 30
caso: nel caso che 16
cattivo 34
ce 64, 70, 111
cento 22
cercare 248
certo 215, 221
che 42, 44, 77, 78, 80, 206, 208, 245
che: che cosa 80, 81, 206, 208
che: followed by the subjunctive 171
che: il che 77
chi 77, 80, 81, 206
chi: di chi 80, 209, 232
chiaro 214
chiunque 74
ci 57, 60, 72, 116, 121, 224
ciascuno 51, 74
come 35, 206, 207, 208, 246
comparative adjectives 33, 34, 35
comparative adverbs 218, 219
comparisons 33, 34, 35, 62, 218
comporre 98
con 240
conditional 130–134
conditional: irregular verbs 133, 134
conjunctions 244–246
consonants 111
contento 69, 174
continuous tenses 103, 136, 163, 165
continuous tense: of reflexives 118

contro 240
convenire 186, 195
cosa 80, 206, 208
cosa: cos'è 206
così 221
could 130
credere 91, 125, 130, 137, 142, 150, 171, 172, 180 see **verb table 27**
credere: followed by **che** 174, 178
credere: followed by **di** 176
cui 77, 78
da 101, 138, 141, 160, 191, 234–236
da + article 16, 229
dagli 16, 229
dai 16, 229
dal 16, 229
dall' 16, 229
dalla 16, 229
dalle 16, 229
dallo 16, 229
dare 60, 108, 172, 180 see **verb table 30**
dates 18, **260**
davanti 225
davanti a 240
days of the week 260
decimal point 258
definite article 14, **15–18**, 33, 45, 46
definite article: with parts of the body 18, 46, 121
definite article: with possessives 45
definite article: combined with other words 16–17, 229
degli 16, 229
dei 16, 229
del 16, 229
dell' 16, 229
della 16, 229
delle 16, 229
dello 16, 229
demonstrative adjectives 38, 39
demonstrative pronouns 53, **83**
describing words see **adjectives**
di 17, 33, 35, 69, 81, 208, 218, **232–234**
di: after verbs 190, 233
di + article 16, 17, 229
di + infinitive 176, 185, 234
di: di cui 77
di: **di meno** 219
di: **di no** 199, 204
di: **di più** 219

di: **di sì** 204
di: **di tutti** 218
dietro 241
difficile 168
dire 60, 108, 126, 133, 136, 142, 164, 172, 180 see **verb table 35**
direct object 57
direct object pronouns 53
direct object pronouns: stressed 62
direct object pronouns: unstressed 57, 58, 60
direct questions 212
diritto 215
dispiacere 186
dispiacere: **mi dispiace** 174, 195
diventare 143, 147, 157
divertirsi 117
doing words see **verbs**
dormire 95, 108
dopo 223, 239
dove 206
dovere 99, 126, 130, 132, 172, 185
doubling of consonants 64, 111
dunque 245
durante 240
e 30, 244
each 50, 74
each other 121
ecco 221
egli 54
either … or 246
ella 54
emphasis 54, 62, 88, 91, 94
endings: adjectives 24, 25, 26, 27, 35
endings: nouns 1, 2, 4, 5, 6, 7, 9, 10, 11
endings: verbs 85, 86
entrare 72, 147
-er 33, 218
-ere verbs 85
-ere verbs: conditional 130
-ere verbs: future 125
-ere verbs: gerund 105, 163
-ere verbs: imperative 108
-ere verbs: imperfect 137
-ere verbs: imperfect subjunctive 180
-ere verbs: past historic 150
-ere verbs: past participle 141
-ere verbs: present continuous 105

-ere verbs: present simple 91, 94
-ere verbs: present subjunctive 171, 172
essere 86, 103, 108, 121, 127, 134, 141, 147, 150, 153, 157, 159, 167, 172, 177 see **verb table 47**
esse 54
essi 54
-est 33, 218
every 50
everybody 75
everything 74, 75
exclamations: **che** used in 22
facile 168, 172
fare 86, 100, 108, 126, 133, 138, 143, 164, 167, 172, 177, 180, 186 see **verb table 49**
feminine adjectives 1, 25, 26, 121
feminine nouns 1, 2, 4, 5, 6, 7, 9
few: a few 22
finire 94, 108, 125, 131, 137, 142, 171, 172, 180
fino a 239
for 101, 138, 228, 235, 238
forse 169, 178, 221
forte 215
fra 240
from 16, 228, 233, 234
from … to 235
future tense 124–127
future tense: irregular verbs 126, 127
future tense: accents 125, 254
gender 1, 2, 4, 5, 14
gerund 105, 136, 163–165, 184
get 115
giusto 215
gli 15, 60, 65, 111, 194
glie 65, 70, 111
gliela 65
gliele 65
glieli 65
glielo 65
grande 27, 34
grave accent 250
he 53
her 45
hers 67
herself 115
him 57
himself 115, 116
his 45, 67
hopes 174, 178

how 206
how long 101, 141, 154, 235, 239
how much/many 42, 69, 80
i 15, 16
i: i loro 45, 67
i: i miei 45, 67
i: i nostri 45, 67
i: i più 34
i: i suoi 45, 67
i: i tuoi 45, 67
i: i vostri 45, 67
l 53
il 1, 14
il: il loro 45, 67
il: il maggiore 35
il: il migliore 35
il: il minore 35
il: il mio 45, 67
il: il nostro 45, 67
il: il peggiore 35
il: il più 34
il: il quale 78
il: il suo 45, 67
il: il superiore 34
il: il tuo 45, 67
il: il vostro 45, 67
imagined situations 181
imperative 107–113
imperative: word order 64, 111
imperfect tense 136–138
imperfect continuous 136
imperfect subjunctive 176, 180, 181
impersonal verbs 167–169
importare 60, 168, 196
in 16, 236–237
in + article 16, 229
in 16, 17, 34, 231, 232, 234, 236, 237
indefinite adjectives 50–51
indefinite article 14, **21–22**
indefinite pronouns 53, **74–75**
indirect object 57
indirect object pronouns 53, 111
indirect object pronouns:
   stressed 62
indirect object pronouns:
   unstressed 58, 60
indirect questions 212
infinitive 64, 65, 69, 72, 85, 98, 113,
   130, **183–187**, 254
infinitives: after adjectives 183
infinitives: after another verb 118,
   183, 185
infinitives: after prepositions 184,

186, 187, 235
infinitives: ending in **–rre** 98
-ing form 72, 105, 163, 165, 184, 185
instructions 183
interessare 60, 195
interrogative adjectives 42
interrogative pronouns 80–81
into 228, 236
invariable adjectives 26, 50
invece 245
io 53
-ire verbs 85
-ire verbs: conditional 131
-ire verbs: future 125
-ire verbs: gerund 105, 164
-ire verbs: imperative 108
-ire verbs: imperfect 137
-ire verbs: imperfect subjunctive
   180
-ire verbs: past historic 151
-ire verbs: past participle 141
-ire verbs: present continuous 105
-ire verbs: present simple 94, 95,
   98
-ire verbs: present subjunctive 171,
   172
irregular comparative and
   superlative adjectives 34
irregular comparative and
   superlative adverbs 218
irregular verbs: conditional 130,
   131, 132, 133, 134
irregular verbs: future tense 126,
   127
irregular verbs: imperative 108
irregular verbs: imperfect 138
irregular verbs: imperfect
   subjunctive 180
irregular verbs: passive 161
irregular verbs: past participle 144
irregular verbs: present
   subjunctive 172, 174
-issimo 35
it 54, 58, 72, 91, 92, 111, 167, 168
its 45
jobs 4, 22
l': definite article 15, 16
l': object pronoun 58
la 1, 15, 57, 58, 65, 144, 154
la loro 45, 67
la meno 34
la mia 45, 67
la nostra 45, 67

la più 33
la quale 78
la sua 45, 67
la tua 45, 67
la vostra 45, 67
là 224, 251
lasciare 186, 248
least 33, 218
le 15, 57, 58, 60, 65, 111, 144, 154
lei 53, 54, 55, 62, 88, 95, 107, 111, 131
Lei 54, 130
le loro 45, 67
le meno 34
le mie 45, 67
le nostre 45, 67
le più 34
le sue 45, 67
le tue 45, 67
le vostre 45, 67
less 33, 218
let's 107, 111
li 57, 58, 65, 144, 154
lì 224, 251
-'ll 124
lo 1, 14, 57, 58, 65, 144, 154
loro 53, 62
lui 53, 54, 62, 131
m' see **mi**
ma 244
mai 199, 223, 224
male 214
malgrado 242
mancare 195
masculine adjectives 1, 24, 25, 26,
   27
masculine and feminine forms of
   words 5, 6, 7
masculine nouns 1, 2, 4, 5, 6, 7, 9,
   10
me 62, 64, 70, 111
me 55, 57
meglio 218
meno 33, 35, 218
mentre 246
mettere 143
mi 57, 60, 116
migliore 34
mille 22
mine 67
minore 34
molto 30, 35, 50, 51, 75, 215,
   222
months 261

more 33, 218
most 33, 218
my 45
myself 115
naming words see **nouns**
nationalities: adjectives 25
ne 69–70, 116
né ... né 246
neanche 54
necessario 169
negatives 22, **198–200**
negli 16, 229
nei 16, 229
neither ... nor 246
nel 16, 229
nell' 16, 229
nella 16, 229
nelle 16, 229
nello 16, 229
nessuno 30, 51, 74, 200
never 198
nevicare 167
niente 74, 167, 200
no 127, 199, 203, 212
nobody 74
noi 53, 62
nulla 74
no longer 199
non 113, 117, 198
non ... da nessuna parte 199
non ... mai 199
non ... né ... né 199
non ... nessuno 199
non ... niente 199
no one 74
non ... più 199
not 198
nothing 74, 198
nouns 1–11, 53
nouns: endings 2, 4, 5
nouns: English,
used in Italian 10
nouns: feminine 1, 2, 4, 5, 6, 7, 9
nouns: masculine 1, 2, 4, 5, 6, 7, 9, 10
nouns: plural 1, 2, 9, 10, 11, 22, 249, 250
nouns: singular 1, 2, 4, 5, 6, 7, 11
numbers 233, **257–259**
nuovo 30
o 199, 244
o ... o 246
object 115, 186

object pronouns 53, 57, 62, 144, 154
object pronouns: word order 57, 58, 60, 62, 64, 65, 69
occorrere 168
of 69, 232
off 234
offers 101, 130
ogni 30, 50, 51
ognuno 74
on 17, 231, 232, 234
one 65, 257
one another 121
oneself 115
opinions Subjunctive
oppure 244
orders and instructions 107, 183
orders and instructions: word order 64, 69, 70, 117, 118
our 45
ours 67
ourselves 115
parecchio 50, 51, 52, 75
parere 168
parlare 88, 124, 125, 130, 137, 142, 150, 153, 172, 180 see **verb table 68**
participles: past 121, 141, 142, 153, 159, 163
partire 95, 108, 147, 150
parts of the body 18, 121
passato remoto 150
passive 159–161
passive: irregular verbs 160
past continuous 163
past historic 150–151
past participles 58, 121, 141, **142**, 153, 159, 163
past participles: irregular verbs 144
past participles: used as adjectives 144
past perfect see **pluperfect**
peccato: è un peccato che 174
peggio 218
peggiore 34
pensare 171
pensare che 174, 178
pensare di 176
per 185, 238
perché 206, 245
perfect conditional 134
perfect infinitive 184
perfect subjunctive 177, 178

perfect tense 58, 121, 122, 137, **141–148**, 167
perfect tense: made with **avere** 142, 143
perfect tense: made with **essere** 147, 148
però 245
personal pronouns 53–65
piacere 60, 148, 157, 184, 186, 194, 195
piccolo 34
piovere 167
più 33, 35, 218, 225
pluperfect tense 153–157
pluperfect tense: made with **avere** 153, 154
pluperfect tense: made with **essere** 157
plural: 1, 2, 9, 10, 11, 14, 26, 258
spelling 249, 250, 251
poco 50, 51, 75, 215, 222
polite plural 107, 108
possession 45, 81, 232
possessive adjectives 18, 30, **45–48**
possessive adjectives: agreement 45, 46
possessive adjectives: with family members 48
possessive pronouns 53, **67**
possibile 168
potere 99, 126, 130, 132, 172, 185
povero 30
predictions 101
prendere 108, 143
preparare 116
prepararsi 116
prepositions 16, 17, 62, 77, 78, 164, 228–242
prepositions: after adjectives 228
prepositions: followed by infinitive 228
prepositions: in questions 81, 208
prepositions + definite article 16, 17, 229
prepositions after verbs 189–191, 194, 195, 196, 228
present conditional 130–134
present continuous 87, 105, 163
present simple 87, **88–99**
present subjunctive 171, 172, 174, 176, 177
present tense 87

present tense: reflexive verbs 116
present tense: used for future 124
prima 223
prima che 177
prima di 177, 239
primo 259
produrre 98
pronouns 53–83, 85, 86
pronouns: reflexive 115, 116
pronouns: word order 111, 113, 165, 203
pronunciation 108
può darsi 169, 174
qualche 30, 50, 51
qualcosa 74
qualcuno 74
quale 31, 42, 80, 207
quale … il quale 78
quale … qual è 80, 207
quali 31, 42, 80, 207
qualsiasi 50, 51
quando 124, 206, 246, 261
quanti 42, 44, 80, 207
quanto 31, 34, 35, 42, 44, 80, 207
quelli 30, 38, 39, 83
quello 30, 38, 39, 83
quello: quello che 78
questions 203–212
questions: indirect 212
question words 22, 31, 203, 206, 207
questo 30, 38, 39, 83
qui 224
quindi 245
reflexive pronouns 115, 116
reflexive pronouns: word order 117, 118
reflexive verbs 65, **115–121**, 154, 157
reflexive verbs: perfect tense 121, 143
reflexive verbs: present tense 117
regular verbs 85
relative pronouns 77–78
restare 196
rimanere 99, 126, 133, 157, 160
rincrescere 196
riuscire 147, 157
-'s 233
s' see si
salire 147
sapere 126, 133, 185
se 181, 245

sè 251
secondo 178
sembrare 168
sempre 219, 225
sentire 95, 108, 186
senza 240
servire 94
scendere 147
several 50
she 53, 55
should 132
si: impersonal 65, 121, 161
si: si passivante 161
si: reflexive pronoun 115, 116, 121
sì 204, 251
sia … che 246
simple past 141, 143, 150
since 235
singular nouns 1, 2, 4, 5, 6, 7, 11, 14
soffrire 95
some 17, 69, 74, 234
somebody 53, 74
someone 74
something 74
sopra 224, 241
sotto 224, 241
spelling 126, 133, **247–251**
spelling: of plurals 10, 11, 249, 250, 251
sperare 171, 174, 178
stare 103, 105, 136, 147, 172, 180 see **verb table 108**
stems 85, 88, 107, 124, 130
stress 125, 253–254
stress: in infinitives 98
stressed pronouns 60, 62
su 17, 237
su + article 17, 229
subject 85, 86, 115, 142, 147, 148, 153, 157, 159, 161, 194
subject pronouns 53, 54, 55, 88, 91, 94
subjunctive 168, **171–181**
subjunctive: imperfect
subjunctive: irregular verbs
subjunctive: perfect
subjunctive: present
succedere 147
suggestions 124
sugli 17, 229
sui 17, 229
sul 17, 229
sull' 17, 229

sulla 17, 229
sulle 17, 229
sullo 17, 229
superlative adjectives 33, 34, 35
superlative adverbs 218, 219
supporre 174
syllable 111, 253
t' see **ti**
tanto 50, 51, 75, 222
te 62, 64, 70, 111
telefonare 60
tenere 126, 133, 172
tense 85
than 33, 218, 234
that 38, 53, 77, 83, 171
that man 83
that one 39, 83
that woman 83
the 1
their 45
theirs 67
them 53, 57, 58, 111
the one 78
these 38, 83
they 53, 88
this 38, 83
this one 39, 83
those 38, 83
ti 57, 58, 60, 116
time 18, 232, 260
time and date 260–262
to 16, 17, 57, 60, 85, 183, 231, 235, 236
tornare 147
towns and cities 231
tra 240
troppo 50, 51, 75, 222
tu 53, 55, 107, 111, 113, 117
tutti 50, 75
tutto 50, 51, 75
un 1, 21, 50, 74, 257
un' 21, 50, 257
una 1, 21, 50, 257
uno 21, 74, 257
unstressed pronouns 57, 60, 64
-urre verbs 98, 183
us 53, 57
uscire 147, 172
v' see **vi**
ve 64, 70, 111
vecchio 30
vedere 99, 126, 133, 143, 186
venire 126, 133, 143, 147, 157, 160, 172
verbal idioms 194–196

verbs 85–196
verbs: active
verbs: ending **–ciare/giare** 126, 133
Spelling verbs: ending **–care/gare** 126, 133
Spelling verbs: followed by **a** 72, 186, 187
verbs: followed by **di** 187, 233
verbs: followed by infinitive 185, 186
verbs: irregular 85, 86
verbs: prepositions after 186, 187
verbs: regular 85
vero 127, 212
verso 241
vi 57, 60, 116, 121
vicino 215
vivere 126
voi 53, 55, 62, 95, 107, 111
volere 126, 131, 171, 172, 176, 185

voler dire 185
vowels: stress 253–255
vowels: following c and g 248
we 53
weather see impersonal verbs
what 42, 80, 81, 208, 209
what (a) …! 44
when 124
where 206
which 42, 77, 80
who 53, 77, 78, 80, 81
whom 77, 80, 81
whose 80, 209, 232
why 206
will 124, 127
with 228
word order: in imperatives 64, 69, 72, 111, 113
word order: in questions 203, 208, 209

word order: with adjectives 24, 30, 31
word order: with adverbs 225
word order: with gerunds 72, 165
word order: with negatives 198
word order: with object pronouns 57, 58, 60, 62, 64, 65, 70
word order: with prepositions 228
word order: with reflexive pronouns 117, 118
would 130
years 18, 261
yes 203
yes: yes/no questions 203, 204
you 53, 54, 65, 121
you: ways of saying 55
your 45
yours 67
yourself 115, 116
yourselves 115

VERB TABLES

Introduction

This section is designed to help you find all the verb forms you need in Italian.

From pages 2-9 you will find a list of 123 regular and irregular verbs with a summary of their main forms, followed on pages 10-25 by some very common regular and irregular verbs shown in full, with example phrases.

Italian verb forms

1 abbattere
Verbs ending in **-tere** don't have alternative forms **-etti**, **-ette**, **-ettero** for past historic

2 accendere
PAST PARTICIPLE acceso
PAST HISTORIC accesi, accendesti, accese, accendemmo, accendeste, accesero

3 accludere
PAST PARTICIPLE accluso
PAST HISTORIC acclusi, accludesti, accluse, accludemmo, accludeste, acclusero

4 accorgersi (*auxiliary* essere)
PAST PARTICIPLE accorto
PAST HISTORIC mi accorsi, ti accorgesti, si accorse, ci accorgemmo, vi accorgeste, si accorsero

5 aggiungere
PAST PARTICIPLE aggiunto
PAST HISTORIC aggiunsi, aggiungesti, aggiunse, aggiungemmo, aggiungeste, aggiunsero

6 andare (*auxiliary* essere)
see full verb table on page 10

7 apparire (*auxiliary* essere)
PAST PARTICIPLE apparso
PRESENT appaio, appari *or* apparisci, appare *or* apparisce, appariamo, apparite, appaiono *or* appariscono
PAST HISTORIC apparvi, apparisti, apparve, apparimmo, appariste, apparvero
PRESENT SUBJUNCTIVE appaia, appaia, appaia, appariamo, appariate, appaiano

8 appendere
PAST PARTICIPLE appeso
PAST HISTORIC appesi, appendesti, appese, appendemmo, appendeste, appesero

9 aprire
PAST PARTICIPLE aperto
PAST HISTORIC aprii, apristi, aprì, aprimmo, apriste, aprirono

10 assistere
PAST PARTICIPLE assistito
PAST HISTORIC assistei *or* assistetti, assistesti, assistette, assistemmo, assisteste, assisterono *or* assistettero

11 assumere
PAST PARTICIPLE assunto
PAST HISTORIC assunsi, assumesti, assunse, assumemmo, assumeste, assunsero

12 avere
see full verb table on page 11

13 baciare
When the verb ending begins with **e**, the **-i-** of the root is dropped → **bacerò** (*not* **bacierò**)

14 bagnare
PRESENT bagniamo, bagniate
PRESENT SUBJUNCTIVE bagniamo, bagniate (*not* **bagnamo**, **bagnate**)

15 bere
PAST PARTICIPLE bevuto
GERUND bevendo
PRESENT bevo, bevi, beve, beviamo, bevete, bevono
FUTURE berrò, berrai, berrà, berremo, berrete, berranno
IMPERFECT bevevo, bevevi, beveva, bevevamo, bevevate, bevevano
PRESENT SUBJUNCTIVE beva, beva, beva, beviamo, beviate, bevano
PAST HISTORIC bevvi *or* bevetti, bevesti, bevve *or* bevette, bevemmo, beveste, bevvero *or* bevettero
PRESENT CONDITIONAL berrei, berresti, berrebbe, berremmo, berreste, berrebbero
IMPERATIVE bevi!, beva!, beviamo!, bevete!, bevano!

16 cadere (*auxiliary* essere)
FUTURE cadrò, cadrai, cadrà, cadremo, cadrete, cadranno
PAST HISTORIC caddi, cadesti, cadde, cademmo, cadeste, caddero
CONDITIONAL cadrei, cadresti, cadrebbe, cadremmo, cadreste, cadrebbero

17 cambiare (*auxiliary* essere/avere)
When 1st person sing. of present doesn't have a stress on the **-i-** of the root and an ending starts with **i** (as in the past historic), then the verb drops the **-i-** of the root (**cambi**, **cambino** and *not* **cambii**, **cambiino** [cf. **inviare**])

18 caricare
When *-c-* in the root is followed by **i** *or* **e**, an **h** should be inserted to retain the hard 'kuh' sound (ie **carichi**, **carichiamo**, **caricherò**)

19 chiedere
PAST PARTICIPLE chiesto
PAST HISTORIC chiesi, chiedesti, chiese, chiedemmo, chiedeste, chiesero

20 chiudere
PAST PARTICIPLE chiuso
PAST HISTORIC chiusi, chiudesti, chiuse, chiudemmo, chiudeste, chiusero

21 cogliere
PAST PARTICIPLE colto
PRESENT colgo, cogli, coglie, cogliamo, cogliete, colgono
PAST HISTORIC colsi, cogliesti, colse, cogliemmo, coglieste, colsero
PRESENT SUBJUNCTIVE colga, colga, colga, cogliamo, cogliate, colgan
IMPERATIVE cogli!, colga!, cogliamo!, cogliete!, colgano!

22 compiere
PAST PARTICIPLE compiuto
PAST HISTORIC compii, compisti, compì, compimmo, compiste, compirono

23 confondere
PAST PARTICIPLE confuso
PAST HISTORIC confusi, confondesti, confuse, confondemmo, confondeste, confusero

24 conoscere
PAST PARTICIPLE conosciuto
PAST HISTORIC conobbi, conoscesti, conobbe, conoscemmo, conosceste, conobbero

25 consigliare
When the ending begins with **i**, then the **-i-** of the root is dropped → **consigli** (*not* **consiglii**)

26 correre (*auxiliary* essere/avere)
PAST PARTICIPLE corso
PAST HISTORIC corsi, corresti, corse, corremmo, correste, corsero

27 credere
see full verb table on page 12

28 crescere (*auxiliary* essere)
PAST PARTICIPLE cresciuto
PAST HISTORIC crebbi, crescesti, crebbe, crescemmo, cresceste, crebbero

29 cuocere
PAST PARTICIPLE cotto
PAST HISTORIC cossi, cuocesti, cosse, cuocemmo, cuoceste, cossero

30 dare
see full verb table on page 13

31 decidere
PAST PARTICIPLE deciso
PAST HISTORIC decisi, decidesti, decise, decidemmo, decideste, decisero

32 deludere
PAST PARTICIPLE deluso
PAST HISTORIC delusi, deludesti, deluse, deludemmo, deludeste, delusero

33 difendere
PAST PARTICIPLE difeso
PAST HISTORIC difesi, difendesti, difese, difendemmo, difendeste, difesero

34 dipingere
PAST PARTICIPLE dipinto
PAST HISTORIC dipinsi, dipingesti, dipinse, dipingemmo, dipingeste, dipinsero

35 dire
see full verb table on page 14

36 dirigere
PAST PARTICIPLE diretto
PAST HISTORIC diressi, dirigesti, diresse, dirigemmo, dirigeste, diressero

37 discutere
PAST PARTICIPLE discusso
PAST HISTORIC discussi, discutesti, discusse, discutemmo, discuteste, discussero

38 disfare
Although it follows the conjugation of fare, it follows the **-are** verb form in the present (**disfo**, etc), future (**disferò**), and in the subjunctive (**disfi**)

39 distinguere
PAST PARTICIPLE distinto
PAST HISTORIC distinsi, distinguesti, distinse, distinguemmo, distingueste, distinsero

40 dividere
PAST PARTICIPLE diviso
PAST HISTORIC divisi, dividesti, divise, dividemmo, divideste, divisero

41 dormire
see full verb table on page 15

42 dovere
see full verb table on page 16

43 esigere
PAST PARTICIPLE esatto (*not common*)
PAST HISTORIC esigei *or* esigetti, esigesti, esigette, esigemmo, esigeste, esigettero

44 espellere
PAST PARTICIPLE espulso
PAST HISTORIC espulsi, espellesti, espulse, espellemmo, espelleste, espulsero

45 esplodere (*auxiliary* essere)
PAST PARTICIPLE esploso
PAST HISTORIC esplosi, esplodesti, esplose, esplodemmo, esplodeste, esplosero

46 esprimere
PAST PARTICIPLE espresso
PAST HISTORIC espressi, esprimesti, espresse, esprimemmo, esprimeste, espressero

47 essere
see full verb table on page 17

48 evadere (*auxiliary* essere)
PAST PARTICIPLE evaso
PAST HISTORIC evasi, evadesti, evase, evademmo, evadeste, evasero

49 fare
see full verb table on page 18

50 fingere
PAST PARTICIPLE finto
PAST HISTORIC finsi, fingesti, finse, fingemmo, fingeste, finsero

51 finire
see full verb table on page 19

52 friggere
PAST PARTICIPLE fritto
PAST HISTORIC frissi, friggesti, frisse, friggemmo, friggeste, frissero

53 immergere
PAST PARTICIPLE immerso
PAST HISTORIC immersi, immergesti, immerse, immergemmo, immergeste, immersero

54 invader
PAST PARTICIPLE invaso
PAST HISTORIC invasi, invadesti, invase, invademmo, invadeste, invasero

55 inviare
When 1st person sing of present has a stress on the **-i-** of the root, the verb keeps the **-i-** of the root even if the ending starts with **i** (**invii**, **inviino**)

56 lavarsi *(auxiliary* essere)
see full verb table on page 20

57 leggere
PAST PARTICIPLE letto
PAST HISTORIC lessi, leggesti, lesse, leggemmo, leggeste, lessero

58 mangiare
When the ending begins with **e**, the **-i-** of the root is no longer needed to soften the **g** and is dropped → **mangerò** (*not* **mangierò**)

59 mettere
PAST PARTICIPLE messo
PAST HISTORIC misi, mettesti, mise, mettemmo, metteste, misero

60 mordere
PAST PARTICIPLE morso
PAST HISTORIC morsi, mordesti, morse, mordemmo, mordeste, morsero

61 morire *(auxiliary* essere)
PAST PARTICIPLE morto
PRESENT muoio, muori, muore, moriamo, morite, muoiono
PRESENT SUBJUNCTIVE muoia, muoia, muoia, moriamo, moriate, muoiano

62 muovere
PAST PARTICIPLE mosso
PAST HISTORIC mossi, muovesti, mosse, muovemmo, muoveste, mossero

63 nascere *(auxiliary* essere)
PAST PARTICIPLE nato
PAST HISTORIC nacqui, nascesti, nacque, nascemmo, nasceste, nacquero

64 nascondere
PAST PARTICIPLE nascosto
PAST HISTORIC nascosi, nascondesti, nascose, nascondemmo, nascondeste, nascosero

65 nuocere
PAST PARTICIPLE nociuto *or* nuociuto
GERUND nocendo *or* nuocendo
PRESENT nuoccio, nuoci, nuoce, nuociamo, nuocete, nuocciono
PAST HISTORIC nocqui, nuocesti, nocque, nuocemmo, nuoceste, nocquero

66 offrire
PAST PARTICIPLE offerto
PAST HISTORIC offrii, offristi, offrì, offrimmo, offriste, offrirono

67 parere (*auxiliary* essere)
PAST PARTICIPLE parso
PRESENT pare, paiono
FUTURE parrà, parranno
PAST HISTORIC parve, parvero
PRESENT SUBJUNCTIVE paia, paiano

68 parlare
see full verb table on page 21

69 perdere
PAST PARTICIPLE perso *or* perduto
PAST HISTORIC persi, perdesti, perse, perdemmo, perdeste, persero

70 piacere (*auxiliary* essere)
PAST PARTICIPLE piaciuto
PRESENT piaccio, piaci, piace, piacciamo *or* piaciamo, piacete, piacciono
PAST HISTORIC piacqui, piacesti, piacque, piacemmo, piaceste, piacquero
PRESENT SUBJUNCTIVE piaccia, piaccia, piaccia, piacciamo, piacciate, piacciano

71 piangere
PAST PARTICIPLE pianto
PAST HISTORIC piansi, piangesti, pianse, piangemmo, piangeste, piansero

72 piovere
PAST PARTICIPLE piovuto
PAST HISTORIC piovve

73 porre
PAST PARTICIPLE posto
PRESENT pongo, poni, pone, poniamo, ponete, pongono
FUTURE porrò, porrai, porrà, porremo, porrete, porranno
PAST HISTORIC posi, ponesti, pose, ponemmo, poneste, posero
PRESENT SUBJUNCTIVE ponga, ponga, ponga, poniamo, poniate, pongano

74 potere
see full verb table on page 22

75 prefiggersi (*auxiliary* essere)
PAST PARTICIPLE prefisso
PAST HISTORIC mi prefissi, ti prefiggesti, si prefisse, ci prefiggemmo, vi prefiggeste, si prefissero

76 pregare
When -**g**- in the root is followed by **i** *or* **e** an **h** should be inserted to keep the hard 'guh' sound (ie **preghi**, **preghiamo**, **pregherò**)

77 prendere
PAST PARTICIPLE preso
PAST HISTORIC presi, prendesti, prese, prendemmo, prendeste, presero

78 prevedere
This verb is conjugated like **vedere** except in the future → **prevederò**, **prevederai** etc (*not* **prevedrò**, **prevedrai** etc) and in the conditional → **prevederei** (*not* **prevedrei** etc)

79 proteggere
PAST PARTICIPLE protetto
PAST HISTORIC protessi, proteggesti, protesse, proteggemmo, proteggeste, protessero

80 pungere
PAST PARTICIPLE punto
PAST HISTORIC punsi, pungesti, punse, pungemmo, pungeste, punsero

81 radere
PAST PARTICIPLE raso
PAST HISTORIC rasi, radesti, rase, rademmo, radeste, rasero

82 reggere
PAST PARTICIPLE retto
PAST HISTORIC ressi, reggesti, resse, reggemmo, reggeste, ressero

83 rendere
PAST PARTICIPLE reso
PAST HISTORIC resi, rendesti, rese, rendemmo, rendeste, resero

84 ridere
PAST PARTICIPLE riso
PAST HISTORIC risi, ridesti, rise, ridemmo, rideste, risero

85 ridurre
PAST PARTICIPLE ridotto
GERUND riducendo
PRESENT riduco, riduci, riduce, riduciamo, riducete, riducono
FUTURE ridurrò, ridurrai, ridurrà, ridurremo, ridurrete, ridurranno
IMPERFECT riducevo, riducevi, riduceva, riducevamo, riducevate, riducevano
PAST HISTORIC ridussi, riducesti, ridusse, riducemmo, riduceste, ridussero
PRESENT SUBJUNCTIVE riduca, riduca, riduca, riduciamo, riduciate, riducano

86 riempire
GERUND riempiendo
PRESENT riempio, riempi, riempie, riempiamo, riempite, riempiono

87 riflettere
PAST PARTICIPLE riflettuto *or* riflesso

88 rimanere *(auxiliary* essere)
PAST PARTICIPLE rimasto
PRESENT rimango, rimani, rimane, rimaniamo, rimanete, rimangono
FUTURE rimarrò, rimarrai, rimarrà, rimarremo, rimarrete, rimarranno
PAST HISTORIC rimasi, rimanesti, rimase, rimanemmo, rimaneste, rimasero
PRESENT SUBJUNCTIVE rimanga, rimanga, rimanga, rimaniamo, rimaniate, rimangano

89 risolvere
PAST PARTICIPLE risolto
PAST HISTORIC risolsi, risolvesti, risolse, risolvemmo, risolveste, risolsero

90 rispondere
PAST PARTICIPLE risposto
PAST HISTORIC risposi, rispondesti, rispose, rispondemmo, rispondeste, risposero

91 rivolgere
PAST PARTICIPLE rivolto
PAST HISTORIC rivolsi, rivolgesti, rivolse, rivolgemmo, rivolgeste, rivolsero

92 rompere
PAST PARTICIPLE rotto
PAST HISTORIC ruppi, rompesti, ruppe, rompemmo, rompeste, ruppero

93 salire *(auxiliary* essere/avere)
PRESENT salgo, sali, sale, saliamo, salite, salgono
PRESENT SUBJUNCTIVE salga, salga, salga, saliamo, saliate, salgano
IMPERATIVE sali!, salga!, saliamo!, salite!, salgano!

94 sapere
see full verb table on page 23

95 scegliere
PAST PARTICIPLE scelto
PRESENT scelgo, scegli, sceglie, scegliamo, scegliete, scelgono
PAST HISTORIC scelsi, scegliesti, scelse, scegliemmo, sceglieste, scelsero
PRESENT SUBJUNCTIVE scelga, scelga, scelga, scegliamo, scegliate, scelgano
IMPERATIVE scegli!, scelga!, scegliamo!, scegliete!, scelgano!

96 scendere (*auxiliary* essere)
PAST PARTICIPLE sceso
PAST HISTORIC scesi, scendesti, scese, scendemmo, scendeste, scesero

97 sciogliere
PAST PARTICIPLE sciolto
PRESENT sciolgo, sciogli, scioglie, sciogliamo, sciogliete, sciolgono
PAST HISTORIC sciolsi, sciogliesti, sciolse, sciogliemmo, scioglieste, sciolsero
PRESENT SUBJUNCTIVE sciolga, sciolga, sciolga, sciogliamo, sciogliate, sciolgano
IMPERATIVE sciogli!, sciolga!, sciogliamo!, sciogliete!, sciolgano!

98 sconfiggere
PAST PARTICIPLE sconfitto
PAST HISTORIC sconfissi, sconfiggesti, sconfisse, sconfiggemmo, sconfiggeste, sconfissero

99 scrivere
PAST PARTICIPLE scritto
PAST HISTORIC scrissi, scrivesti, scrisse, scrivemmo, scriveste, scrissero

100 scuotere
PAST PARTICIPLE scosso
PAST HISTORIC scossi, scuotesti, scosse, scuotemmo, scuoteste, scossero

101 sedere
PRESENT siedo, siedi, siede, sediamo, sedete, siedono
PRESENT SUBJUNCTIVE sieda, sieda, sieda, sediamo, sediate, siedano

102 sorgere (*auxiliary* essere)
PAST PARTICIPLE sorto
PAST HISTORIC sorse, sorsero

103 spargere
PAST PARTICIPLE sparso
PAST HISTORIC sparsi, spargesti, sparse, spargemmo, spargeste, sparsero

104 sparire (*auxiliary* essere)
PAST HISTORIC sparii, sparisti, sparì, sparimmo, spariste, sparirono

105 spegnere
PAST PARTICIPLE spento
PRESENT spengo, spegni, spegne, spegniamo, spegnete, spengono
PAST HISTORIC spensi, spegnesti, spense, spegnemmo, spegneste, spensero
PRESENT SUBJUNCTIVE spenga, spenga, spenga, spegniamo, spegniate, spengano

106 spingere
PAST PARTICIPLE spinto
PAST HISTORIC spinsi, spingesti, spinse, spingemmo, spingeste, spinsero

107 sporgersi (*auxiliary* essere)
PAST PARTICIPLE sporto
PAST HISTORIC mi sporsi, ti sporgesti, si sporse, ci sporgemmo, vi sporgeste, si sporsero

108 stare
see full verb table on page 24

109 stringere
PAST PARTICIPLE stretto
PAST HISTORIC strinsi, stringesti, strinse, stringemmo, stringeste, strinsero

110 succedere (*auxiliary* essere)
PAST PARTICIPLE successo
PAST HISTORIC successi, succedesti, successe, succedemmo, succedeste, successero

111 tacere
PAST PARTICIPLE taciuto
PRESENT taccio, taci, tace, tacciamo, tacete, tacciono
PAST HISTORIC tacqui, tacesti, tacque, tacemmo, taceste, tacquero
PRESENT SUBJUNCTIVE taccia, taccia, taccia, tacciamo, tacciate, tacciano

112 tendere
PAST PARTICIPLE teso
PAST HISTORIC tesi, tendesti, tese, tendemmo, tendeste, tesero

113 tenere
PAST PARTICIPLE tenuto
PRESENT tengo, tieni, tiene, teniamo, tenete, tengono
FUTURE terrò, terrai, terrà, terremo, terrete, terranno
PAST HISTORIC tenni, tenesti, tenne, tenemmo, teneste, tennero
PRESENT SUBJUNCTIVE tenga, tenga, tenga, teniamo, teniate, tengano
CONDITIONAL terrei, terresti, terrebbe, terremmo, terreste, terrebbero

114 togliere
PAST PARTICIPLE tolto
PRESENT tolgo, togli, toglie, togliamo, togliete, tolgono
PAST HISTORIC tolsi, togliesti, tolse, togliemmo, toglieste, tolsero
PRESENT SUBJUNCTIVE tolga, tolga, tolga, togliamo, togliate, tolgano
IMPERATIVE togli!, tolga!, togliamo!, togliete!, tolgano!

115 trarre
PAST PARTICIPLE tratto
GERUND traendo
PRESENT traggo, trai, trae, traiamo, traete, traggono
FUTURE trarrò, trarrai, trarrà, trarremo, trarrete, trarranno
IMPERFECT traevo, traevi, traeva, traevamo, traevate, traevano
PAST HISTORIC trassi, traesti, trasse, traemmo, traeste, trassero
PRESENT SUBJUNCTIVE tragga, tragga, tragga, traiamo, traiate, traggano

116 ungere
PAST PARTICIPLE unto
PAST HISTORIC unsi, ungesti, unse, ungemmo, ungeste, unsero

117 uscire (*auxiliary* essere)
PRESENT esco, esci, esce, usciamo, uscite, escono
PRESENT SUBJUNCTIVE esca, esca, esca, usciamo, usciate, escano

118 valere (*auxiliary* essere)
PAST PARTICIPLE valso
PRESENT valgo, vali, vale, valiamo, valete, valgono
FUTURE varrò, varrai, varrà, varremo, varrete, varranno
PAST HISTORIC valsi, valesti, valse, valemmo, valeste, valsero
PRESENT SUBJUNCTIVE valga, valga, valga, valiamo, valiate, valgano

119 vedere
PAST PARTICIPLE visto
FUTURE vedrò, vedrai, vedrà, vedremo, vedrete, vedranno
PAST HISTORIC vidi, vedesti, vide, vedemmo, vedeste, videro

120 venire (*auxiliary* essere)
PAST PARTICIPLE venuto
PRESENT vengo, vieni, viene, veniamo, venite, vengono
FUTURE verrò, verrai, verrà, verremo, verrete, verranno
PAST HISTORIC venni, venisti, venne, venimmo, veniste, vennero
PRESENT SUBJUNCTIVE venga, venga, venga, veniamo, veniate, vengano
IMPERATIVE vieni!, venga!, veniamo!, venite!, vengano!

121 vincere
PAST PARTICIPLE vinto
PAST HISTORIC vinsi, vincesti, vinse, vincemmo, vinceste, vinsero

122 vivere (*auxiliary* essere)
PAST PARTICIPLE vissuto
PAST HISTORIC vissi, vivesti, visse, vivemmo, viveste, vissero

123 volere
see full verb table on page 25

andare (to go)

	PRESENT		FUTURE
io	**vado**	io	**andrò**
tu	**vai**	tu	**andrai**
lui/lei/Lei	**va**	lui/lei/Lei	**andrà**
noi	**andiamo**	noi	**andremo**
voi	**andate**	voi	**andrete**
loro	**vanno**	loro	**andranno**

	IMPERFECT		CONDITIONAL
io	**andavo**	io	**andrei**
tu	**andavi**	tu	**andresti**
lui/lei/Lei	**andava**	lui/lei/Lei	**andrebbe**
noi	**andavamo**	noi	**andremmo**
voi	**andavate**	voi	**andreste**
loro	**andavano**	loro	**andrebbero**

	PERFECT		PRESENT SUBJUNCTIVE
io	**sono andato/a**	io	**vada**
tu	**sei andato/a**	tu	**vada**
lui/lei/Lei	**è andato/a**	lui/lei/Lei	**vada**
noi	**siamo andati/e**	noi	**andiamo**
voi	**siete andati/e**	voi	**andiate**
loro	**sono andati/e**	loro	**vadano**

	PAST HISTORIC
io	**andai**
tu	**andasti**
lui/lei/Lei	**andò**
noi	**andammo**
voi	**andaste**
loro	**andarono**

GERUND

andando

PAST PARTICIPLE

andato

IMPERATIVE

va' *or* **vai / andiamo / andate**

EXAMPLE PHRASES

Ci **vado** spesso. I go there often.
Andate via! Go away!
Spero che **vada** bene. I hope it goes well.

Remember that subject pronouns are not used very often in Italian.

avere (to have)

	PRESENT		FUTURE
io	**ho**	io	**avrò**
tu	**hai**	tu	**avrai**
lui/lei/Lei	**ha**	lui/lei/Lei	**avrà**
noi	**abbiamo**	noi	**avremo**
voi	**avete**	voi	**avrete**
loro	**hanno**	loro	**avranno**

	IMPERFECT		CONDITIONAL
io	**avevo**	io	**avrei**
tu	**avevi**	tu	**avresti**
lui/lei/Lei	**aveva**	lui/lei/Lei	**avrebbe**
noi	**avevamo**	noi	**avremmo**
voi	**avevate**	voi	**avreste**
loro	**avevano**	loro	**avrebbero**

	PERFECT		PRESENT SUBJUNCTIVE
io	**ho avuto**	io	**abbia**
tu	**hai avuto**	tu	**abbia**
lui/lei/Lei	**ha avuto**	lui/lei/Lei	**abbia**
noi	**abbiamo avuto**	noi	**abbiamo**
voi	**avete avuto**	voi	**abbiate**
loro	**hanno avuto**	loro	**abbiano**

	PAST HISTORIC
io	**ebbi**
tu	**avesti**
lui/lei/Lei	**ebbe**
noi	**avemmo**
voi	**aveste**
loro	**ebbero**

GERUND

avendo

PAST PARTICIPLE

avuto

IMPERATIVE

abbi / abbiamo / abbiate

EXAMPLE PHRASES

Ha un fratello e una sorella. He has a brother and a sister.
Avevo la febbre. I had a temperature.
Domani **avranno** più tempo. They'll have more time tomorrow.

Remember that subject pronouns are not used very often in Italian.

credere (to believe)

	PRESENT		FUTURE
io	credo	io	crederò
tu	credi	tu	crederai
lui/lei/Lei	crede	lui/lei/Lei	crederà
noi	crediamo	noi	crederemo
voi	credete	voi	crederete
loro	credono	loro	crederanno

	IMPERFECT		CONDITIONAL
io	credevo	io	crederei
tu	credevi	tu	crederesti
lui/lei/Lei	credeva	lui/lei/Lei	crederebbe
noi	credevamo	noi	crederemmo
voi	credevate	voi	credereste
loro	credevano	loro	crederebbero

	PERFECT		PRESENT SUBJUNCTIVE
io	ho creduto	io	creda
tu	hai creduto	tu	creda
lui/lei/Lei	ha creduto	lui/lei/Lei	creda
noi	abbiamo creduto	noi	crediamo
voi	avete creduto	voi	crediate
loro	hanno creduto	loro	credano

	PAST HISTORIC
io	credei or credetti
tu	credesti
lui/lei/Lei	credè or credette
noi	credemmo
voi	credeste
loro	credettero

GERUND

credendo

PAST PARTICIPLE

creduto

IMPERATIVE

credi / crediamo / credete

EXAMPLE PHRASES

Credo di sì. I think so.
Gli **ho creduto**. I believed him.
Non ci posso **credere**! I can't believe it!

Remember that subject pronouns are not used very often in Italian.

dare (to give)

PRESENT

io	**do**
tu	**dai**
lui/lei/Lei	**dà**
noi	**diamo**
voi	**date**
loro	**danno**

FUTURE

io	**darò**
tu	**darai**
lui/lei/Lei	**darà**
noi	**daremo**
voi	**darete**
loro	**daranno**

IMPERFECT

io	**davo**
tu	**davi**
lui/lei/Lei	**dava**
noi	**davamo**
voi	**davate**
loro	**davano**

CONDITIONAL

io	**darei**
tu	**daresti**
lui/lei/Lei	**darebbe**
noi	**daremmo**
voi	**dareste**
loro	**darebbero**

PERFECT

io	**ho dato**
tu	**hai dato**
lui/lei/Lei	**ha dato**
noi	**abbiamo dato**
voi	**avete dato**
loro	**hanno dato**

PRESENT SUBJUNCTIVE

io	**dia**
tu	**dia**
lui/lei/Lei	**dia**
noi	**diamo**
voi	**diate**
loro	**diano**

PAST HISTORIC

io	**diedi** *or* **detti**
tu	**desti**
lui/lei/Lei	**diede** *or* **dette**
noi	**demmo**
voi	**deste**
loro	**diedero** *or* **dettero**

GERUND

dando

PAST PARTICIPLE

dato

IMPERATIVE

da' *or* **dai** / **diamo** / **date**

EXAMPLE PHRASES

Zia Maria ci **dà** le caramelle. Aunt Maria gives us sweets.
Mi **ha dato** un libro. He gave me a book.
Mi **daranno** una risposta domani. They'll give me an answer tomorrow.

Remember that subject pronouns are not used very often in Italian.

dire (to say)

	PRESENT		FUTURE
io	**dico**	io	**dirò**
tu	**dici**	tu	**dirai**
lui/lei/Lei	**dice**	lui/lei/Lei	**dirà**
noi	**diciamo**	noi	**diremo**
voi	**dite**	voi	**direte**
loro	**dicono**	loro	**diranno**

	IMPERFECT		CONDITIONAL
io	**dicevo**	io	**direi**
tu	**dicevi**	tu	**diresti**
lui/lei/Lei	**diceva**	lui/lei/Lei	**direbbe**
noi	**dicevamo**	noi	**diremmo**
voi	**dicevate**	voi	**direste**
loro	**dicevano**	loro	**direbbero**

	PERFECT		PRESENT SUBJUNCTIVE
io	**ho detto**	io	**dica**
tu	**hai detto**	tu	**dica**
lui/lei/Lei	**ha detto**	lui/lei/Lei	**dica**
noi	**abbiamo detto**	noi	**diciamo**
voi	**avete detto**	voi	**diciate**
loro	**hanno detto**	loro	**dicano**

	PAST HISTORIC
io	**dissi**
tu	**dicesti**
lui/lei/Lei	**disse**
noi	**dicemmo**
voi	**diceste**
loro	**dissero**

GERUND

dicendo

PAST PARTICIPLE

detto

IMPERATIVE

di / diciamo / dite

EXAMPLE PHRASES

Dice sempre quello che pensa. She always says what she thinks.
Mi **ha detto** una bugia. He told me a lie.
Diranno che è colpa mia. They'll say it's my fault.

Remember that subject pronouns are not used very often in Italian.

dormire (to sleep)

PRESENT

io	**dormo**
tu	**dormi**
lui/lei/Lei	**dorme**
noi	**dormiamo**
voi	**dormite**
loro	**dormono**

FUTURE

io	**dormirò**
tu	**dormirai**
lui/lei/Lei	**dormirà**
noi	**dormiremo**
voi	**dormirete**
loro	**dormiranno**

IMPERFECT

io	**dormivo**
tu	**dormivi**
lui/lei/Lei	**dormiva**
noi	**dormivamo**
voi	**dormivate**
loro	**dormivano**

CONDITIONAL

io	**dormirei**
tu	**dormiresti**
lui/lei/Lei	**dormirebbe**
noi	**dormiremmo**
voi	**dormireste**
loro	**dormirebbero**

PERFECT

io	**ho dormito**
tu	**hai dormito**
lui/lei/Lei	**ha dormito**
noi	**abbiamo dormito**
voi	**avete dormito**
loro	**hanno dormito**

PRESENT SUBJUNCTIVE

io	**dorma**
tu	**dorma**
lui/lei/Lei	**dorma**
noi	**dormiamo**
voi	**dormiate**
loro	**dormano**

PAST HISTORIC

io	**dormii**
tu	**dormisti**
lui/lei/Lei	**dormì**
noi	**dormimmo**
voi	**dormiste**
loro	**dormirono**

GERUND

dormendo

PAST PARTICIPLE

dormito

IMPERATIVE

dormi / dormiamo / dormite

EXAMPLE PHRASES

I bambini **dormono**. The children are sleeping.
Quando ha telefonato **dormivo**. I was sleeping when he phoned.
Hai dormito bene? Did you sleep well?

Remember that subject pronouns are not used very often in Italian.

dovere (to have to)

PRESENT

io	**devo**
tu	**devi**
lui/lei/Lei	**deve**
noi	**dobbiamo**
voi	**dovete**
loro	**dovono**

FUTURE

io	**dovrò**
tu	**dovrai**
lui/lei/Lei	**dovrà**
noi	**dovremo**
voi	**dovrete**
loro	**dovranno**

IMPERFECT

io	**dovevo**
tu	**dovevi**
lui/lei/Lei	**doveva**
noi	**dovevamo**
voi	**dovevate**
loro	**dovevano**

CONDITIONAL

io	**dovrei**
tu	**dovresti**
lui/lei/Lei	**dovrebbe**
noi	**dovremmo**
voi	**dovreste**
loro	**dovrebbero**

PERFECT

io	**ho dovuto**
tu	**hai dovuto**
lui/lei/Lei	**ha dovuto**
noi	**abbiamo dovuto**
voi	**avete dovuto**
loro	**hanno dovuto**

PRESENT SUBJUNCTIVE

io	**deva** or **debba**
tu	**deva** or **debba**
lui/lei/Lei	**deva** or **debba**
noi	**dobbiamo**
voi	**dobbiate**
loro	**devano** or **debbano**

PAST HISTORIC

io	**dovetti**
tu	**dovesti**
lui/lei/Lei	**dovette**
noi	**dovemmo**
voi	**deveste**
loro	**dovettero**

GERUND

dovendo

PAST PARTICIPLE

dovuto

IMPERATIVE

not used

EXAMPLE PHRASES

Ho **dovuto** dirglielo. I had to tell him.
Dev'essere tardi. It must be late.
Dovresti aiutarlo. You should help him.

Remember that subject pronouns are not used very often in Italian.

essere (to be)

PRESENT

io	**sono**
tu	**sei**
lui/lei/Lei	**è**
noi	**siamo**
voi	**siete**
loro	**sono**

FUTURE

io	**sarò**
tu	**sarai**
lui/lei/Lei	**sarà**
noi	**saremo**
voi	**sarete**
loro	**saranno**

IMPERFECT

io	**ero**
tu	**eri**
lui/lei/Lei	**era**
noi	**eravamo**
voi	**eravate**
loro	**erano**

CONDITIONAL

io	**sarei**
tu	**saresti**
lui/lei/Lei	**sarebbe**
noi	**saremmo**
voi	**sareste**
loro	**sarebbero**

PERFECT

io	**sono stato/a**
tu	**sei stato/a**
lui/lei/Lei	**è stato/a**
noi	**siamo stati/e**
voi	**siete stati/e**
loro	**sono stati/e**

PRESENT SUBJUNCTIVE

io	**sia**
tu	**sia**
lui/lei/Lei	**sia**
noi	**siamo**
voi	**siate**
loro	**siano**

PAST HISTORIC

io	**fui**
tu	**fosti**
lui/lei/Lei	**fu**
noi	**fummo**
voi	**foste**
loro	**furono**

GERUND

essendo

PAST PARTICIPLE

stato

IMPERATIVE

sii / siamo / siate

EXAMPLE PHRASES

Sono italiana. I'm Italian.
Siete mai **stati** in Africa? Have you ever been to Africa?
Quando è arrivato **erano** le quattro in punto. When he arrived it was exactly four o'clock.
Spero che **sia** vero. I hope it is true.

Remember that subject pronouns are not used very often in Italian.

fare (to do, to make)

	PRESENT		FUTURE
io	**faccio**	io	**farò**
tu	**fai**	tu	**farai**
lui/lei/Lei	**fa**	lui/lei/Lei	**farà**
noi	**facciamo**	noi	**faremo**
voi	**fate**	voi	**farete**
loro	**fanno**	loro	**faranno**

	IMPERFECT		CONDITIONAL
io	**facevo**	io	**farei**
tu	**facevi**	tu	**faresti**
lui/lei/Lei	**faceva**	lui/lei/Lei	**farebbe**
noi	**facevamo**	noi	**faremmo**
voi	**facevate**	voi	**fareste**
loro	**facevano**	loro	**farebbero**

	PERFECT		PRESENT SUBJUNCTIVE
io	**ho fatto**	io	**faccia**
tu	**hai fatto**	tu	**faccia**
lui/lei/Lei	**ha fatto**	lui/lei/Lei	**faccia**
noi	**abbiamo fatto**	noi	**facciamo**
voi	**avete fatto**	voi	**facciate**
loro	**hanno fatto**	loro	**facciano**

	PAST HISTORIC
io	**feci**
tu	**facesti**
lui/lei/Lei	**fece**
noi	**facemmo**
voi	**faceste**
loro	**fecero**

GERUND

facendo

PAST PARTICIPLE

fatto

IMPERATIVE

fa' *or* **fai / facciamo / fate**

EXAMPLE PHRASES

Cosa stai **facendo**? What are you doing?
Ho fatto i letti. I've made the beds.
Ieri non **abbiamo fatto** niente. We didn't do anything yesterday.

Remember that subject pronouns are not used very often in Italian.

finire (to finish)

	PRESENT		**FUTURE**
io	**finisco**	io	**finirò**
tu	**finisci**	tu	**finirai**
lui/lei/Lei	**finisce**	lui/lei/Lei	**finirà**
noi	**finiamo**	noi	**finiremo**
voi	**finite**	voi	**finirete**
loro	**finiscono**	loro	**finiranno**

	IMPERFECT		**CONDITIONAL**
io	**finivo**	io	**finirei**
tu	**finivi**	tu	**finiresti**
lui/lei/Lei	**finiva**	lui/lei/Lei	**finirebbe**
noi	**finivamo**	noi	**finiremmo**
voi	**finivate**	voi	**finireste**
loro	**finivano**	loro	**finirebbero**

	PERFECT		**PRESENT SUBJUNCTIVE**
io	**ho finito**	io	**finisca**
tu	**hai finito**	tu	**finisca**
lui/lei/Lei	**ha finito**	lui/lei/Lei	**finisca**
noi	**abbiamo finito**	noi	**finiamo**
voi	**avete finito**	voi	**finiate**
loro	**hanno finito**	loro	**finiscano**

	PAST HISTORIC
io	**finii**
tu	**finisti**
lui/lei/Lei	**finì**
noi	**finimmo**
voi	**finiste**
loro	**finirono**

GERUND

finendo

PAST PARTICIPLE

finito

IMPERATIVE

finisci / finiamo / finite

EXAMPLE PHRASES

Le lezioni **finiscono** alle tre. Classes finish at three.
Finisci i compiti! Finish your homework!
Ho finito. I've finished.

Remember that subject pronouns are not used very often in Italian.

lavarsi (to wash oneself)

PRESENT

io	**mi lavo**
tu	**ti lavi**
lui/lei/Lei	**si lava**
noi	**ci laviamo**
voi	**vi lavate**
loro	**si lavano**

FUTURE

io	**mi laverò**
tu	**ti laverai**
lui/lei/Lei	**si laverà**
noi	**ci laveremo**
voi	**vi laverete**
loro	**si laveranno**

IMPERFECT

io	**mi lavavo**
tu	**ti lavavi**
lui/lei/Lei	**si lavava**
noi	**ci lavavamo**
voi	**vi lavavate**
loro	**si lavavano**

CONDITIONAL

io	**mi laverei**
tu	**ti laveresti**
lui/lei/Lei	**si laverebbe**
noi	**ci laveremmo**
voi	**vi lavereste**
loro	**si laverebbero**

PERFECT

io	**mi sono lavato/a**
tu	**ti sei lavato/a**
lui/lei/Lei	**si è lavato/a**
noi	**ci siamo lavati/e**
voi	**vi siete lavati/e**
loro	**si sono lavati/e**

PRESENT SUBJUNCTIVE

io	**mi lavi**
tu	**ti lavi**
lui/lei/Lei	**si lavi**
noi	**ci laviamo**
voi	**vi laviate**
loro	**si lavino**

PAST HISTORIC

io	**mi lavai**
tu	**ti lavasti**
lui/lei/Lei	**si lavò**
noi	**ci lavammo**
voi	**vi lavaste**
loro	**si lavarono**

GERUND

lavandosi

PAST PARTICIPLE

lavatosi

IMPERATIVE

lavati / laviamoci / lavatevi

EXAMPLE PHRASES

Si sta **lavando**. He's washing.
Ti sei lavato le mani? Did you wash your hands?
Lavati i denti. Brush your teeth.

Remember that subject pronouns are not used very often in Italian.

parlare (to speak)

PRESENT

io	**parlo**
tu	**parli**
lui/lei/Lei	**parla**
noi	**parliamo**
voi	**parlate**
loro	**parlano**

FUTURE

io	**parlerò**
tu	**parlerai**
lui/lei/Lei	**parlerà**
noi	**parleremo**
voi	**parlerete**
loro	**parleranno**

IMPERFECT

io	**parlavo**
tu	**parlavi**
lui/lei/Lei	**parlava**
noi	**parlavamo**
voi	**parlavate**
loro	**parlavano**

CONDITIONAL

io	**parlerei**
tu	**parleresti**
lui/lei/Lei	**parlerebbe**
noi	**parleremmo**
voi	**parlereste**
loro	**parlerebbero**

PERFECT

io	**ho parlato**
tu	**hai parlato**
lui/lei/Lei	**ha parlato**
noi	**abbiamo parlato**
voi	**avete parlato**
loro	**hanno parlato**

PRESENT SUBJUNCTIVE

io	**parli**
tu	**parli**
lui/lei/Lei	**parli**
noi	**parliamo**
voi	**parliate**
loro	**parlino**

PAST HISTORIC

io	**parlai**
tu	**parlasti**
lui/lei/Lei	**parlò**
noi	**parlammo**
voi	**parlaste**
loro	**parlarono**

GERUND

parlando

PAST PARTICIPLE

parlato

IMPERATIVE

parla / parliamo / parlate

EXAMPLE PHRASES

Non **parlo** francese. I don't speak French.
Ho parlato con tuo fratello ieri. I spoke to your brother yesterday.
Parlerò con lei stasera. I'll speak to her this evening.

Remember that subject pronouns are not used very often in Italian.

potere (to be able)

	PRESENT		FUTURE
io	**posso**	io	**potrò**
tu	**puoi**	tu	**potrai**
lui/lei/Lei	**può**	lui/lei/Lei	**potrà**
noi	**possiamo**	noi	**potremo**
voi	**potete**	voi	**potrete**
loro	**possono**	loro	**potranno**

	IMPERFECT		CONDITIONAL
io	**potevo**	io	**potrei**
tu	**potevi**	tu	**potresti**
lui/lei/Lei	**poteva**	lui/lei/Lei	**potrebbe**
noi	**potevamo**	noi	**potremmo**
voi	**potevate**	voi	**potreste**
loro	**potevano**	loro	**potrebbero**

	PERFECT		PRESENT SUBJUNCTIVE
io	**ho potuto**	io	**possa**
tu	**hai potuto**	tu	**possa**
lui/lei/Lei	**ha potuto**	lui/lei/Lei	**possa**
noi	**abbiamo potuto**	noi	**possiamo**
voi	**avete potuto**	voi	**possiate**
loro	**hanno potuto**	loro	**possano**

	PAST HISTORIC
io	**potei**
tu	**potesti**
lui/lei/Lei	**potè**
noi	**potemmo**
voi	**poteste**
loro	**poterono**

GERUND

potendo

PAST PARTICIPLE

potuto

IMPERATIVE

not used

EXAMPLE PHRASES

Puoi venire con noi? Can you come with us?
Potrebbe succedere. It could happen.
Non **ho potuto** farlo ieri. I couldn't do it yesterday.

Remember that subject pronouns are not used very often in Italian.

sapere (to know)

	PRESENT		**FUTURE**
io	**so**	io	**saprò**
tu	**sai**	tu	**saprai**
lui/lei/Lei	**sa**	lui/lei/Lei	**saprà**
noi	**sappiamo**	noi	**sapremo**
voi	**sapete**	voi	**saprete**
loro	**sanno**	loro	**sapranno**

	IMPERFECT		**CONDITIONAL**
io	**sapevo**	io	**saprei**
tu	**sapevi**	tu	**sapresti**
lui/lei/Lei	**sapeva**	lui/lei/Lei	**saprebbe**
noi	**sapevamo**	noi	**sapremmo**
voi	**sapevate**	voi	**sapreste**
loro	**sapevano**	loro	**saprebbero**

	PERFECT		**PRESENT SUBJUNCTIVE**
io	**ho saputo**	io	**sappia**
tu	**hai saputo**	tu	**sappia**
lui/lei/Lei	**ha saputo**	lui/lei/Lei	**sappia**
noi	**abbiamo saputo**	noi	**sappiamo**
voi	**avete saputo**	voi	**sappiate**
loro	**hanno saputo**	loro	**sappiano**

	PAST HISTORIC	**GERUND**
io	**seppi**	**sapendo**
tu	**sapesti**	
lui/lei/Lei	**seppe**	**PAST PARTICIPLE**
noi	**sapemmo**	**saputo**
voi	**sapeste**	
loro	**seppero**	**IMPERATIVE**

IMPERATIVE

sappi / sappiamo / sappiate

EXAMPLE PHRASES

Non lo **so**. I don't know.
Non ne **sapeva** niente. He didn't know anything about it.
Non **ha saputo** cosa fare. He didn't know what to do.

Remember that subject pronouns are not used very often in Italian.

stare (to be)

PRESENT

io	**sto**
tu	**stai**
lui/lei/Lei	**sta**
noi	**stiamo**
voi	**state**
loro	**stanno**

FUTURE

io	**starò**
tu	**starai**
lui/lei/Lei	**starà**
noi	**staremo**
voi	**starete**
loro	**staranno**

IMPERFECT

io	**stavo**
tu	**stavi**
lui/lei/Lei	**stava**
noi	**stavamo**
voi	**stavate**
loro	**stavano**

CONDITIONAL

io	**starei**
tu	**staresti**
lui/lei/Lei	**starebbe**
noi	**staremmo**
voi	**stareste**
loro	**starebbero**

PERFECT

io	**sono stato/a**
tu	**sei stato/a**
lui/lei/Lei	**è stato/a**
noi	**siamo stati/e**
voi	**siete stati/e**
loro	**sono stati/e**

PRESENT SUBJUNCTIVE

io	**stia**
tu	**stia**
lui/lei/Lei	**stia**
noi	**stiamo**
voi	**stiate**
loro	**stiano**

PAST HISTORIC

io	**stetti**
tu	**stesti**
lui/lei/Lei	**stette**
noi	**stemmo**
voi	**steste**
loro	**stettero**

GERUND

stando

PAST PARTICIPLE

stato

IMPERATIVE

sta' *or* **stai** / **stiamo** / **state**

EXAMPLE PHRASES

Come **stai**? How are you?
Sto leggendo un libro. I'm reading a book.
Sei mai **stato** a Firenze? Have you ever been to Florence?

Remember that subject pronouns are not used very often in Italian.

volere (to want)

PRESENT		FUTURE	
io	**voglio**	io	**vorrò**
tu	**vuoi**	tu	**vorrai**
lui/lei/Lei	**vuole**	lui/lei/Lei	**vorrà**
noi	**vogliamo**	noi	**vorremo**
voi	**volete**	voi	**vorrete**
loro	**vogliono**	loro	**vorranno**

IMPERFECT		CONDITIONAL	
io	**volevo**	io	**vorrei**
tu	**volevi**	tu	**vorresti**
lui/lei/Lei	**voleva**	lui/lei/Lei	**vorrebbe**
noi	**volevamo**	noi	**vorremmo**
voi	**volevate**	voi	**vorreste**
loro	**volevano**	loro	**vorrebbero**

PERFECT		PRESENT SUBJUNCTIVE	
io	**ho voluto**	io	**voglia**
tu	**hai voluto**	tu	**voglia**
lui/lei/Lei	**ha voluto**	lui/lei/Lei	**voglia**
noi	**abbiamo voluto**	noi	**vogliamo**
voi	**avete voluto**	voi	**vogliate**
loro	**hanno voluto**	loro	**vogliano**

PAST HISTORIC			
io	**volli**	**GERUND**	
tu	**volesti**	**volendo**	
lui/lei/Lei	**volle**	**PAST PARTICIPLE**	
noi	**volemmo**	**voluto**	
voi	**voleste**	**IMPERATIVE**	
loro	**vollero**	**not used**	

EXAMPLE PHRASES

Cosa **vuoi**? What do you want?
Vorrei andare in Australia. I'd like to go to Australia.
Non **ha voluto** ammetterlo. He didn't want to admit it.

Remember that subject pronouns are not used very often in Italian.